2. Sample Student Assignment: Informal Assessment of a Child

A practical and enjoyable assignment for students taking a course in learning disabilities is to give informal tests to assess a child. Several informal assessment procedures suggested in this book can be used for this assignment. To use all of the assessment procedures, several children of different ages may be needed. The assignment can require students to give the informal assessments, report on the results of the assessments, provide samples of the child's responses, evaluate the child's level of achievement, and make further interpretations based on their observations of the child. The sections of the book that can be used for the informal assessment assignment are as follows:

Area of Assessment	Location of Assessment Procedure in Text
1. Motor skills: visual-motor, gross-motor, fine-motor	Chapter 7, Soft Neurological Signs, pp. 234–236
2. Rating scale of student behavior	Chapter 3, Figure 3.2, p. 82
3. Informal phonological awareness test	Chapter 10, Table 10.1, Informal Test of Phonological Awareness, p. 332
4. Informal reading	Chapter 3, Table 3.4, Informal Graded Word-Recognition Test, p. 84
5. Informal survey of arithmetic skills	Chapter 3, Figure 3.3, Informal Survey Test: Sixth-Grade Level, p. 84 (or use directions to make an arithmetic survey test for another grade level)
6. Informal spelling test	Chapter 13, Figure 13.4, Informal Spelling Test, p. 477
7. Informal test of phonics generalizations	Appendix B, Phonics, Nonsense Words Quiz, p. 586

3. Videotapes

Several of the videotapes listed below can be purchased from the Learning Disabilities Association of America (LDA), 4156 Library Road, Pittsburgh, PA 15234. Phone (412) 341-1515. In addition, the LDA can provide a list of videotapes that are available for a small rental fee.

ADHD: Inclusive Instruction and Collaborative Practices. This videotape is a presentation by Sandra Rief that shows ways that general education teachers can serve children with diverse needs in the regular classroom. 38 minutes. $99 + $5 shipping and handling. National Professional Resources, 25 S. Regent St., Port Chester, NY 10573. Phone (800) 453-7461. FAX (914) 937-9327.

ALL CHILDREN LEARN DIFFERENTLY. Narrated by Steve Allen. Interviews 12 specialists in medicine, perception, language, and education. It takes a nutritional/educational approach to the remediation of learning disabilities, calling for the right professional team for each child. 30 minutes. $42. Learning Disabilities Association of America.

A CHILD'S FIRST WORDS. How speech and language development in children under age 4 can affect their ability to learn. Alerts parents to the milestones of good speech and language acquisition in children under age 4 and tells them how to get help if they need it. 18 minutes. $21. Learning Disabilities Association of America.

GIFTS OF GREATNESS. The lives of great people who overcame dyslexia, starring Ed Asner, Danny Thomas, and others. $125 + $15 handling fee. Educator's Publishing Service, 75 Moulton Street, Cambridge, MA 02138. Phone (800) 225-5750.

HOMEWORK AND LEARNING DISABILITIES. Offers practical techniques for solving homework problems. Clarifies responsibilities of teachers, students, and parents. 34 minutes. $99. The Menninger Clinic and Center for Learning Disabilities, Box 829, Topeka, KS 66601-0820. Phone (800) 345-6036.

HOW DIFFICULT CAN THIS BE? F.A.T. CITY. Rick Lavoie explores the world of difficulties faced by children with learning disabilities through a simulation. 45 minutes. $39.95 + shipping and handling. CACLD (Connecticut Association for Children with Learning Disabilities), 18 Marshall St., South Norwalk, CT 06834. Phone (203) 838-5010.

I'M NOT STUPID. Depicts the constant battle of the child with learning disabilities in school. It points out how the child is often misdiagnosed as slow, retarded, emotionally disturbed, or lazy. Recommended for parents, teachers, administrators, or students. $22. Learning Disabilities Association.

LAST ONE PICKED. FIRST ONE PICKED ON. Rick Lavoie addresses the social problems children with learning disabilities face and offers some practical solutions for teachers and parents. 40 minutes. $49.95 + $8.50 shipping and handling. Public Broadcasting Service. Phone (800) 344-3337.

Instructor's Resource Manual with Test Items

LEARNING DISABILITIES: THEORIES, DIAGNOSIS, AND TEACHING STRATEGIES

A Guide to Your Examination of *Learning Disabilities: Theories, Diagnosis, and Teaching Strategies, Seventh Edition*

Audience

Learning Disabilities: Theories, Diagnosis, and Teaching Strategies is an introductory text written for both undergraduate and graduate students who are taking a first course in learning disabilities. It is designed to provide a broad view of the field for present and future special and regular educators, school psychologists, administrators, related professionals, and others preparing to work with individuals with learning disabilities. This book is geared for elementary and secondary teachers who will be working with students with learning disabilities in their classrooms and collaborating with special educators about these students. In addition, the text can serve parents who are seeking the necessary background information to better understand the problems their children face.

Scope and Focus

Teachers need to understand the characteristics of students with learning disabilities, appreciate the historical evolvement of the field, be familiar with underlying theories, know assessment procedures and approaches to teaching these students, and be familiar with strategies and methods. Thus the text is eclectic in its approach to offer the reader a comprehensive view of the field—its various theories, assessment procedures, and teaching strategies and methods.

This text has up-to-date information on and coverage of new issues and topics in the field of learning disabilities. It incorporates features of the Individuals with Disabilities Education Act (IDEA), such as the individualized education program (IEP), procedural safeguards, and alternative placement arrangements. The text gives the reader a background in learning disabilities, special education, and pertinent aspects of regular education. There is a chapter on young children with learning disabilities and one on adolescents and adults with learning disabilities. The text includes illustrative case examples and detailed case studies.

Organization

The book is organized into four major parts. Part One is an overview of learning disabilities. Chapter 1 presents the field of learning disabilities as one in transition. Chapter 2 looks at the historical evolvement of the field and emerging directions.

Part Two deals with the assessment and teaching processes. Assessment and teaching are viewed as interrelated parts of a continuous process of trying to understand students and help them learn. Assessment is discussed in Chapter 3, with special emphasis on the development of the individualized education program. Chapter 4 examines instruction and the elements that make teaching successful. Chapter 5 reviews various systems for delivering education services.

Part Three deals with theoretical issues and expanding directions. Chapter 6 analyzes underlying psychological theories of learning disabilities. Chapter 7 presents medical aspects of research, assessment, and treatment. Chapter 8 looks at the problems of young children with learning disabilities. Chapter 9 focuses on adolescents and adults with learning disabilities.

Part Four links the theories to instruction; it thus deals with the heart of the problem—teaching children and youth with learning disabilities. The chapters are organized by academic area. Each chapter has two sections: the first section reviews the theoretical issues for teaching that particular content area, and the second section offers practical suggestions for teaching strategies. Chapter 10 discusses developmental and preacademic learning. Chapter 11 looks at oral language, specifically listening and speaking. Chapter 12 analyzes the area of reading—both reading skills and reading comprehension. Chapter 13 reviews written language, including written expression, spelling, and handwriting. Chapter 14 analyzes disorders in mathematics—concepts, skills, and problem solving. Chapter 15 discusses the social and emotional implications of learning disabilities.

Writing Style

This book provides a clear and fair presentation of topics and issues. The previous editions achieved a style that students reported was readable and easy to understand. This edition retains this style of presentation.

Pedagogical Features

In order to make this text easy to study and more appealing to use, the following features are included:

Chapter outlines begin each chapter, present the major headings, and provide a handy checklist or organization aid for students to use in learning chapter material.

Summaries conclude each chapter and highlight, in a clear point-by-point format, the major ideas in the chapter.

Key terms, listed at the end of each chapter, highlight the most important terminology and provide an opportunity for students to review their knowledge of key chapter concepts. These terms are defined in the glossary in Appendix E.

Questions for discussion and reflection are included at the end of each chapter to promote class discussion or for use as essay examination questions. Sample responses to these questions are included in this *Instructor's Resource Manual.*

Case examples are short illustrative vignettes and discussions interspersed throughout all chapters to add real life situations.

Case studies provide longer, more comprehensive examples and are designed to show practical applications. One extended case study is contained in Chapters 3, 4, and 5. Another extended case study is in Appendix A.

Appendixes contain useful information for teachers. Appendix A is an extended case study. Appendix B consists of a phonics quiz and a brief review of basic phonics generalizations. Appendix C is a listing and brief description of commonly used tests. Appendix D contains a listing of publishers' addresses. Appendix E is a glossary of key terms.

Study Guide with Cases

The *Study Guide with Cases* is a supplementary manual to help students learn the content and concepts present in the text. Each chapter is divided into seven parts: (1) Objectives, (2) Terms You Should Know, (3) Key Points, (4) Seeing the System, (5) Application and Synthesis, (6) Rapid Review Questions, and (7) Case Study.

Instructor's Resource Manual with Test Items

This *Instructor's Resource Manual* accompanies the text *Learning Disabilities: Theories, Diagnosis, and Teaching Strategies.* Its purpose is to provide assistance for instructors who teach the course. It has four parts: (1) Chapter Guides, (2) Test Questions: Short-Answer and Essay-Discussion Questions, (3) Multiple-Choice Questions, and (4) Additional Teaching Resources.

1. *Chapter guides* provide for each chapter objectives, focus, chapter outline, key terms and definitions, suggested activities, and materials for transparency presentation.

2. *Test questions:*

    a. *Short-answer questions* are given for each chapter, along with answers.

    b. *Essay-discussion questions* are provided for each chapter, along with the answers.

3. *Multiple-choice questions* are grouped together in one section for ease of use. There is a set of "A" questions and a comparable set of "B" questions for each chapter. Answers to the multiple-choice questions are also provided. There is a computer disk available to help instructors use the multiple-choice questions.

4. *Additional teaching resources* contain professional resources that can support class instruction. Included are videotapes, selected references, a student assignment for informal assessment of children, and some sample syllabi.

Instructor's Resource Manual with Test Items

LEARNING DISABILITIES: THEORIES, DIAGNOSIS, AND TEACHING STRATEGIES

Seventh Edition

Janet W. Lerner
Northeastern Illinois University

HOUGHTON MIFFLIN COMPANY   BOSTON   NEW YORK

Senior Sponsoring Editor: Loretta Wolozin
Associate Editor: Lisa A. Mafrici
Associate Project Editor: Elena Di Cesare
Editorial Assistant: Angela Schoenherr
Associate Production Coordinator: Deborah Frydman
Senior Manufacturing Coordinator: Priscilla J. Bailey
Marketing Manager: Pamela Laskey

Printed in the U.S.A.

ISBN: 0-395-79487-0

123456789-BB-00 99 98 97 96

Contents

Part Four   Additional Teaching Resources   323

Changes in the Seventh Edition of *Learning Disabilities: Theories, Diagnosis, and Teaching Strategies*

If you have used the sixth edition of *Learning Disabilities: Theories, Diagnosis, and Teaching Strategies,* you will find the transition to the seventh edition easy, because the basic organization of the chapters has been retained. The changes are discussed below, but you will not have to make major rearrangements of your syllabi.

Some general revisions in the text should make it even more helpful for your classes. This edition includes up-to-date information about new issues and expands the coverage of key contemporary topics:

- *Updating of material.* Material has been thoroughly revised to contain the most recent references, up-to-date data, and validated practices in the field.

- *Inclusion.* More students with learning disabilities are placed in inclusive general education classrooms for services. This edition expands information about inclusion practices and offers suggestions for responsible inclusion procedures.

- *Attention deficit disorders.* The revision expands the coverage of ADD/ADHD to meet the needs of an increasing number of students who are being diagnosed with this disability.

- *Collaboration.* The need for collaboration is becoming more apparent as the inclusion movement expands. Suggestions for collaboration between regular and special education teachers are made throughout the text.

- *Early precursors of learning disabilities.* The revision examines the early signs of learning disabilities exhibited by young children, such as problems in phonological awareness or rapid naming.

- *Computer technology.* The dizzying pace of change in computer technology and the growing availability of computers means that teachers must have knowledge about computer use for students with learning disabilities. The revision in several chapters considers how the new advances in computer technology can be used for students with learning disabilities: for example, in early childhood, for reading, writing, and mathematics.

- *The value of explicit decoding instruction in the teaching of reading.* The text integrates the contributions of whole-language instruction in reading and the teaching of decoding skills for students with learning disabilities.

- *Assessment.* The revision explores new assessment approaches such as authentic assessment, discusses recent information about the use of intelligence tests in the identification process, and provides alternatives to using eligibility criteria formulas for identification. New approaches to assessment include alternative and authentic evaluation procedures.

- *Linguistically and culturally diverse children who have learning disabilities.* The revision expands the methods for teaching the growing number of students with learning disabilities who come from diverse cultural and linguistic environments.

- *Recent brain research.* The text updates the neuroscience information on the brain, with recent studies that have implications for learning disabilities.

- *Adolescents and Transition.* The revision addresses the issue of transition from school to adult life and expands the discussion of adolescents and adults with learning disabilities.

- *The role of parents.* The text emphasizes the essential role of parents and the importance of establishing a healthy home-school partnership.

- *Computer software.* A computer software disk is available for instructors that contains the testing program.

Chapter 1. The information and data about children with learning disabilities have been brought up to date, and the discussion of characteristics of children and youth with learning disabilities has been reorganized. New information about inclusion practices and collaboration is included. A discussion of multiple intelligences has been added.

Chapter 2. The information about emerging directions and the "current phase" of the history of learning disabilities has been revised. The emerging directions section contains information about inclusion, cultural and linguistic diversity, attention deficit disorders, the education reform movement, and the use of computer technology.

Chapter 3. More information about traditional and alternative assessment procedures is given in this chapter. In addition, all the information about formal tests is brought up to date.

Chapter 4. Clinical teaching remains the key to instructing students with learning disabilities. New teaching strategies and ways to bring clinical teaching into the inclusive classroom are added.

Chapter 5. This chapter now reflects the changing placement of students with learning disabilities. The implications of more students with learning disabilities in general education classes are examined in this chapter. The section on working with families is expanded.

Chapter 6. This chapter examines new theories for teaching students with learning disabilities. It includes new information from developmental psychology, behavioral psychology, cognitive psychology, and learning strategy instruction.

Chapter 7. This chapter describes the new research from the neurosciences and the study of the brain. It also expands on the most recent information about attention deficit disorders and attention deficit hyperactivity disorders from the *Diagnostic and Statistical Manual of Mental Disorders,* 4th edition.

Chapter 8. The important strides in early childhood special education are included in this chapter. It adds the recent findings about the precursors of learning disabilities in young children and information about developmentally appropriate practice (DAP). The section on using computers with young children is updated.

Chapter 9. This chapter highlights new information about adolescents and adults with learning disabilities. The chapter expands and updates the section on transition planning for secondary students with learning disabilities.

Chapter 10. New information about the precursors of learning disabilities in developmental and preacademic learning is added to this chapter. The chapter updates the section on phonological awareness with the most recent research and strategies for teaching this skill to young children with learning disabilities.

Chapter 11. The information on oral language—listening and speaking—is updated in this chapter. New ideas have been added about the innatist theory of language acquisition and emergent literacy. The discussions of the integrated language core and strategies for teaching listening and speaking are expanded.

Chapter 12. New views about teaching reading are added to this chapter. The explicit code-emphasis approach is added and whole-language instruction is expanded. The teaching strategies for teaching word recognition, improving fluency, improving reading comprehension, and building vocabulary are reorganized. The section on computers and reading is updated.

Chapter 13. This chapter updates the discussion of written language: written expression, spelling, and handwriting. The sections on keyboarding skills, word processing, and multisensory approaches to spelling are expanded.

Chapter 14. This chapter expands the discussion of changing views on the teaching of mathematics and the implication for students with learning disabilities. Updated are the sections on precursors of learning disabilities, secondary students, and the use of computers for teaching mathematics.

Chapter 15. In this chapter the sections on social skills, emotional problems, and behavioral considerations are updated. Teaching strategies for social competencies, self-esteem, and behavior management are reorganized. A special section on accommodations for inclusive classrooms is added.

Preface

Preparing to teach a course in learning disabilities is an arduous task. The breadth and scope of the topics in this field require many hours of preparation and broad experience. In this preparation process, the ideas and experiences of instructors who have taught such courses can be of considerable value.

The purpose of this *Instructor's Resource Manual* is to offer suggestions and assistance to instructors who are using the seventh edition of *Learning Disabilities: Theories, Diagnosis, and Teaching Strategies*. It also provides information for instructors whose students are using the *Study Guide* that accompanies the text. The four major parts are (1) chapter guides, (2) test questions: short-answer questions and essay-discussion questions, (3) multiple-choice questions, and (4) additional teaching resources.

For the benefit of users of earlier editions of this book, the changes for the seventh edition of this text are highlighted on page x of this *Instructor's Resource Manual*.

Part One.   Chapter Guides

For each chapter, the guide is divided into the following sections:

1. *Learning Objectives*—what students should learn in this chapter

2. *Focus*—an overview of the material in the chapter

3. *Lecture-Discussion Outline*—a detailed outline of the major points in the chapter

4. *Key Terms and Definitions*—important vocabulary used in the chapter

5. *Suggested Activities*—activities requiring out-of-class research

6. *Pages for Making Transparencies*—pages that can be made into transparencies and used with an overhead projector for instruction

Part Two.   Short-Answer Questions and Essay-Discussion Questions

Several different types of questions are provided for each chapter. Answers are given following each question.

1. *Short-Answer Questions*—questions requiring concise answers, along with sample responses

2. *Essay-Discussion Questions*—comprehensive questions for class discussion or for essay examinations, along with sample responses

Part Three.   Multiple-Choice Questions

There are two sets of multiple-choice test questions for each chapter. The multiple-choice questions are grouped together to make them easier to use. They are also available to instructors on a computer test bank.

Answers for multiple-choice questions are grouped together.

Part Four.   Additional Teaching Resources

Part Four contains information and professional resources for instruction. These include a suggested syllabus, a suggested assignment for the informal assessment of children, videotapes, learning disabilities organizations, and selected references and professional journals.

Teaching a preservice or an in-service course in learning disabilities can be an exciting, challenging, and rewarding experience. I hope that you have a successful adventure using *Learning Disabilities: Theories, Diagnosis, and Teaching Strategies*. I welcome your comments, criticisms, or suggestions. An instructor evaluation form is provided at the end of the book for this purpose.

Janet W. Lerner

PART ONE
Chapter Guides

CHAPTER 1

Learning Disabilities: A Field in Transition

Learning Objectives

1. Identify some accomplished people who have had severe difficulty in learning as children.

2. Recognize the common characteristics of learning disabilities.

3. Specify four age groupings of individuals with learning disabilities and the characteristics of each age group.

4. Recognize the cross-cultural nature of learning disabilities and the implications for culturally and linguistically diverse children.

5. List the common elements in the definitions of learning disabilities and the problems involved in each of these elements.

6. Describe the prevalence rates of learning disabilities and explain the reasons for an increase in the number of students identified as having learning disabilities.

7. Describe the trend in placements for children with learning disabilities and the importance of collaboration because of this trend.

8. Describe the various disciplines contributing to the field of learning disabilities.

Focus

This chapter serves as an introduction to the field of learning disabilities. It discusses the puzzle of learning disabilities, characteristics of learning disabilities, the age span and traits at different ages, the cross-cultural nature of learning disabilities, common elements in the definitions, the prevalence of learning disabilities, changing trends in placement (especially inclusion), collaboration, and disciplines that contribute to the field of learning disabilities.

Lecture-Discussion Outline

I. The enigma of learning disabilities. The puzzling condition of learning disabilities can affect many different areas of learning.

II. Some eminent people with learning disabilities. Many accomplished and successful people have learning disabilities.

III. Characteristics of learning disabilities.

   A. Diverse characteristics. Individuals with learning disabilities are a diverse group, and each individual displays different traits.

   B. More boys than girls are identified in the schools, but research suggests that there are many girls who are not identified.

   C. Multiple intelligences. Schools call upon linguistic and mathematics intelligences, but individuals with learning disabilities often have talents in other areas.

IV. The widening age span of the learning disabilities population. Four different age levels are considered, and each encounters different types of problems.

   A. Preschool level

   B. Elementary level

   C. Secondary level

   D. Adult years

V. The cross-cultural nature of learning disabilities. The condition of learning disabilities is universal, occurring across all cultures, languages, and economic classes. Some children in our schools who are culturally and linguistically diverse also have learning disabilities.

VI. Definitions of learning disabilities.

   A. The federal definition of learning disabilities in the reauthorization of the Individuals with Disabilities Education Act is widely used.

   B. There are other suggested definitions, including those of the Interagency Committee on Learning Disabilities and the National Joint Committee on Learning Disabilities.

   C. There is a need for several different definitions of learning disabilities.

VII. Common elements in the definitions. Even though there are several different definitions of learning disabilities, there are several common elements among them.

   A. Central nervous system dysfunction

   B. Uneven growth pattern and psychological processing differences

   C. Difficulty in academic and learning tasks

   D. Discrepancy between potential and achievement

   E. Exclusion of other causes

VIII. Prevalence of learning disabilities

    A. The number of students identified as having learning disabilities has increased over the years. About half of all students with disabilities are identified under the category of learning disabilities.

    B. The percentage of children and youth with learning disabilities in the United States is over 5 percent.

IX. Shifts in the settings for delivering services. A growing trend in placement is inclusion, in which children with learning disabilities receive instruction in the general education classroom.

X. Collaboration: the new role for learning disabilities teachers. General education teachers and special education teachers must learn to work together in a collaborative arrangement.

XI. Disciplines contributing to the study of learning disabilities. Many different disciplines contribute to the research, assessment, and treatment of learning disabilities.

    A. Education

    B. Psychology

    C. Language disciplines

    D. Medicine

    E. Other professions

Key Terms and Definitions

Students should take note of the following terms as they appear in this chapter. Students who have difficulty should refer to the glossary in Appendix E of the text or to the text page on which the term is discussed.

central nervous system dysfunction   A disorder in learning caused by an impairment in brain function.

current achievement level   A student's present stage of performance in an academic area.

heterogeneous   A term referring to students who exhibit a variety of characteristics, as opposed to a single set of characteristics. The population of students with learning disabilities is heterogeneous because individuals exhibit many different behaviors.

inclusion   The placement of children with disabilities in the general education classroom for instruction.

Individuals with Disabilities Education Act (IDEA)   A federal law to protect the rights of children and youth with disabilities. It was reauthorized in 1996.

Interagency Committee on Learning Disabilities   A committee commissioned by the U.S. Congress and made up of representatives from twelve agencies of the Department of Health and Human Services and the Department of Education to develop a federal definition of learning disabilities.

learning disabilities   A disorder in one or more of the basic psychological processes involved in understanding or using language, spoken or written, that may manifest itself in an imperfect ability to listen, speak, read, write, spell, or do mathematics calculations. The term includes such conditions as perceptual disabilities, brain injury, minimal brain dysfunction, and developmental aphasia. The term does not apply to children who have learning problems that are primarily the result of visual, hearing, or motor disabilities, of mental retardation, of emotional disturbance, or of environmental, cultural, or economic disadvantage. Individuals with learning disabilities encounter difficulty in one or more of seven areas: (1) receptive language, (2) expressive language, (3) basic reading skill, (4) reading comprehension, (5) written expression, (6) mathematics calculations, or (7) mathematics reasoning.

Multiple Intelligences   Various kinds of intelligences: verbal/linguistic, logical/mathematical, visual/spatial, musical/rhythmic, body/kinesthetic, intrapersonal, and interpersonal.

National Joint Committee on Learning Disabilities (NJCLD)   An organization of representatives from several organizations and disciplines involved with learning disabilities.

potential for learning   A term that refers to intellectual ability, whether measured by an intelligence test; a test of cognitive abilities, clinical judgment, or other means.

Public Law 94-142   The Education for All Handicapped Children Act, passed in 1975 and reauthorized in 1990.

Public Law 101-476   IDEA, passed by Congress in 1990. It updated PL94-142 and is to be reauthorized for implementation in 1997.

Severe discrepancy   A significant difference between a child's current achievement and intellectual potential.

Suggested Activities

The following activities can extend a student's experience with learning disabilities.

1. Read a biography of an individual who seems to have had learning disabilities as a child.

2. Interview a parent, a teacher, or an individual with a learning disability.

3. Read an article on learning disabilities and write a review.

4. Obtain definitions of learning disabilities used by various authors, school districts, state legislatures, and parent organizations.

5. Obtain copies of your state's laws on special education. How are children with learning disabilities identified?

6. Attend a meeting of an organization concerned with students with learning disabilities.

Pages for Making Transparencies

These pages can be transferred to transparencies for use with an overhead projector during class instruction.

1. Common Elements in the Definitions of Learning Disabilities

2. Multiple Intelligences (Figure 1.1)

3. Age Distribution of Students with Learning Disabilities (Figure 1.2)

4. Percentage of Students with Learning Disabilities in Enrolled School Population (Figure 1.3)

5. Percentage of Children with Disabilities Ages 6–17, School Year 1993–94 (Table 1.1)

6. Composition of Students with Disabilities (Figure 1.4)

COMMON ELEMENTS IN THE DEFINITIONS OF LEARNING DISABILITIES

- **Neurological dysfunction**

- **Uneven growth pattern**

- **Difficulty in academic and learning tasks**

- **Discrepancy between achievement and potential**

- **Exclusion of other causes**

Figure 1.1
Multiple Intelligences

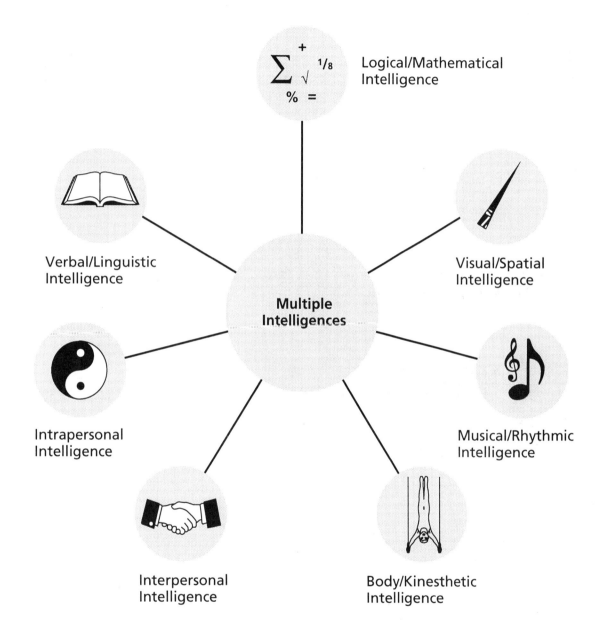

Figure 1.2
Age Distribution of Students with Learning Disabilities

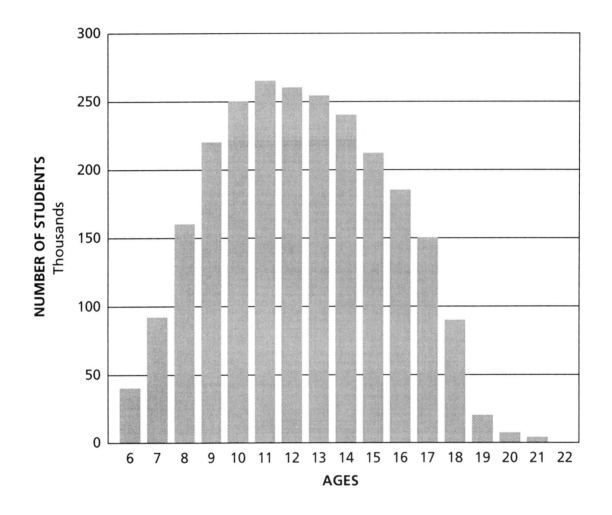

Source: From *To Assure the Free Appropriate Public Education of All Children with Disabilities.* Seventeenth Annual Report to Congress on the Implementation of the Individuals with Disabilities Education Act, by the U.S. Department of Education, 1995, Washington, DC: U.S. Government Printing Office.

Figure 1.3
Percentage of Students with Learning Disabilities in Enrolled School Population

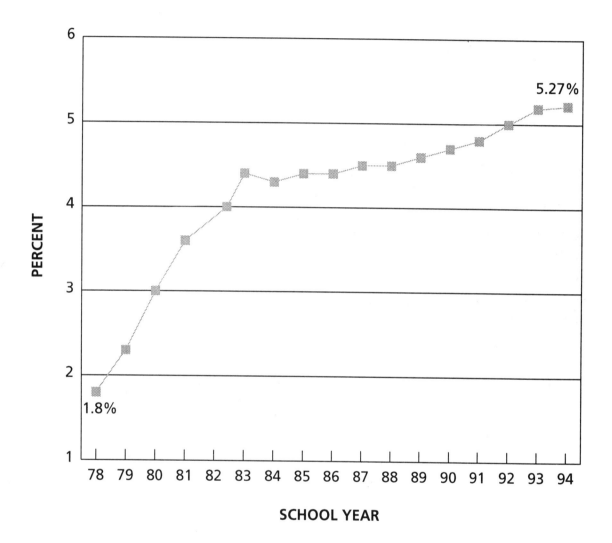

Table 1.1
Percentage of Children with Disabilities Ages 6–17, School Year 1993–94

CATEGORY OF DISABILITY	PERCENT OF ENROLLMENT	PERCENT OF ALL DISABILITIES
LEARNING DISABILITIES	5.27	51.1
SPEECH OR LANGUAGE DISABILITIES	2.28	22.1
MENTAL RETARDATION	1.11	10.8
SEVERE EMOTIONAL DISTURBANCE	.89	8.6
MULTIPLE DISABILITIES	.22	2.1
OTHER HEALTH IMPAIRED	.18	1.7
HEARING DISABILITIES	.14	1.3
ORTHOPEDIC DISABILITIES	.12	1.2
VISUAL DISABILITIES	.05	.5
AUTISM	.04	.4
TRAUMATIC BRAIN INJURY	.01	< .1
DEAF BLIND	< .01	< .1
TOTAL	10.31	100.0

Source: From *To Assure the Free Appropriate Public Education of All Children with Disabilities.* Seventeenth Annual Report to Congress on the Implementation of the Individuals with Disabilities Education Act, by the U.S. Department of Education, 1995, Washington, DC: U.S. Government Printing Office.

Figure 1.4
Composition of Students with Disabilities

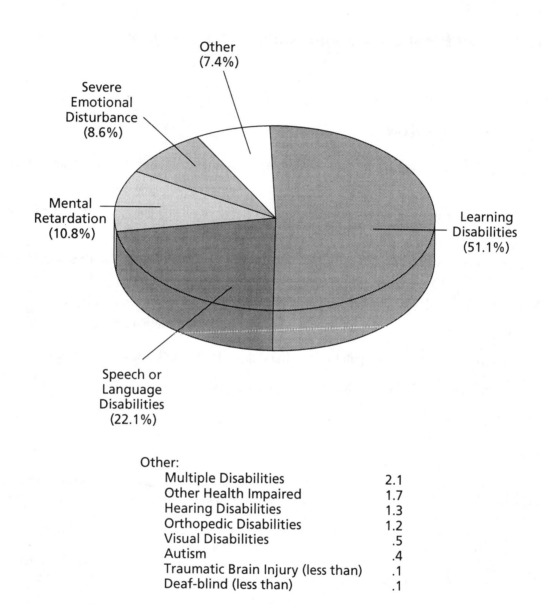

Other:

Multiple Disabilities	2.1
Other Health Impaired	1.7
Hearing Disabilities	1.3
Orthopedic Disabilities	1.2
Visual Disabilities	.5
Autism	.4
Traumatic Brain Injury (less than)	.1
Deaf-blind (less than)	.1

Source: From *To Assure the Free Appropriate Public Education of All Children with Disabilities.* Seventeenth Annual Report to Congress on the Implementation of the Individuals with Disabilities Education Act, by the U.S. Department of Education, 1995, Washington, DC: U.S. Government Printing Office.

CHAPTER 2
Historical Perspectives and Emerging Directions

Learning Objectives

1. Describe the growth of the field of learning disabilities, highlighting the various historical phases.

2. Know the major milestones, laws, and events that have shaped our understanding of learning disabilities.

3. Discuss the changes in placements for providing services and educating students with learning disabilities, including the inclusion movement, and how these placements affect students with learning disabilities.

4. Describe the emerging directions of the current phase of learning disabilities.

5. Describe the value of computers for instructing students with learning disabilities.

6. Explain the philosophy of the full inclusion movement.

Focus

The relatively short history of the field of learning disabilities is traced in this chapter. The major phases of its development are the *foundation phase,* the *transition phase,* the *integration phase,* and the *contemporary phase.* The foundation phase (1800–1930) was an early era of scientific research on the brain and its disorders. In the transition phase (1930–1960), the focus shifted to clinical studies of children who had learning difficulties and who were identified as brain-injured. Alfred Strauss conducted pioneering work with children he called *brain-injured.* The integration phase (1960–1980) was a period of implementation of school programs across the nation. William Cruickshank
applied the Strauss-Lehtinen concepts in public school settings. In the current phase (1980 to the present), there are many new concerns: inclusion, collaboration, cultural and linguistic diversity, attention deficit disorders, the educational reform movement, Goals 2000, and computer technology.

Objections to Strauss's term *brain-injured children* led to the use of other terms to describe these children. The suggested terms included *Strauss syndrome, minimal brain dysfunction,* and finally *learning disabilities.*

Lecture-Discussion Outline

I. The foundation phase: brain research. The early research on functions and dysfunctions of the brain was conducted in the period of 1800–1930. Researchers studied the brains of people who had lost some function because of brain damage and subsequently had died. This information provided the foundation for the field of learning disabilities.

II. The transition phase: clinical study of children. During this period (1930–1960), the focus shifted to the study of children thought to have suffered brain damage that resulted in learning difficulties.

   A. The brain-injured child

   B. Search for other terminology

   C. Learning disabilities

III. The integration phase: rapid expansion of school programs. During this period (1960–1980), public school programs were implemented across the country for students with learning disabilities.

   A. Rapid growth of public school learning disabilities programs

   B. Increased legislative support for teacher training

   C. Special education laws

IV. The current phase: emerging directions. During this period, 1980 to the present, the field of learning disabilities has been expanding in many directions.

   A. The inclusion movement

   B. Cultural and linguistic diversity

   C. Attention deficit disorders

   D. The education reform movement

   E. Using computer technology

   F. Learning disabilities organizations

   G. Journals and periodicals

Key Terms and Definitions

Students should take note of the following terms as they appear in this chapter. Students who have difficulty should refer to the glossary in Appendix E of the text or to the text page on which the term is discussed.

aphasia   Impairment of the ability to use or understand oral language, usually associated with an injury or abnormality of the speech centers of the brain. Several classifications are used, including expressive aphasia, receptive aphasia, developmental aphasia, and acquired aphasia.

may or may not

attention deficit disorder (ADD)   Difficulty in concentrating and staying on task. It may or may not be accompanied by hyperactivity. This is the term used by the U.S. Department of Education.

attention deficit hyperactivity disorder (ADHD)   Difficulty in concentrating and staying on task, accompanied by hyperactivity. This criteria for ADHD are given in the *Diagnostic and Statistical Manual of Mental Disorders,* fourth edition (DSM-IV). It is the term used by psychiatrists and psychologists to refer to ADD.

brain-injured child   A child who before, during, or after birth has received an injury to or suffered an infection of the brain. As a result of such organic impairment, there are disturbances that prevent or impede the normal learning process.

collaboration   The process of working together that is used by regular and general education teachers as they develop a plan for a child.

conceptual disorders   Difficulty in thinking and organizing thoughts.

cultural and linguistic diversity   Representation by many different cultures and language groups.

distractibility   The tendency to attend to irrelevant external stimuli, which detracts from attending to the task at hand.

educational reform movement   A general movement throughout the United States to improve education in schools. As a result of educational reform, curriculum requirements in high schools have become more stringent.

Individuals with Disabilities Education Act (IDEA)   The special education law ensuring that students with disabilities have a free, appropriate, public education.

minimal brain dysfunction   A mild or minimal neurological abnormality that causes learning difficulties in the student.

perceptual disorder   A disturbance in the ability to perceive objects, relations, or qualities; difficulty in the interpretation of sensory stimulation.

perseveration   The behavior of being locked into continually performing an action.

soft neurological signs   Minimal or subtle neurological deviations that some neurologists use as indicators of mild neurological dysfunction.

Suggested Activities

1. Read a selection by a writer from one of the major periods: the foundation phase, the transition phase, the integration phase, or the contemporary phase. Write a brief report on your reaction.

2. Discuss the relation of cultural and linguistic diversity to learning disabilities. Interview a teacher who teaches culturally and linguistically diverse children who have learning disabilities.

3. Locate the parent group for children with learning disabilities in your community. You might find a group affiliated with the Learning Disabilities Association (LDA). (See addresses in Appendix D.) Attend a meeting and write a brief report on your reaction.

4. Observe a learning disabilities student using a computer program and interview the student about his or her reaction to computers.

5. Attend a meeting in your community on one of the emerging directions in the field of learning disabilities. Write a report on the meeting.

Pages for Making Transparencies

These pages can be transferred to transparencies for use with an overhead projector during class instruction.

1. Major Phases in the Field of Learning Disabilities

2. Perceptual Confusion (Figure 2.1)

3. A young girl or an old woman? (Figure 2.2)

4. Current Phase: Emerging Directions

5. National Education Goals for the Year 2,000

MAJOR PHASES IN THE FIELD OF LEARNING DISABILITIES

1. Foundation phase: 1800–1930
   Brain research

2. Transition phase: 1930–1960
   Clinical study of children

3. Integration phase: 1960–1980
   School programs

4. Current phase: 1980–present
   Emerging Directions

Figure 2.1
Perceptual Confusion

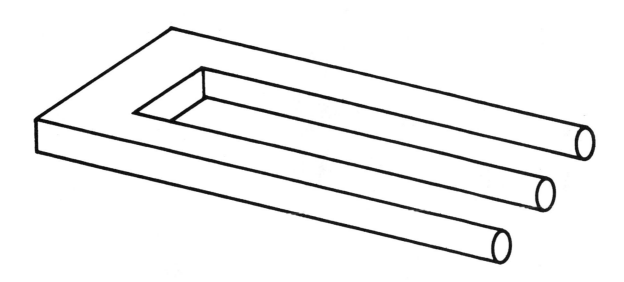

Figure 2.2
Do you see a young girl or an old woman in this picture?

CURRENT PHASE: EMERGING DIRECTIONS

- **Inclusion**

- **Collaboration**

- **Cultural and linguistic diversity**

- **Attention deficit disorders (ADDs)**

- **Education reform movement**

- **Goals 2000: Educate America Act**

- **Computer technology**

National Education Goals for the Year 2000

1. All children in America will start school ready to learn.

2. The high school graduation rate will increase to at least 90 percent.

3. American students in grades 4, 8, and 12 will demonstrate competencies in subject matter.

4. U.S. students will be first in the world in science and mathematics achievement.

5. Teachers will have the knowledge and skills to teach students for the next century.

6. Every adult will be literate and will possess the knowledge and skills to compete in a global economy.

7. Every school in America will be free of drugs, violence, firearms, and alcohol and will have a disciplined environment.

8. Every school will promote parental involvement.

CHAPTER 3
Assessment

Learning Objectives

1. Describe how assessment and teaching constitute an interrelated process.

A 2. Describe the uses of assessment.

A 3. Know the models of traditional assessment and alternative assessment.

A 4. Describe the effects of the Individuals with Disabilities Education Act (IDEA) on the assessment process.

A 5. Know the procedural safeguards that protect the rights of students with disabilities.

A 6. Know the six stages of the assessment/teaching process.

7. Identify and give an example of the four methods of obtaining assessment information.

8. Describe the ways the schools use discrepancy formulas to determine eligibility for learning disabilities services.

Focus

This chapter looks at assessment procedures. Assessment is used for screening, referral, classification, instructional planning, and monitoring of student progress.

There are two different models of assessment. Traditional assessment uses standardized norm-referenced tests. Alternative assessment uses informal methods, which are based on what the student does in the curriculum.

The individualized education program (IEP) is part of the assessment process. There are six phases of the IEP: (1) prereferral, (2) referral and initial planning, (3) multidisciplinary evaluation, (4) the case conference, (5) teaching to implement the IEP plan, and (6) review and monitoring of student progress.

The participants in the case conference, or the IEP meeting, and the contents of the IEP itself are designated in the Individuals with Disabilities Education Act (IDEA). Among the issues that must be addressed are (1) the student's present level of educational performance, (2) the need for additional information, (3) the discrepancy between potential and achievement, (4) whether the student has learning disabilities, (5) annual goals and short-term objectives, (6) services to be provided, (7) how progress will be measured, and (8) a plan for teaching.

Assessment information is obtained through (1) case history and interview, (2) observations, (3) informal measures, and (4) formal standardized tests.

Eligibility criteria are used to determine whether the student's problem warrants placement in the school's learning disabilities program. There is some criticism of the use of IQ scores as the only measure of potential for learning.

Lecture-Discussion Outline

[handwritten notes: Assessment defined - collecting info on a student for the purposes of making decisions about that student]

[handwritten: A.I. Major reasons for assessment in Special Ed ① Classification ② Planning Instruction]

I. Uses of assessment information. Assessment information has several different uses: screening for students who may have problems, making a referral for a special education evaluation, classifying the nature of the student's disability, making plans for teaching a student, and monitoring the progress made by the student.

[handwritten margin: Uses or Purposes]

A. Screening *[handwritten: Detecting students within a large group who may need a more comprehensive evaluation]*

B. Referral *[handwritten: Requesting a further evaluation of a student for special education services]*

C. Classification *[handwritten: Determining a student's eligibility for special ed. services]*

D. Instructional planning *[handwritten: Using the assessment information in making of educational plans]*

E. Monitoring pupil progress *[handwritten: Reviewing a student's achievement + gains]*

II. Models of assessment. Assessment procedures can follow different assessment models. Traditional assessment uses standardized tests. Alternative assessment uses methods based on what students learn in the classroom, such as authentic and performance assessment, portfolio assessment, and dynamic assessment.

[handwritten margin: Models & Give Examples]

A. Traditional assessment *[handwritten: Standardized Tests]*

B. Alternative Assessment *[handwritten: Authentic, Performance, Portfolio, Dynamic]*

III. The influence of the law on the assessment process. The law (IDEA) regulates much of the assessment process, especially the individualized education program and the procedural safeguards to protect the student's rights.

A. The individualized education program (IEP) as an assessment/teaching process

[handwritten: i. Written plan for a particular student]

[handwritten: 2. Management tool for entire assessment-teaching process - appropriate education is planned, executed, monitored]

B. Procedural safeguards

[handwritten margin: Transparency]

IV. Stages of the assessment/teaching process. There are different stages of the assessment process, including prereferral, referral, assessment and developing the IEP, instruction, and review.

[handwritten margin: Transparency]

A. Prereferral

B. Referral and initial planning

C. Case conference (or IEP meeting)—writing the IEP

D. Implementation of the teaching plan

E. Review and monitoring of student progress

Make transparency   V. Assessment decisions. A number of different decisions <u>must</u> be made during the assessment. Many of these are determined by the law (IDEA). *Must be included, mandated by law*

IEP   A.1 Determining present levels of performance

B.2 Gathering additional information

C.3 Measuring discrepancy

D.4 Determining eligibility

IEP   E.5 Setting annual goals

IEP   F.6 Deciding on services

G.7 Developing a teaching plan

IEP   H.8 Monitoring progress

VI. Obtaining assessment information. Four ways of obtaining information about the student are using the case history, observing the student in the class, using informal measures, and using *put on board* standardized tests.

A. Case history

B. Observation

C. Informal measures

D. Formal standardized tests

Study WISC to become familiar

VII. Eligibility criteria. Eligibility criteria help to determine if the student has learning disabilities and is eligible for services within the schools. Different methods for determining this eligibility are discussed here.

A. Methods for determining the eligibility score

B. Combining qualitative and quantitative data

VIII. Testing pressures in the schools. There is a great deal of pressure and concern in the schools about students' test scores.

IX. Case Study: Rita G.—Part I. An extended case study is begun here. The case continues into the next two chapters.

Key Terms and Definitions

Students should take note of the following terms as they appear in this chapter. Students who have difficulty should refer to the glossary in Appendix E of the text or to the text page on which the term is discussed.

annual goals General estimates of what the student will achieve in one year. These goals should represent the most essential needs of the student. Annual goals are part of the written individualized education program.

alternative assessment Alternative assessment assesses the child in the natural setting, uses the school curriculum, and capitalizes on what the student actually does in the classroom.

authentic assessment Assessment that makes realistic demands and that is set in real-life contexts, such as at school or at home.

case history A compilation of the student's background, development, and other information. Case history information is usually obtained from parents and the student's school and medical histories. Often this information is obtained by interview.

criterion-referenced tests Tests that measure abilities in specific tasks (rather than tests that compare a student to others in a norm group).

curriculum-based assessment Assessment designed to measure student performance on the student's curriculum activities and materials. The student's performance on an academic task is repeatedly measured and charted to assess changes in learning performance.

diagnostic teaching Teaching designed for the purpose of gathering further information about a student.

discrepancy score Quantitative data that measure the gap between performance and potential.

dynamic assessment Evaluation of a student by noting how that student performs during instruction in an interactive teaching environment.

eligibility criteria Standards for determining whether a student can be classified as having learning disabilities and will be eligible for learning disabilities services.

formal standardized tests Commercially prepared tests that have been used with and standardized on large groups of students. Manuals that accompany the tests provide derived scores on student performance, such as grade scores, age scores, percentiles, and standard scores.

individualized education program (IEP) The written plan for the education of an individual student with learning disabilities. The plan must meet requirements specified in the rules and regulations of the Individuals with Disabilities Education Act.

informal assessment measures Ways of evaluating performance that are not formal standardized tests. These can include teacher-made tests, diagnostic teaching, commercial nonstandardized tests, curriculum-based assessment, and so on.

multidisciplinary evaluation   The assessment process in which specialists from several disciplines evaluate a child and coordinate their findings.

norm-referenced tests   Standardized tests that compare a child's performance to that of other children of the same age.

observation   Careful watching of a student's behavior, usually in the classroom setting.

performance assessment   A method of assessing students by observing and assessing what they actually do in the classroom.

portfolio assessment   A method of evaluating student progress by analyzing samples of the student's classroom work.

prereferral activities   Preventive procedures taken prior to referral for special education evaluation and intended to help regular teachers work more successfully with the child in the regular classroom.

present levels of educational performance   The levels at which the student is currently achieving in various developmental and academic areas. The written individualized education program must include a statement of the child's present levels of educational performance.

procedural safeguards   Regulations in federal law that are designed to protect the rights of students with learning disabilities and their families.

rating scales   A ranking of student behavior as judged by a parent, teacher, or other informant.

referral   The initial request to consider a student for a special education evaluation.

short-term instructional objectives   Specific steps to be accomplished to reach the annual goal written in the individualized education program.

test-wiseness   Knowledge skills for effective test taking.

traditional assessment   An evaluation procedure that measures students with standard norm-referenced tests.

Suggested Activities

1. Observe an evaluation being conducted in a public school or clinic. If a staff meeting is held following the assessment, ask to observe it as well. Keep a record of the tests that are used, other kinds of data obtained, reactions of the child, interaction and communication of the staff, and decisions made.

2. Administer to a student the motor test (described in Chapter 3), the informal word-recognition test, and others. Analyze the results.

3. Design an informal test of one area (such as motor development, language, reading, or arithmetic). Try it out on students of various ages.

4. Read a research report on a standardized test such as the WISC III, Key Math—Revised; the Woodcock-Johnson Psychoeducational Battery—Revised; or the Brigance Comprehensive Inventory of Basic Skills, a reading test. Write a review of the test.

5. Role-play a parent interview, with students playing the interviewer and the child's mother and father.

Pages for Making Transparencies

These pages can be transferred to transparencies and used with an overhead projector during class instruction.

1. Alternative or Informal Assessment

2. Stages of the IEP Process (Figure 3.1)

3. Procedural Safeguards

4. Contents of the IEP

5. Methods of Obtaining Assessment Information

6. A Curriculum-Based Assessment Chart Monitoring an Individual Student's Progress (Figure 3.4)

ALTERNATIVE OR INFORMAL ASSESSMENT

- **Authentic/performance assessment**

- **Teacher-made tests**

- **Portfolio assessment**

- **Dynamic assessment**

- **Diagnostic teaching**

- **Curriculum-based assessment**

- **Rating scales**

- **Criterion-referenced tests**

Figure 3.1
Stages of the IEP Process

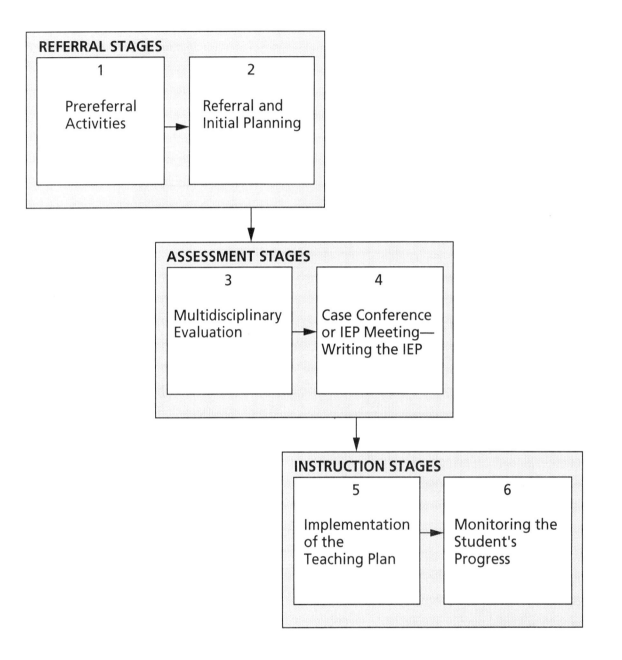

Source: From *Cases in Learning and Behavior Problems: A Guide to Individualized Education Programs,* by J. Lerner, D. Dawson, and L. Horvath, 1980, Salem, WI: Sheffield Publishing Co., p. 3.

PROCEDURAL SAFEGUARDS

1. Parents must consent in writing to the evaluation.

2. Tests must be conducted in the student's native language and reported in the parents' native language.

3. Tests must be free of racial and cultural bias.

4. Parents have the right to see all information.

5. The student and the parents have the right to impartial due process procedures.

6. Confidentiality is protected.

7. No single test can be used.

CONTENTS OF THE IEP

1. **Present level of educational performance**

2. **Annual goals and short-term objectives**

3. **Special education and related services; extent to which child will be able to participate in regular education programs**

4. **Projected date of initiation of services; anticipated duration of services**

5. **Objective criteria and evaluation procedures; schedule of determining, at least annually, if short-term objectives are met**

METHODS OF OBTAINING ASSESSMENT INFORMATION

- ## Case history/interview

- ## Observation

- ## Informal measures

- ## Formal tests

Figure 3.4
A Curriculum-Based Assessment Chart Monitoring an Individual Student's Progress

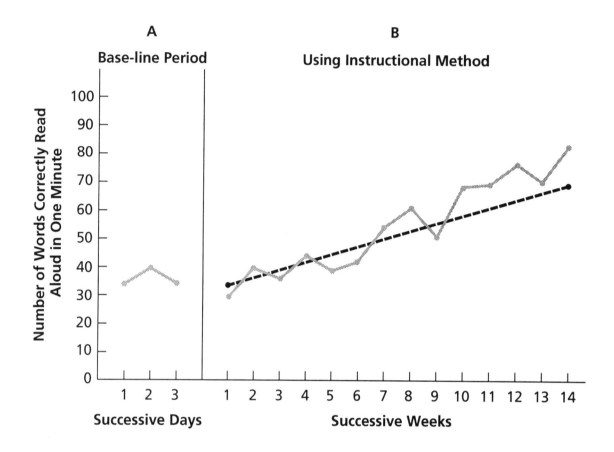

CHAPTER 4
Clinical Teaching

Learning Objectives

1. Specify the steps in the clinical teaching cycle.

2. Identify the different environments of the student's ecological system and recognize how the interactions of the environmental systems affect the student.

3. Classify teaching methods according to analysis of the student, analysis of content, and analysis of environmental conditions.

4. Identify modifications and adjustments the clinical teacher may make in the variables of difficulty level, space, time, language, and interpersonal relationships.

5. Describe ways to establish and maintain the student's self-esteem and motivation.

6. Describe the elements of task analysis.

Focus

Clinical teaching differs from regular teaching in that it tailors learning experiences to the unique needs of the individual student. Clinical teaching requires continual decision making and can be viewed as a cycle whose stages are (1) assessment, (2) planning, (3) implementation, and (4) evaluation, leading to (5) a modification of the diagnosis and then new planning.

It is also important to consider the ecological systems in which the students live and learn. These include the home environment, school environment, social environment, and cultural environment.

The classification of remedial approaches includes the following categories: analysis of the student (cognitive processing, stages of child development, and learning strategies approaches); analysis of the curriculum (mastery learning, specialized techniques, and materials approaches); and analysis of environmental conditions (behavioral, psychotherapeutic, and pedagogical approaches).

Some variables that interfere with teaching cannot be modified by clinical teaching. Therefore, learning disabilities teachers should focus on those areas that can be changed or manipulated, including (1) difficulty level, (2) space, (3) time, (4) language, and (6) interpersonal relationships.

Teaching can build a student's self-esteem and motivation. The teacher can build a relationship with the student by establishing rapport, sharing responsibility, structuring lessons, providing success, and creating interest.

Current trends for instruction include accommodations in the general education classroom, effective teaching procedures, promotion of active learning, reciprocal teaching, learning strategies instruction, and collaboration between general education and special education teachers.

Task analysis is used to provide further information through an analysis of the curriculum or content to be learned.

Lecture-Discussion Outline

I. Clinical teaching cycle

II. Ecological considerations. The ecological systems are the environments in which the student lives and learns.

    A. Home environment

    B. School environment

    C. Social environment

    D. Cultural and language environment

III. Classification of teaching methods. For purposes of categorization, the many different teaching methodologies are grouped as methods that analyze the student, methods that analyze the curriculum or content to be taught, and methods that analyze the environment.

    A. Analysis of the student

        1. Cognitive processing approach

        2. Stages of child development approach

        3. Learning strategies approach

    B. Analysis of the curriculum

        1. Mastery learning approach

        2. Specialized techniques approach

        3. Materials approach

    C. Analysis of the environment

        1. Behavioral approach

        2. Psychotherapeutic approach

        3. Pedagogical approach

    D. Implications of the classification system

IV. Controlling instructional variables in clinical teaching. Teachers can do little about many variables, but certain ones can be modified, including difficulty level, space, time, language, and interpersonal relationships.

    A. Adjusting the difficulty level of the work

    B. Changing the space in which the student works

    C. Changing the time limits given to the student

    D. Modifying the language used with the student

    E. Establishing interpersonal relationships

V. Building self-esteem and motivation. The relationship between teacher and student is extremely important, and ways to build this relationship are described in this section.

    A. Building rapport between the student and the teacher

    B. Sharing responsibility between the student and teacher in planning lessons

    C. Providing structure to the student's life

    D. Establishing the teacher's sincerity

    E. Building successful experiences

    F. Developing interest and motivation

VI. Current trends for instruction

    A. Accommodations for students with learning disabilities in the general education classroom

    B. Effective teaching practices

    C. Promoting active learning

    D. Reciprocal teaching

    E. Learning strategies instruction

    F. Collaboration between general and special educators

VII. Task analysis. Task analysis is a way of analyzing the task the student is expected to learn.

VIII. Case Study: Rita G.—Part II. This is the second part of the extended case study that was begun in Chapter 3.

Key Terms and Definitions

Students should take note of the following terms as they appear in this chapter. Students who have difficulty should refer to the glossary in Appendix E of the text or to the text page on which the term is discussed.

behavioral approach   An approach to teaching that concentrates on the sequence of learning skills and on changing a child's behavior through contingencies (such as reward and punishment).

bibliotherapy   A technique of using characters in books to help children work through personal problems.

clinical teaching   A method of teaching that tailors learning experiences to the unique needs of a particular child.

cognitive processing   The mental processing involved in thinking and learning, such as perception, memory, language, attention, concept formation, and problem solving.

collaboration   Two or more people working together to find solutions to mutual problems.

direct instruction   A method associated with behavioral theories of instruction. The focus is directly on the curriculum or task to be taught and the steps needed to learn that task.

ecological system   The several environments within which an individual lives and grows, including home and school, as well as social and cultural environments.

learning strategies approach   A series of methods to help students direct their own learning, focusing on how students learn rather than on what they learn.

mastery learning   An approach that is compatible with instructional methods advocated by behavioral psychologists. It is based on sequential steps. Instructional programs using this approach are highly structured and carefully sequenced. They require very directive teaching.

pedagogy   The art of teaching.

psychological processing disorders   A phrase in the federal definition of learning disabilities that refer to disabilities in visual or auditory perception, memory, or language.

psychotherapeutic approach   An approach to teaching that concentrates on the student's feelings and relationship with the teacher.

rapport   A close relationship between teacher and child that is based on total acceptance of the child as a human being worthy of respect.

reasonable accommodations   Modifications that classroom teachers can make for students with disabilities in the general education classroom. Complies with Section 504 of the Rehabilitation Act of 1973.

reciprocal teaching   A method of teaching through a social interactive dialogue between teacher and student, which emphasizes the development of thinking processes.

self-esteem   Feelings of self-worth, self-confidence, and self-concept that provide an experience of success.

skills sequence   The sequence of steps involved in learning a task.

task analysis   An approach to teaching that analyzes an activity by breaking it down into a sequence of steps.

Suggested Activities

1. Select a page from the workbook accompanying a basal reader series. Analyze the task the student is supposed to perform from the student's perspective. What abilities are needed to understand the task? What abilities are needed to perform the task? Is it a verbal or nonverbal task, a social or nonsocial task?

2. Select a single task (such as buttoning a button) and analyze it as a sequence of sequential skills. What individual steps must be taken to perform the task? Teach someone to perform the task by following the steps you have outlined.

3. Observe three teaching methods being used in a classroom. Describe each method and classify it within the classification system of teaching approaches.

4. Observe a student with learning disabilities in a classroom setting. Analyze how the student's home, school, and social and cultural environments affect his or her learning.

Pages for Making Transparencies

These pages can be transferred to transparencies for use with an overhead projector during class instruction.

1. The Five Phases of the Clinical Teaching Cycle (Figure 4.1)

2. A Classification of Teaching Methods (Figure 4.2)

3. Controlling Instructional Variables

4. Building Self-Esteem

5. Current Trends for Instruction

6. Flow Chart Showing the Relationship Between the Provisions of IDEA and Section 504 of the Rehabilitation Act (Figure 4.4)

Figure 4.1
The Five Phases of the Clinical Teaching Cycle

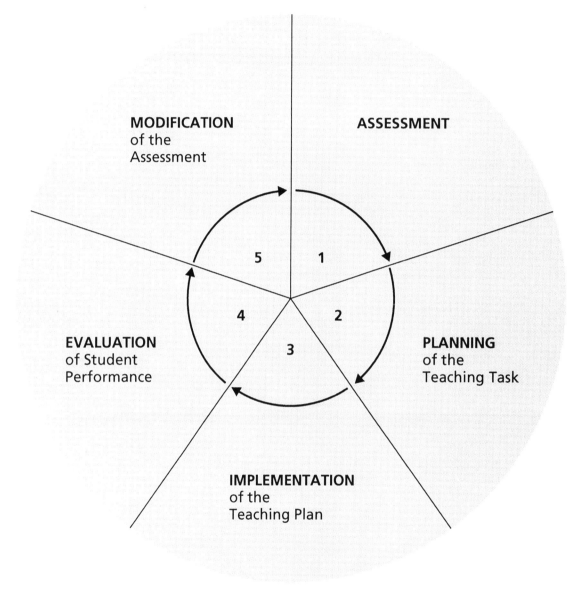

Figure 4.2
A Classification of Teaching Methods

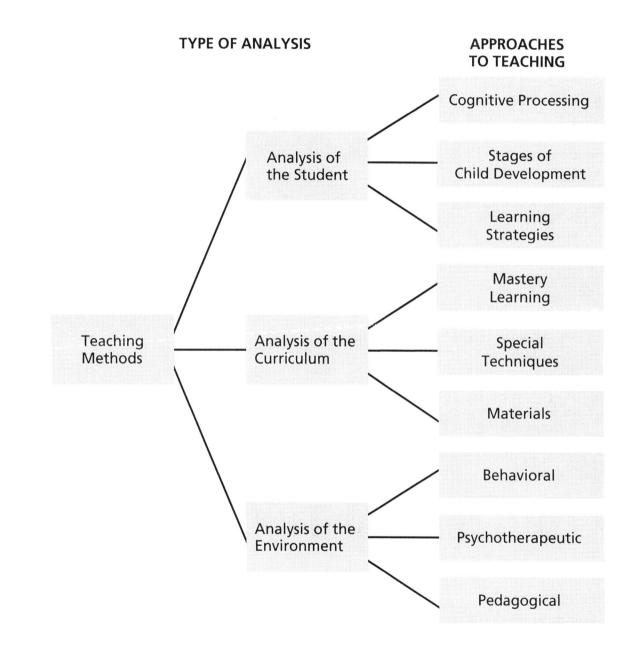

CONTROLLING INSTRUCTIONAL VARIABLES

- **Difficulty level**

- **Space**

- **Time**

- **Language**

- **Interpersonal relationships**

BUILDING SELF-ESTEEM

- ## Establishing rapport

- ## Sharing responsibility

- ## Providing structure

- ## Conveying sincerity

- ## Indicating success

- ## Capitalizing on interests

CURRENT TRENDS FOR INSTRUCTION

- **Accommodations in the general education classroom**

- **Effective teaching practices**

- **Active learning**

- **Reciprocal teaching**

- **Learning strategies**

- **Collaboration between general education and special education teachers**

Figure 4.4
Flow Chart Showing the Relationship Between the Provisions of IDEA and Section 504 of the Rehabilitation Act

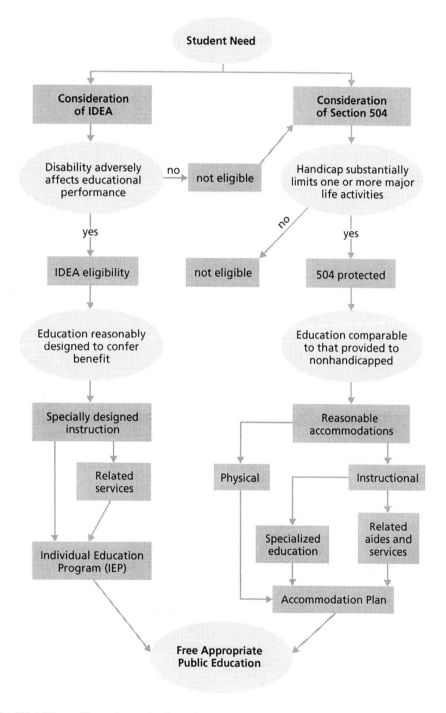

Source: IDEA/504 Flow Chart from *Student Access: A Resource Guide for Educators,* 1992. Reprinted by permission.

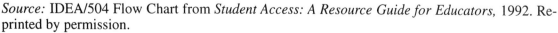

CHAPTER 5

Systems for Delivering Educational Services

Learning Objectives

1. Describe the features of the Individuals with Disabilities Education Act (IDEA) that pertain to placement or the delivery of education services, including the continuum of alternative placements and the least restrictive environment.

2. Discuss the advantages and disadvantages of the various placement options for students with learning disabilities, ranging from the most restrictive to the least restrictive option.

3. Describe the differences among some of the placement options, such as inclusion, full inclusion, mainstreaming, and the regular education initiative.

4. Describe the various roles of the learning disabilities teacher in specific situations.

5. Know activities to promote collaboration between general education and special education teachers.

6. Describe methods and programs for working with parents. Relate the advantages of parent education groups.

Focus

This chapter examines topics related to placement and provision of services.

Important concepts regarding the placement of students in the schools and how services are delivered to them stem from the Individuals with Disabilities Education Act (IDEA) and the state counterparts of this law. Two important features of the law are *the continuum of alternative placements* and *the least restrictive environment.* Mainstreaming and the regular education initiative are also important considerations.

Alternative placements include general education classrooms, resource rooms, separate classes, separate schools, and residential schools, hospitals, homebound instruction, and one-to-one instruction.

As students with learning disabilities are increasingly placed in general education classrooms, it is important to promote partnerships between general and special educators.

In today's schools, the learning disabilities teacher has an expanding role. This includes the technical and professional competencies needed for assessment and teaching, and skills in human relations needed to engage in working with others.

The family system concept is that what happens to one member of a family affects all members of the family. Parents often go through a mourning process as they accept that their child has learning disabilities.

The parent-school relationship is particularly important for guiding parents of learning disabled students. This includes parent conferences, counseling, and parent education groups.

Lecture-Discussion Outline

I. Important concepts for placement or delivery of special education services. Legislation in the Individuals with Disabilities Education Act requires adherence to features related to the placement of students for services: the continuum of alternative placements and the least restrictive environment. Recent placement options focus on integrating general and special education: inclusion, mainstreaming, and the regular education initiative. Several cautions about inclusion for all students with learning disabilities are important to consider.

   A. Continuum of alternative placements

   B. Least restrictive environment

   C. Integrating general and special education

   D. Responsible placement practices

II. Placement options. Most students with learning disabilities are in the resource room, the general education classroom, or separate classes. Other placements are separate schools and residential schools.

   A. Current education placements of students with learning disabilities

   B. General education classroom

   C. Resource room

   D. Separate classes

   E. Separate schools

   F. Residential schools

   G. Other placement considerations

III. It is important to promote partnerships between general and special educators.

   A. Peer tutoring

   B. Collaboration

   C. Co-teaching

   D. Cooperative Learning

IV. Competencies for learning disabilities teachers. The roles and responsibilities of learning disabilities teachers are expanding. In addition to the competencies in professional knowledge and skills, learning disabilities teachers need human relationship competencies. Suggested competencies for collaboration are provided.

A. Professional knowledge and skills

B. Human relationship abilities

V. The parent-school relationship. Schools are recognizing the important role of parents in the child's school learning. Parents must learn how to cope with a child with learning disabilities and may need the help of support groups and other professionals.

A.   The family system

B.   Stages of acceptance

C.   Parent support groups and family counseling

D.   Parent-teacher conferences

E.   Suggestions for parents

VI. Case Study: Rita G.—Part III. This is the third and final part of the case study begun in Chapter 3.

Key Terms and Definitions

Students should take note of the following terms as they appear in this chapter. Students who have difficulty should refer to the glossary in Appendix E of the text or to the text page on which the term is discussed.

collaboration   Two or more people working together to find solutions to mutual problems.

continuum of alternative placements   An array of different placements that should be available in a school system to meet the varied needs of students with disabilities.

co-teaching   A form of partnership between regular and special education teachers in which both share the teaching of a diverse group of students in one space.

full inclusion   The policy of placing and instructing all children, including all categories of disability and levels of severity, in their neighborhood school and the general education classroom.

general education classroom   The class in which most students in school receive instruction.

least restrictive environment   The term referring to the placement of students with learning disabilities, to the extent appropriate, in settings with students who do not have any disabilities.

mainstreaming   Placing children with disabilities in the regular classroom.

one-to-one instruction   Teaching with one teacher and one student.

parent support groups   Small groups of parents who meet to obtain information about their children with disabilities and to discuss common problems.

peer tutoring   A method of instruction in which the student is taught by peers or classmates.

placement   The selection of the appropriate setting for teaching a child.

regular education initiative (REI)   A proposal advanced by the Office of Special Education and Rehabilitation Services (OSERS) that students with many types of learning problems and low achievers can be served effectively through the general education classroom.

residential facility (school)   An educational institution in which students live away from home and receive their education. A residential school may be sponsored by a government agency or may be privately managed.

resource room   A special instructional setting, usually a room within a school. In this room, small groups of children meet with a special education teacher for special instruction for a portion of the day. Children usually spend the remainder of the day in their regular classrooms.

separate class   A special class for children with disabilities, taught by a teacher with special training. Children in a special class usually spend most of the day in this setting.

separate school   A school for students with learning disabilities that students attend during the day. They return home after school.

stages of acceptance   The different emotions parents go through when they learn they have a child with disabilities.

Suggested Activities

1. Talk with the special education teacher in a nearby school district and discuss the placements available. Into which of the categories described in this chapter do the available services fall?

2. Select one of the placements. Research its advantages and disadvantages.

3. Investigate the placements mandated or suggested for students with learning disabilities by your state laws, the state's education agency, and your local school district.

4. Read an article on co-teaching or collaboration in special education. Describe activities that can be used by the learning disabilities teacher to promote the partnership between regular and special educators.

Pages for Making Transparencies

These pages can be transferred to transparencies for use with an overhead projector during class instruction.

1. Continuum of Alternative Placements

2. A Model of the Continuum of Alternative Placements (Figure 5.1)

3. Placement of Students with Learning Disabilities (Figure 5.2)

4. Collaboration

5. Stages of Parent Reaction

CONTINUUM OF ALTERNATIVE PLACEMENTS

- **General education classroom**

- **Resource room**

- **Separate class**

- **Separate school**

- **Residential school/hospital facility**

Figure 5.1
A Model of the Continuum of Alternative Placements

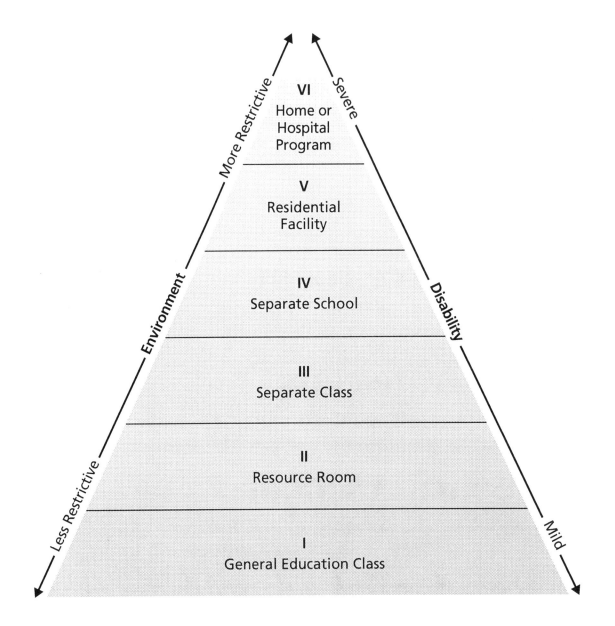

Figure 5.2
Placement of Students with Learning Disabilities

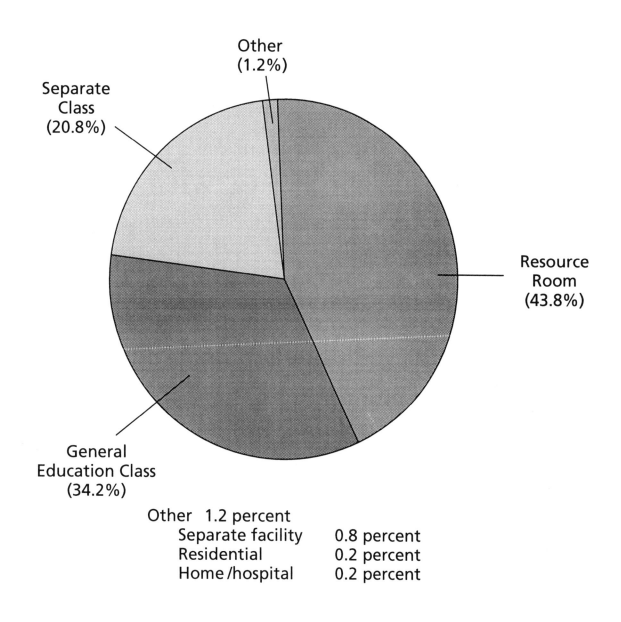

Other
(1.2%)

Separate
Class
(20.8%)

Resource
Room
(43.8%)

General
Education Class
(34.2%)

Other 1.2 percent
    Separate facility   0.8 percent
    Residential   0.2 percent
    Home /hospital   0.2 percent

Source: From *To Assure the Free Appropriate Public Education of All Children with Disabilities.*
Seventeenth Annual Report to Congress on the Implementation of the Individuals with Disabilities
Act, by the U.S. Department of Education, 1995, Washington, DC: U.S. Government Printing
Office.

COLLABORATION

- **Assist in all phases of instruction**

- **Help regular teacher with modifications**

- **Work with parents, administrators, support staff**

- **Give direct instruction in regular class**

- **Implement IEP with classroom teachers**

- **Work with vocational teachers and employers**

STAGES OF PARENT REACTION

- **Shock**

- **Disbelief**

- **Anger**

- **Bargaining**

- **Depression**

- **Acceptance**

CHAPTER 6

Theories of Learning: Implications for Learning Disabilities

Learning Objectives

1. Discuss the role of theory in planning services for students with learning disabilities.

2. Know the implications of developmental psychology for learning disabilities.

3. Know the implications of behavioral psychology for learning disabilities.

4. Know the implications of cognitive psychology for learning disabilities.

5. Explain the information-processing model and its implications for learning disabilities.

6. Compare and contrast direct instructional and cognitive instructional approaches.

7. Describe the concepts of learning strategies, metacognition, and styles of learning, and discuss their implications for students with learning disabilities.

8. Discuss how the social context affects learning.

Focus

The purpose of theory is to bring form, coherence, and meaning to what we observe in the real world. Theory serves as a guide for activities and for structural thought. Theories are meant to be working statements, not eternal truths. Theory building implies the development of conceptual frameworks that take into account the shortcomings of earlier theories.

Developmental theories of learning disabilities stress the relationship of the natural progression of child growth to the sequential development of cognitive abilities. A state of readiness is needed before the child can acquire certain abilities. Forcing a child to learn before he or she has reached the state of readiness can lead to academic failure and create learning disabilities.

Behavioral theories of learning disabilities emphasize direct teaching and mastery of academic skills. These theories analyze each academic task in terms of the subskills that lead to achievement of that task and of direct instruction in each of the subskills.

Cognitive psychology deals with the way human beings learn, think, and know. Concepts in cognitive psychology have been broadly elaborated over the years, and ideas in the field of learning disabilities reflect these changes. Theories of psychological-processing and information-processing models, and cognitive learning theories are reviewed.

Learning strategies instruction teaches students with learning disabilities how to use the learning approaches used by good learners. Students learn how to learn. The methods involve metacognition (or directing one's learning). Styles of learning and the social context of learning are also discussed in this section.

Lecture-Discussion Outline

I. Theories in learning disabilities. Theory is useful because it brings coherence and meaning to what we experience.

   A. The need for theory

   B. The purpose of theory

II. Developmental psychology and maturation theories of learning disabilities. Maturation and developmental theories stress the natural growth of cognitive abilities.

   A. Maturational lag

   B. Piaget's maturational stages of development

   C. Implications for learning disabilities

1. Entrance tests/assessments
2. Cautions of "birth date effect" when enrolling students
3. Design experiences that enhance child's natural developmental growth
4. Teach readiness to LD
5. Give ample opportunities + experiences to stabilize thought + behavior

III. Behavioral psychology and direct instruction. Behavioral psychology emphasizes instruction that is direct, structured, sequenced, and continuously monitored.

   A. The behavioral unit Stimulus Response Reinforcement

   B. Direct instruction p.137 Instructional practices resulting from the behavioral theory

   C. Behavioral analysis Characteristics p.195.

   analysis of task behaviors needed to learn task
   Pretest of skills?

   task analysis

   analyze academic tasks in terms of the skills needed to accomplish the task logical progression
   1. give direct instruction in academic tasks
   2. Team direct instruction w/ knowledge of style of learning + specific difficulties

   D. Stages of learning

   E. Implications for learning disabilities

   LD 3. Determine stage of learning - realize each stage

IV. Cognitive psychology and learning. Cognitive psychology deals with the thinking, problem-solving, and knowing aspects of learning. Concepts stemming from cognitive psychology have changed over the years.

   will take longer than w/ direct instruction

   A. Disorders of psychological processing

   B. The information-processing model of learning

   C. Cognitive learning theories

   D. Implications for learning disabilities

V. Learning strategies. Learning strategies instruction is an application of cognitive learning theories, focusing on how students learn.

   A. Metacognition

   B. Learning strategies

   C. Styles of learning

   D. The social context of strategies instruction

   E. Implications for learning disabilities

Key Terms and Definitions

Students should take note of the following terms as they appear in this chapter. Students who have difficulty should refer to the glossary in Appendix E of the text or to the text page on which the term is discussed.

antecedent event   In behavioral psychology, the situation that precedes the target behavior.

automaticity   In cognitive learning theory, the condition in which learning has become almost subconscious and so requires little processing effort.

behavior analysis   The process of determining the subskills or steps needed to accomplish a task.

behavioral unit   In behavioral psychology, the core unit that constitutes an action and its environment: the antecedent event, the target behavior, and the consequent event.

cognitive abilities   The mental processes involved in thinking and learning, such as perception, memory, language, attention, concept formation, and problem solving.

concrete operations stage   In Piaget's theory, the stage at which children can systematize and organize thoughts on the basis of past sensual experience.

consequent event   In behavioral psychology, the reinforcement that follows the target behavior.

direct instruction   A method associated with behavioral theories of instruction. The focus is directly on the curriculum or task to be taught and the steps needed to learn that task.

executive control   A component in the information-processing model that refers to the ability to control and direct one's own learning. It is also referred to as *metacognition*.

formal operations stage   In Piaget's theory, the stage at which children can work with abstractions.

information processing   A theory of cognitive processing that incorporates and expands the concepts of cognitive processing. It emphasizes the flow of information and a systems approach to analyzing the interrelationships of the elements of cognitive processes.

learned helplessness   A trait of students with learning disabilities in which they exhibit passiveness and do not take on the responsibility for their own learning.

learning strategies approach   A series of methods to help students direct their own learning, focusing on how students learn rather than on what they learn.

long-term memory   Permanent memory storage that retains information for an extended period of time.

maturational lag   A slowness in specialized aspects of development.

metacognition   The ability to facilitate learning by taking control and directing one's own thinking process.

multistore memory system   A concept of the flow of information among three types of memory: sensory register, short-term memory (or working memory), and long-term memory.

passive learning style   A characteristic of students with learning disabilities who tend to wait until the teacher directs them and tells them what to do. A lack of interest in learning. (See *learned helplessness.*)

preoperational stage   One of Piaget's developmental stages of learning. During this stage, children make intuitive judgments about relationships and also begin to think with symbols.

psychological-processing disorders   A phrase in the federal definition of learning disabilities that refers to disabilities in visual or auditory perception, memory, or language.

readiness   The state of maturational development that is needed before some desired skill can be learned.

reciprocal teaching   A method of teaching through a social interactive dialogue between teacher and student, which emphasizes the development of thinking processes.

sensorimotor period   One of Piaget's developmental stages of learning. During this stage, children learn through senses and movements and by interacting with the physical environment.

sensory register   The first memory system in the information-processing model that interprets and maintains information long enough for it to be perceived and analyzed.

short-term (working) memory   A second memory storage within the information-processing model. It is a temporary storage facility, serving as working memory as a problem receives one's conscious attention.

stages of learning   The stages a person goes through in mastering material, such as acquisition, proficiency, maintenance, and generalization.

underlying abilities   The student's facility in areas that provide the prerequisites for academic learning—for example, language, memory, motor, and perception skills.

zone of proximal development (ZPD)   A term, used by Vygotsky, envisioning a range of levels of difficulty for a student. The lower end is very easy, the upper end beyond the student's capacity. The ZPD is the midpoint and appropriate level for learning.

Suggested Activities

1. In a book, article, or other source on learning disabilities or special education, find a theory or model of learning disorders, of assessment, of teaching, of a service delivery system, or of a related area. Explain the theory or model.

2. Give examples of analyzing a task using behavioral analysis for direct instruction. Select an academic task (spelling, arithmetic, handwriting) or a nonacademic task (cleaning your desk, meeting new friends).

3. Demonstrate how to teach a learning strategy.

4. Explain how a maturational lag can lead to learning disabilities.

Pages for Making Transparencies

These pages can be transferred to transparencies for use with an overhead projector during class instruction.

1. Theories of Learning

2. Components of the Behavioral Unit (Figure 6.1)

3. The Computer System (Figure 6.2)

4. The Human Information-Processing System (Figure 6.3)

5. An Information-Processing Model of Learning (Figure 6.4)

6. Graphic Organizer

7. Learning Strategies

THEORIES OF LEARNING

- ## Why theory is important

- ## Developmental psychology and maturational theories

- ## Behavioral psychology and direct instruction

- ## Cognitive psychology: psychological-processing and information-processing models

- ## Metacognition and learning strategies

Figure 6.1
Components of the Behavioral Unit

Figure 6.2
The Computer System

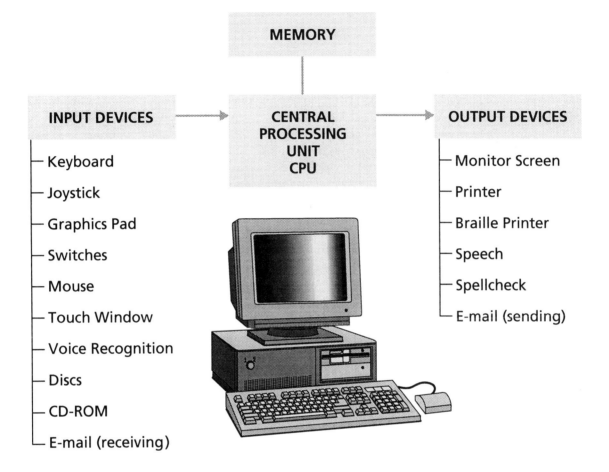

Figure 6.3
The Human Information-Processing System

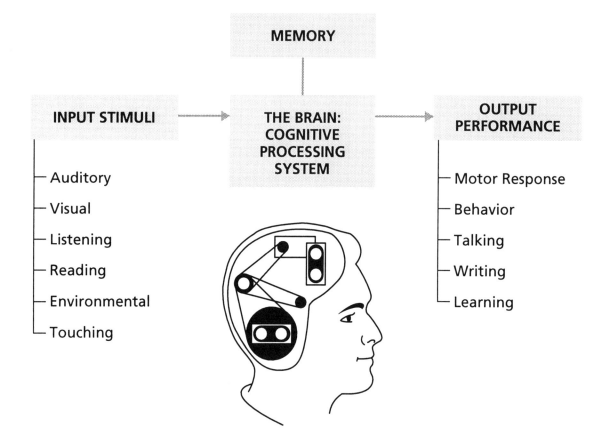

MEMORY

INPUT STIMULI

- Auditory
- Visual
- Listening
- Reading
- Environmental
- Touching

THE BRAIN: COGNITIVE PROCESSING SYSTEM

OUTPUT PERFORMANCE

- Motor Response
- Behavior
- Talking
- Writing
- Learning

Figure 6.4
An Information-Processing Model of Learning

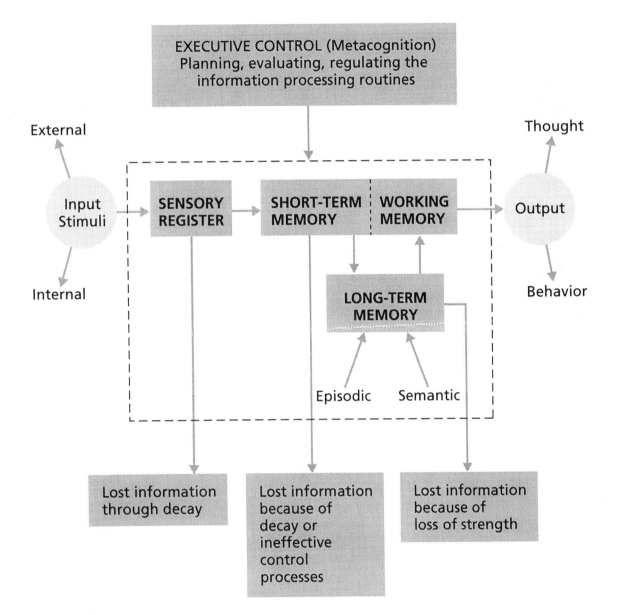

GRAPHIC ORGANIZER

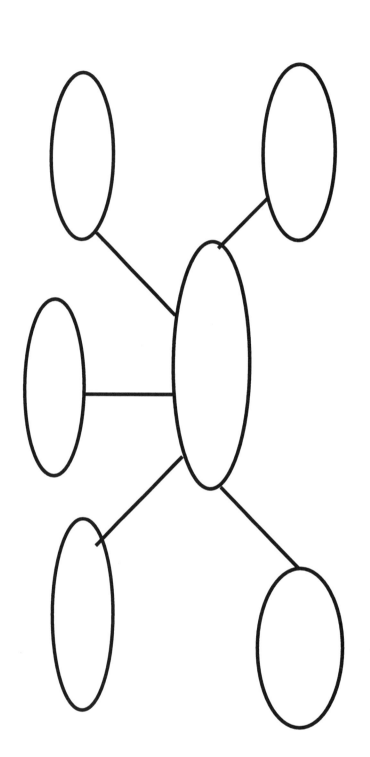

LEARNING STRATEGIES

- ## Metacognition

- ## Learning strategies instruction

- ## Styles of learning

- ## Social context of strategies instruction

CHAPTER 7

Medical Aspects of Learning Disabilities

Learning Objectives

1. Discuss the value of knowing the medical aspects of learning disabilities.

2. Describe the major structures of the brain.

3. Describe the neurological examination, including the examination for soft signs.

4. Describe some of the findings of recent brain research and its relationship to learning disabilities.

5. Describe the three major characteristics of attention deficit disorders. How are children with ADD or ADHD served in the schools?

6. Describe the major medical treatments for individuals with attention deficit disorders and learning disabilities.

7. List the major medical specialties involved with learning disabilities and explain their functions.

Focus

The medical profession plays an important role in the field of learning disabilities. Teachers should understand medical vocabulary, assessment, and common treatments.

Learning occurs within the brain; what happens in the central nervous system affects the relationship between the brain and learning. The two halves of the brain are the right and left hemispheres. Each hemisphere controls a different kind of learning.

Neurological examinations are conducted by several different medical specialists. Two neurological examinations are significant for children with learning disabilities: the conventional neurological examination and the examination for soft signs.

The condition of attention deficit disorder is called ADD (attention deficit disorder) by the U.S. Department of Education, and is called ADHD (attention deficit hyperactivity disorder) in the *Diagnostic and Statistical Manual of Mental Disorders,* fourth edition. The key characteristics are inattention, impulsiveness, and hyperactivity. An individual with ADD can have problems with attention but not be impulsive or hyperactive. A statement of the U.S. Department of Education clarifies that children with ADD can be eligible for special education services under the categories of other health impaired, learning disabilities, emotional disturbance, or Section 504 of the Rehabilitation Act.

Suggested medical treatments include medication, diet control, allergy treatment, and megavitamins.

Medical specialists who diagnose or treat learning disabilities include pediatricians, family practitioners, pediatric neurologists, and pediatric psychiatrists.

Lecture-Discussion Outline

I. The value of medical information for educators. Learning occurs within the brain. Physicians are part of the assessment and treatment team. Teachers are important in providing feedback about medical effects. There are many new advances in medical research.

II. Neuroscience and study of the brain. The neurosciences are various disciplines that study the brain, its structure and functions, and its relation to learning.

A. The brain: its structure and function

B. Recent brain research

C. Neuropsychology

III. The neurological examination. The neurological examination can be conducted by several medical specialists and consists of the conventional neurological examination and the examination for soft signs.

A. Conventional neurological examination

B. Examination for neurological soft signs

IV. Attention deficit disorders. Attention deficit disorders can include problems with attention, impulsivity, and hyperactivity. Children with ADD can be eligible for special education services under the categories of learning disabilities, emotional disturbance, or other health impaired.

A. Evolving views of attention deficit disorders

B. *Diagnostic and Statistical Manual of Mental Disorders,* fourth edition

C. ADD and coexisting conditions

D. U.S. Department of Education Clarification Memorandum

E. Assessment

F. Treatment

V. Medical treatments for learning disabilities. The medically related treatments include medication, nutrition, and diet control.

    A. Medication therapy

    B. Nutrition

    C. Diet control

VI. Medical specialists involved with learning disabilities. Many medical specialties are involved with the diagnosis and treatment of individuals with learning disabilities.

    A. Pediatrics and family practice

    B. Neurology

    C. Ophthalmology

    D. Otology

    E. Psychiatry

    F. Other medical specialties

Key Terms and Definitions

Students should take note of the following terms as they appear in this chapter. Students who have difficulty should refer to the glossary in Appendix E of the text or to the text page on which the term is discussed.

attention deficit disorder (ADD)   Difficulty in concentrating and staying on a task. It may or may not be accompanied by hyperactivity.

attention deficit hyperactivity disorder (ADHD)   Difficulty in concentrating and staying on task, accompanied by hyperactivity. The condition of ADHD is identified and defined by the American Psychiatric Association's *Diagnostic and Statistical Manual of Mental Disorders,* fourth edition.

audiology   A discipline that spans a number of functions, including the testing and measurement of hearing, the diagnosis and rehabilitation of those who are deaf or hard-of-hearing, the scientific study of the physical process of hearing, and the broadening of knowledge and understanding of the hearing process.

brain electrical activity mapping (BEAM)   A procedure using a machine to monitor brain wave activity.

central nervous system   The organic system comprising the brain and the spinal cord.

cerebral dominance   The theory that one hemisphere of the brain controls major functions. In most individuals, the left side of the brain controls language function and, in this theory, is considered the dominant hemisphere.

cerebral hemisphere   One of the two halves (the right hemisphere and the left hemisphere) that make up the human brain.

coexisting conditions   A term used to describe conditions that exist along with an attention deficit disorder. Cormorbidity.

developmental pediatrics   A medical specialty that combines expertise in child development with medical knowledge. The medical areas of pediatrics, genetics, neurology, and psychiatry are particularly important.

dyslexia   A severe reading disorder in which the individual cannot learn to read or does not acquire fluent and efficient reading skills. Research suggests that there is a connection between dyslexia and neurological dysfunction.

Feingold diet   A diet that eliminates artificial flavors, artificial preservatives, and artificial colors in an attempt to control hyperactivity in children.

food additives   Artificial flavors, artificial preservatives, and artificial colors that are put into food.

functional magnetic resonance imaging   A new MRI method for studying the live human brain at work.

hyperactivity   A condition characterized by uncontrollable, haphazard, and poorly organized motor behavior. In young children, excessive gross motor activity makes them appear to be on the go, and they have difficulty sitting still. Older children may be extremely restless or fidgety, may talk too much in class, or may constantly fight with friends, siblings, and classmates.

lateral preference   A tendency to use either the right or left side of the body or to favor using the hand, foot, eye, or ear of one side of the body.

magnetic resonance imaging (MRI)   An advanced neurology procedure using a scanner that converts signals into a shape on a video screen, thereby permitting the study of the living brain.

megavitamins   Orally administered pills, capsules, or liquids containing massive doses of vitamins, sometimes given to children with learning disabilities.

neurology   A medical specialty concerned with the development and functioning of the central nervous system.

neuropsychology   A discipline that combines neurology and psychology and studies the relationship between brain function and behavior.

neurosciences   Disciplines that are involved with the study of the brain and its functions.

neurotransmitters   The chemicals that transmit messages from one cell to another across the synapse (a microscopic space between nerve cells).

ophthalmologist   A medical specialist concerned with the physiology of the eye, its organic aspects, diseases, and structure.

otitis media   Middle-ear infection that may cause temporary hearing loss and may impede language development.

otologist   The medical specialist responsible for the diagnosis and treatment of auditory disorders.

positron emission tomography (PET)   A procedure that permits one to measure metabolism within the brain.

scotopic sensitivity   A difficulty in processing full-spectrum light efficiently, which causes a reading disorder.

soft neurological signs   Minimal or subtle neurological deviations that some neurologists use as indicators of mild neurological dysfunction.

Suggested Activities

1. Examine the case study of a student who has a medical diagnosis. Which medical specialist examined the student? Translate the medical findings into your own words.

2. Look at the records of students with learning disabilities in your school to determine how many students are currently on medication. What medication is each student taking? The school nurse might be helpful in conducting this survey.

3. Research and write a report on one of the controversial medical aspects of learning disabilities, such as the role of visual defects in reading problems, the use of drugs in the treatment of learning disabilities, or food additives as a cause of learning disabilities.

4. Interview a parent whose child has seen medical specialists. How does the parent feel the medical specialists helped or did not help to understand and treat the child?

Pages for Making Transparencies

These pages can be transferred to transparencies for use with an overhead projector during class instruction.

1. The Brain (Figure 7.1)

2. Recent Brain Research

3. Examination for Soft Neurological Signs

4. Historical Overview of ADD

5. Subtypes of ADHD in DSM-IV

6. Medications

Figure 7.1
The Brain

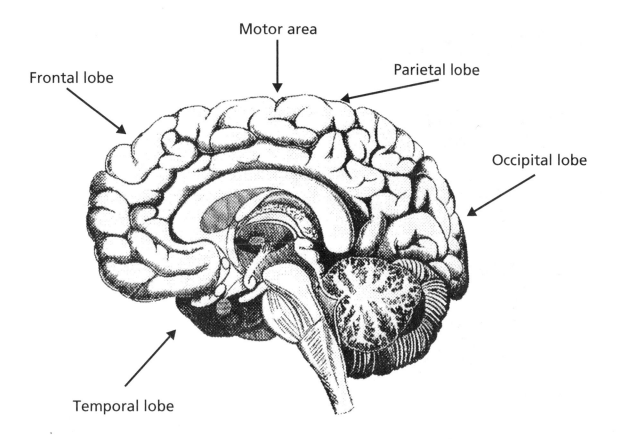

Motor area

Frontal lobe

Parietal lobe

Occipital lobe

Temporal lobe

RECENT BRAIN RESEARCH

- ## Dyslexia research

- ## Postmortem studies

- ## Imaging techniques

  - ### Magnetic resonance imaging (MRI)

  - ### Functional MRI

  - ### Brain electrical activity mapping (BEAM)

  - ### Positron emission tomography (PET)

- ## Genetic studies

  - ### Family studies

  - ### Twin studies

EXAMINATION FOR SOFT NEUROLOGICAL SIGNS

- ## VISUAL MOTOR TESTS
  Copying Designs

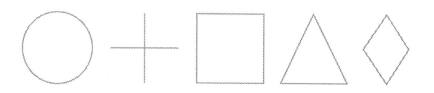

- ## GROSS MOTOR TESTS
  Hopping
  Standing on one foot
  Tandem walking
  Nose–ear test
  Finger–nose test

- ## FINE MOTOR TESTS
  Finger agnosia
  Finger dexterity

HISTORICAL OVERVIEW OF ADD

Year	Description	Source
1941	**Brain damage syndrome**	**Werner, Strauss**
1966	**Minimal brain dysfunction (MBD)**	**Clements et al.**
1968	**Hyperkinetic reaction of childhood**	**DSM II**
1980	**Attention deficit disorder with hyperactivity (ADDH)**	**DSM III**
	Attention deficit disorder without hyperactivity (ADD/noH)	
1987	**Attention deficit hyperactivity disorder (ADHD)**	**DSM III-R**
	Undifferentiated attention deficit disorder (U-ADD)	
1991	**Attention deficit disorder (ADD)**	**Policy memo, U.S. Dept. of Ed.**
1994	**Attention deficit hyperactivity disorder (ADHD), 3 subtypes**	**DSM-IV**

SUBTYPES OF ADHD
IN DSM-IV

1. ADHD-IA: primarily inattentive

2. ADHD-HI: primarily hyperactive and impulsive

3. ADHD-C: combined

MEDICATIONS

- **Psychostimulant medications**
  - ✓ **Ritalin**
  - ✓ **Dexedrine**
  - ✓ **Cylert**

- **Antidepressant medications**
  - ✓ **Norpramin**
  - ✓ **Tofranil**
  - ✓ **Elavil**
  - ✓ **Prozac**

- **Hypertension medication**
  - ✓ **Clonidine**

CHAPTER 8
Young Children with Disabilities

Learning Objectives

1. Discuss the reasons for early identification of and intervention for young children who have disabilities or who are at risk for disabilities.

2. Describe the precursors of learning disabilities in young children.

3. Describe the features of the law that support early childhood special education and the nature of federal support for various early childhood programs.

4. Describe the stages of assessment of young children and the methods and instruments used at each stage.

5. Describe the kinds of placements for delivering services to young children and their families.

6. Compare and contrast four early childhood curricula and describe the integrated or combined curriculum model.

7. Discuss the use of computer technology with young children with disabilities.

Focus

The preschool years are critical years for learning. Early detection of disabilities in young children and the provision of an intervention program for them are effective ways of preventing or lessening later failure.

Precursors of learning disabilities are evident in young children with disabilities. Precursors include deficits in phonological awareness, the ability to analyze and synthesize language sounds, rapid naming skills, knowledge of letter names and sounds, visual-perceptual matching, and visual-motor integration.

The legislation of the reauthorized IDEA incorporates the features of earlier special education legislation for young children with disabilities. The features of the law address services for preschoolers (ages 3–5), infants and toddlers (ages birth–2), and children at risk for academic failure. Among the programs are the Early Education Program for Children with Disabilities (EEPCD), Head Start, and compensatory education programs.

The identification and assessment of young children with disabilities include four phases: locating, screening, diagnosing, and evaluating. Consideration should be given to a number of problems related to early assessment. Services are provided to young children and their families through home-based programs, center-based programs, and combination programs. Transition, the least restrictive environment, and case management must also be considered.

Several different types of curriculum models have been used in early childhood special education programs: developmentally appropriate practice (DAP), the traditional whole-child enrichment approach, the direct teaching approach for teaching basic skills, and the cognitive emphasis curriculum. Most early childhood special education programs include elements of each type of curriculum and teach motor skills, language skills, cognitive skills, and social skills.

Computer technology offers a useful, very effective tool for young children with disabilities.

Lecture-Discussion Outline

I. The importance of the preschool years. The early childhood years are critical learning years for all children. For children with learning disabilities, it is especially important not to lose this precious learning time with its opportunities for early intervention.

II. Young children with disabilities. When a child's problems are recognized early, school failure might be prevented or reduced.

   A. Effectiveness of early intervention

   B. Prevalence of disabilities in young children

III. Learning disabilities in preschool children. Young children with learning disabilities have not yet failed, but they do exhibit precursors of learning disabilities in several essential areas.

IV. Legislation for young children with disabilities. The reauthorized Individuals with Disabilities Education Act (IDEA) incorporates earlier special education laws for young children with disabilities. The law provides comprehensive services to preschool children and supports states in providing services to infants, toddlers, and their families.

   A. Preschool children with disabilities: ages 3–5

   B. Infants and toddlers with disabilities: birth–2

   C. Children at risk

V. Services and programs. A wide variety of different programs offer services to young children with disabilities.

   A. Inclusionary setting for young children with disabilities

   B. The Early Education Program for Children with Disabilities (EEPCD)

   C. Head Start

   D. Compensatory education programs

VI. Early identification and assessment. There are four phases of assessment for young children with disabilities: locating, screening, diagnosing, and evaluating. Each serves a different purpose.

A. Phases of identification and assessment

B. Areas of testing

C. Problems related to early identification and assessment

VII. Placements for delivering services to young children. Services include several models: home-based, center-based, and combination services.

A. Home-based services

B. Center-based services

C. Combination services

VIII. Transition to other placements. Ending one type of program and moving to another can be traumatic for the child and for the family.

A. Transition for preschool children (ages 3–5)

B. Transition for infants and toddlers (ages birth–2)

IX. Early childhood curriculum models. Curriculum models include enrichment, direct instruction, cognitive emphasis, and combination early childhood curriculum models.

A. Developmentally appropriate practice (DAP)

B. Enrichment curriculum

C. Direct teaching curriculum

D. Cognitive emphasis curriculum

E. Combination early childhood curriculum

X. Using computers with young children with disabilities. For many areas of learning, computers are extremely effective with young children with disabilities.

Key Terms and Definitions

Students should take note of the following terms as they appear in this chapter. Students who have difficulty should refer to the glossary in Appendix E of the text or to the text page on which the term is discussed.

center-based program   A program offered at a central facility for comprehensive services for young children and delivered by staff members with expertise in disciplines related to intervention and therapy for young children.

children at risk   Children at risk for poor development and learning failure. Three categories of *at risk* are established risk, biological risk, and environmental risk.

cognitive emphasis curriculum   A curriculum that focuses on helping children develop thinking and cognitive abilities. Many of the concepts and curriculum programs of this approach stem directly from the ideas of Jean Piaget.

developmental delay   A term designating a child's lag in cognitive, physical, communication, social/emotional, or adaptive development. It is considered a noncategorical assessment term for identifying a child with disabilities for services.

developmentally appropriate practice (DAP)   Guidelines for a curriculum for young children based on a constructivist philosophy emphasizing child-initiated learning, exploratory play, and the child's interests.

direct teaching curriculum   A curriculum based on direct instruction of specific preselected learning and academic skills.

enrichment curriculum   A preschool curriculum based on a maturational view of child development. This "traditional" program of nursery schools assumes a natural growth sequence for the young child's abilities within a nurturing environment.

Head Start   A preschool program intended to provide compensatory educational experiences for children from low-income families who might otherwise come to school unprepared and unmotivated to learn. Head Start is sponsored by the Office of Child Development.

home-based program   A system delivering intervention services to very young children in their homes. The parent(s) becomes the child's primary teacher. A professional child-care provider goes to the child's home, typically one to three times per week, to train the parent(s) to work with the child.

Individuals with Disabilities Education Act (IDEA)   This is the special education law and was reauthorized by Congress in 1996. It provides a free appropriate public education for children and youth with disabilities ages 3 through 21.

lead agency   The agency with primary responsibility for programs for young children. The governor of each state appoints the lead agency for infants and toddlers ages birth through 2 years. The state education agency is the lead agency for preschoolers ages 3 through 5.

least restrictive environment   The term referring to the placement of students with learning disabilities, to the extent appropriate, in settings with students who do not have such disabilities.

Part B   The part of IDEA that refers to regulations for children with disabilities. In reference to early childhood, Part B covers preschoolers with disabilities ages 3 through 5.

Part H   The part of IDEA that covers infants and toddlers from birth through 2 years.

screening   A type of assessment using ways to survey many children quickly to identify those who may need special services.

service coordinator   The professional who serves as a case manager for children ages birth through 2 years and their families.

transition   The process of moving from one type of program to another. In early childhood programs it can be from the birth through 2 program to the age 3 through 5 program, or from the age 3 through 5 program to another educational placement. For adolescents, *transition* refers to the passage from school to the world of work.

Suggested Activities

1. Visit a preschool program in your area. Observe the children and note the typical development behaviors of preschoolers ages 3 through 5 years.

2. Visit a day-care program in your area. Observe the behaviors of infants and toddlers ages birth through 2 years.

3. Develop an informal screening test for young children. You might use the motor tests described in Chapter 7. Use your test to assess a young child.

4. Develop a lesson for young children. Plan to teach some skills (language, color, number, size, social skills) to a preschool child.

5. Investigate the services available in your area for children ages 3 through 5 with special needs and also for children ages birth through 2 years.

Pages for Making Transparencies

These pages can be transferred to transparencies for use with an overhead projector during class instruction.

1. Benefits of Early Intervention

2. Learning Disabilities in Preschool Children

3. Legislation for Young Children with Disabilities

4. Phases of Assessment

5. Programs for Young Children with Disabilities

BENEFITS OF EARLY INTERVENTION

- ## Helps children with disabilities
  - ✓ Gains in cognitive, physical, language, and social skills

- ## Benefits families
  - ✓ Helps families manage the child
  - ✓ Reduces stress

- ## Benefits society
  - ✓ Reduces need for institutional placement
  - ✓ Reduces need for special education
  - ✓ Saves money

LEARNING DISABILITIES IN PRESCHOOL CHILDREN

PRECURSORS OF ACADEMIC FAILURE—
DEFICITS IN THE FOLLOWING:

- **Communication and oral language skills**

- **Phonological awareness**

- **Rapid naming skills**

- **Knowledge of the alphabet**

- **Visual-perceptual matching**

- **Visual-motor integration**

- **Fine- and gross-motor skills**

- **Social skills**

LEGISLATION FOR YOUNG CHILDREN WITH DISABILITIES

	Preschoolers	Infants/Toddlers
Law	Part B Mandatory	Part H Permissive
Age	3 through 5	Birth through 2
Plan	IEP or IFSP	IFSP
Lead agency	State education agency	Agency appointed by governor
Transition	To general or special program	To preschool program
Orientation	Developmental learning of child	Family, parent/infant interaction

PHASES OF ASSESSMENT

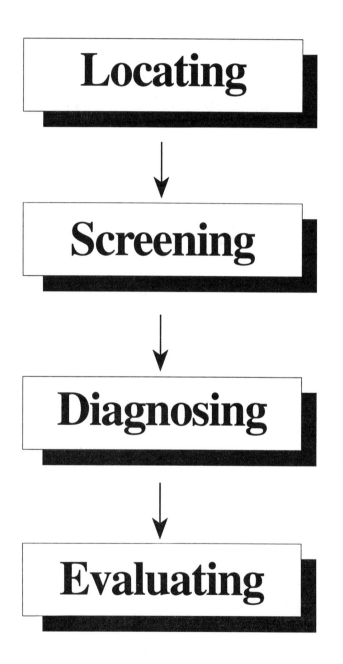

Locating

↓

Screening

↓

Diagnosing

↓

Evaluating

PROGRAMS FOR YOUNG CHILDREN WITH DISABILITIES

- ## Inclusion placements

- ## Head Start program

- ## Early Education Programs for Young Children with Disabilities (EEPCD)

- ## Compensatory programs
  - ### Perry Preschool Project

CHAPTER 9

Adolescents and Adults with Learning Disabilities

Learning Objectives

1. Identify the characteristics of the period of adolescence and the characteristics of adolescents who have learning disabilities.

2. Describe specific problems found at the secondary level of schooling that are not found at the elementary level.

3. Know the requirements within IDEA concerning transition plans for helping students go from school to adult life.

4. Describe approaches to instruction that are used with adolescents with learning disabilities.

5. Describe the philosophy of learning strategies instruction and give examples of learning strategies.

6. Discuss what is happening at the college level for young adults with learning disabilities.

Focus

Adolescents with learning disabilities need special services at the secondary level of schooling. Programs for them are provided in most junior and senior high schools today.

All adolescents must cope with dramatic changes in their lives caused by puberty. Those with learning disabilities face additional problems. Special characteristics of adolescents with learning disabilities include passive learning styles, poor self-concept, social ineptitude, attentional disorders, and problems with motivation.

The secondary school poses different problems than the elementary school. Only one-half of students receive a high school diploma, and another 10 percent receive a certificate of completion. Other special issues at the secondary level include minimum competency tests as a requirement for graduation and the educational reform movement. There are heavier curriculum demands at the high school level, and high school teachers tend to be more content oriented. Collaboration between the learning disabilities teacher and the content-area teachers is essential to serve adolescents with learning disabilities.

The transition from school to adult life is full of complexities for all adolescents, but especially for those with learning disabilities. The Individuals with Disabilities Education Act requires that an individualized transition plan be developed for adolescents with disabilities, beginning at age 14.

Post-high school plans for students can be made for competitive employment, vocational training, college attendance, or supported employment.

There are several different approaches to teaching students with learning disabilities at the secondary level. Models include basic skills instruction, functional skills programs, tutorial programs, work-study programs, and learning strategies programs. Collaboration programs are important because almost 80 percent of students with learning disabilities ages 12 to 18 receive at least some instruction in regular classrooms.

Instruction in learning strategies offers a viable approach for helping adolescents with learning disabilities learn to take control of their own learning. The strategies intervention model (SIM) is a widely used approach for strategies instruction with adolescents with learning disabilities.

Post–high school and college programs for young adults with learning disabilities are increasing. In addition, it is recognized that, for some individuals, learning disabilities may be a lifelong problem continuing into the adult years.

Lecture-Discussion Outline

   I. Characteristics of adolescents with learning disabilities. The period of adolescence is one of dramatic change and turmoil. If the adolescent also has learning disabilities, this period is particularly trying.

   A. Characteristics of the stage of adolescence

   B. Special characteristics of adolescents with learning disabilities

      1. Passive learning

      2. Poor self-concept

      3. Social and behavioral problems

      4. Attention deficits

      5. Lack of motivation

   II. Special issues at the secondary level. The high school poses many problems that are not encountered at the elementary level.

   A. Challenges for adolescents with learning disabilities

      1. What happens to students with learning disabilities in secondary school?

      2. Diverse problems of adolescents with learning disabilities

   B. Increasing high school demands and requirements

   C. Secondary teachers

   III. Transition planning: the transition from school to adult life. Going from school to the world of work is a very important step, and the IDEA contains regulations that attend to transition.

A. Transition legislation

    1. Content of the transition plan

    2. Developing transition plans

    3. Transition questions

B. Transition guidelines

    1. Other legislation for transition

IV. Approaches to teaching students with learning disabilities in secondary school. There are many different instructional approaches for teaching adolescents with learning disabilities.

    A. Components of effective secondary programs

        1. Intensive instruction in reading and mathematics

        2. Explicit instruction in survival skills

        3. Successful completion of courses needed for high school graduation

    B. Curriculum models for serving adolescents with learning disabilities at the secondary level

        1. Basic skills instruction

        2. Tutorial instruction

        3. Functional skills instruction

        4. Work-study programs

        5. Collaboration programs

V. Learning strategies instruction. Many special educators believe that instruction in learning strategies is particularly beneficial for adolescents with learning disabilities.

    A. Guidelines for teaching learning strategies

    B. Strategies intervention model (SIM)

    C. Steps in teaching learning strategies

VI. Into the adult years. The condition of learning disabilities can affect one's adult years. Many college programs are available today for adults with learning disabilities.

    A. Postsecondary and college programs

        1. Section 504 of the Rehabilitation Act

2. College entrance testing for individuals with learning disabilities

3. Special problems at the college level

4. Finding colleges for students with learning disabilities

B. Adults with learning disabilities.

C. Essential life skills

Key Terms and Definitions

Students should take note of the following terms as they appear in this chapter. Students who have difficulty should refer to the glossary in Appendix E of the text or to the text page on which the term is discussed.

accommodations   Refers to adjustments and modifications within a program to meet the needs of students with disabilities. Required under Section 504 of the Rehabilitation Act.

basic skills instruction   Instruction focusing on direct teaching, especially in reading and mathematics. Students receive instruction at a level that approximates their achievement or instructional level.

collaboration   The process of two or more professionals working together to seek a joint solution. Often refers to the joint efforts of the learning disabilities teacher and the general education or content-area teachers.

content-area teachers   High school teachers whose primary orientation and expertise are in the subject matter of their specialty. In contrast, elementary teachers tend to have an orientation and more expertise in child development.

functional skills instruction   Teaching survival skills to enable students to get along in the outside world.

learned helplessness   A trait of students with learning disabilities in which they exhibit passiveness and do not take on the responsibility for their own learning.

learning strategies instruction   A series of methods to help students direct their own learning, focusing on how students learn rather than on what they learn.

life skills   The knowledge and abilities that a student needs to adapt to real-life situations.

minimum competency tests   Tests of academic skills that must be passed before a student receives a high school diploma or passes to the next grade.

passive learning style   A characteristic of students with learning disabilities who tend to wait until the teacher directs them and tells them what to do. A lack of interest in learning.

Section 504 of the Rehabilitation Act   Federal law that covers all agencies and institutions receiving financial assistance and that requires that no otherwise qualified handicapped individual shall be excluded from participation.

strategies intervention model (SIM)   An instructional method for teaching learning strategies to adolescents with learning disabilities.

transition planning   Planning for making the change from being a student to being an adult. Students with learning disabilities need help in this process.

tutorial instruction   Teaching designed to help students meet requirements in their specific academic-content subjects and to achieve success in the regular curriculum. This teaching is usually accomplished through one-to-one instruction or in small groups.

work-study program   A high school program in which students work on a job for a portion of the day and go to school for a portion of the day.

Suggested Activities

1. Check with a high school to determine how students with learning disabilities are being served (placements, special classes for content-area subjects, IEP modifications, transition plans).

2. Read an article on a topic related to secondary learning disabilities (for example, characteristics of adolescents with learning disabilities, adults with learning disabilities, a delivery system in a high school, or learning strategies instruction).

3. Examine instructional materials designed for adolescents with learning disabilities.

4. Interview an adolescent who has learning disabilities and have the student describe his or her secondary school program.

Pages for Making Transparencies

These pages can be transferred to transparencies for use with an overhead projector during class instruction.

1. Characteristics of Adolescents with Learning Disabilities

2. Reasons why Students with Learning Disabilities Leave High School

3. The Transition Plan

4. Placement of Adolescents with Learning Disabilities

5. Accommodations for College Students

CHARACTERISTICS OF ADOLESCENTS WITH LEARNING DISABILITIES

- **Passive learning**

- **Poor self-concept**

- **Social and behavioral problems**

- **Attention deficits**

- **Lack of motivation**

REASONS WHY STUDENTS WITH LEARNING DISABILITIES LEAVE HIGH SCHOOL

Reason for Leaving School	% of LD Adolescents
High school diploma	49.7 %
Certificate of completion	10.8
Reached maximum age	0.5
Dropped out of school	21.3
Status unknown	17.7
Total	100.0 %

Source: From *To Assure the Free Appropriate Public Education of All Children with Disabilities.* Sixteenth Annual Report to Congress on the Implementation of the Individuals with Disabilities Education Act, by the U.S. Department of Education, 1994, Washington, DC: U.S. Government Printing Office.

THE TRANSITION PLAN

1. Current levels of performance

2. Interests and aptitude

3. Postschool goals

4. Transition activities

5. Designate responsible persons

6. Review

PLACEMENT OF ADOLESCENTS WITH LEARNING DISABILITIES

Educational Environment	Percent of Adolescents with Learning Disabilities
General education class	33%
Resource room	46
Separate class	20
Other placements	1
Total	100%

Source: Table 9.5. U.S. Department of Education (1995). Seventeenth Annual Report to Congress on the Implementation of the Individuals with Disabilities Education Act. Washington, DC: U.S. Government Printing Office.

ACCOMMODATIONS FOR COLLEGE STUDENTS

- **Extending time to complete program**

- **Adapting the method of instruction**

- **Substituting alternative course for required course**

- **Modifying or substituting for the foreign language requirement**

- **Allowing for part-time rather than full-time study**

- **Modifying examination procedures**

- **Providing audiotapes of student textbooks**

- **Providing note takers to help students with lectures**

- **Offering counseling services**

CHAPTER 10

Developmental and Preacademic Learning

Learning Objectives

1. Know the differences between developmental learning disabilities and academic learning disabilities.

2. Describe the precursors of learning disabilities in young children.

3. Describe the six senses used for obtaining information about the world.

4. Know how problems in perception relate to learning disabilities.

5. Describe sensory-motor integration theory.

6. Know how problems in auditory perception, including phonological awareness, relate to learning disabilities.

7. Describe three basic presumptions underlying motor theories.

Focus

Theories

Developmental learning disabilities include deficits in the precursor skills—motor, perceptual, linguistic, and cognitive—that a child needs to learn academic subjects. This chapter concentrates on the motor and perceptual skills and theories.

Theories of motor development were particularly influential in the early stages of the field of learning disabilities. Three underlying concepts of motor learning are as follows: (1) human learning begins with motor learning; (2) there is a natural sequence of developmental motor stages; and (3) academic and cognitive performances are based on successful gross-motor development and fine-motor skills and coordination. Gross-motor development involves the large body muscles, and fine-motor development involves the small muscles. The motor theories discussed in this section include (1) motor learning through play and adapted physical education, (2) perceptual-motor theory formulated by Newell Kephart, and (3) sensory integration theory, which involves the field of occupational therapy.

Perceptual learning is another consideration in preacademic skills. *Perception* refers to the recognition of sensory information or the ability of the intellect to extract meaning from sensory stimulation. The perceptual modality concept suggests that each student has a preferred perceptual modality for learning and that individual learning styles can be matched to appropriate teaching methods. Constructs of perception that have implications for learning disabilities include the perceptual modality concept, overloading the perceptual modalities, whole and part perception, auditory perception, visual perception, tactile perception, and kinesthetic perception. The auditory skill of phonological awareness is increasingly recognized as an essential precursor for reading.

Perception is a learned skill and can be taught. Teaching procedures can modify and strengthen perceptual learning.

Teaching Strategies

The teaching strategies section of the chapter offers a sampling of activities used in motor and perception teaching.

Lecture-Discussion Outline

Theories

I. Precursors of Learning Disabilities in young children. Developmental learning disabilities are the precursors of later academic learning disabilities. The focus is on prevention and early intervention. Precursors include deficits in motor development, perceptual ability, language skills, and social skills. Motor and perceptual development are considered in this chapter.

II. Motor development and learning. Many children with learning disabilities exhibit severe motor incoordination problems and significant delays in motor development. The several theories of motor disabilities stem from different disciplines.

A. Historical interest in motor development and physical fitness

B. The value of motor development

C. Concepts of motor development

   1. Gross- and fine-motor development

   2. Motor learning through play

   3. Perceptual-motor theory

   4. Sensory integration

D. Tests of motor development

III. Perceptual development. Many essential learning skills are developed during the preschool years, before the child enters first grade. Considered here are the development of the perceptual systems and disabilities related to perceptual development.

A. The perceptual systems and their impact on learning

B. Perceptual modality concept

C. Overloading of the perceptual system

D. Auditory perception

    1. Phonological awareness

    2. Auditory discrimination

    3. Auditory memory

    4. Auditory blending

E. Visual perception

    1. Visual discrimination

    2. Figure-ground discrimination

    3. Visual closure

    4. Spatial relations

    5. Object and letter recognition

    6. Visual perception and reversals

    7. Whole-part perception

F. Tactile and kinesthetic perception

    1. Tactile perception

    2. Kinesthetic perception

G. Tests of perception

Teaching Strategies

IV. Activities to promote motor development. Teachers often must take the responsibility for motor development. Activities in gross motor skills, body image and awareness, and fine-motor skills are suggested.

A. Gross-motor activities

B. Body image and awareness activities

C. Fine-motor activities

V. Activities for intervention for perceptual precursors of learning disabilities. Intervention activities include strategies in auditory perception and phonological awareness, visual perception, and tactile and kinesthetic perception.

   A. Phonological awareness and auditory perception activities

   B. Visual perception activities

   C. Tactile and kinesthetic perception activities

   D. Integrating perceptual system activities

Key Terms and Definitions

Students should take note of the following terms as they appear in this chapter. Students who have difficulty should refer to the glossary in Appendix E of the text or to the text page on which the term is discussed.

adapted physical education   Physical education programs that have been modified to meet the needs of students with disabilities.

auditory blending   The ability to synthesize the phonemes of a word in recognizing the entire word. In an auditory blending test, the individual sounds of a word are pronounced with separations between each phoneme sound. The child must combine the individual sounds to say and recognize the word.

auditory discrimination   The ability to recognize a difference between phoneme sounds; also the ability to identify words that are the same and words that are different when the difference is a single phoneme element (for example, *big-pig*).

auditory perception   The ability to recognize or interpret what is heard.

developmental learning disabilities   Deficits in the requisite skills that a child needs to learn academic subjects. It includes motor, perceptual, language, and thinking skills.

kinesthetic perception   Perception obtained through body movements and muscle feeling, such as the awareness of positions taken by different parts of the body and bodily feelings of muscular contraction, tension, and relaxation.

occupational therapist   A therapist who is trained in brain physiology and function and who prescribes exercises to improve motor and sensory integration.

perception   The process of recognizing and interpreting information received through the senses.

perceptual modality concept   The notion that individuals have preferred channels for learning (for example, auditory or visual). Information on the child's perceptual strengths and weaknesses is used in planning instruction.

perceptual-motor match   Kephart's term for the process of comparing and collating the two kinds of input information. Perceptual data become meaningful when correlated with previously learned motor information.

perceptual-motor skill　A behavior that requires the efficient interaction of visual perception with motor actions.

perceptual-motor theory　The theory that a stable concept of the world depends on being able to correlate perceptions and motor development.

phonological awareness　A child's recognition of the sounds of language. The child must understand that speech can be segmented into syllables and phonemic units.

precursor skills　Skills that are necessary for academic learning, such as motor and perceptual skills and language skills.

sensory integration theory　A theory expounded by occupational therapists emphasizing the relationship between the neurological process and human behavior. The theory highlights three sensory systems—tactile, vestibular, and proprioceptive.

sound counting　Activities to help students count the number of sounds in a word. Counters (such as popsicle sticks or tongue depressors) are often used.

splinter skill　A motor skill that is not within a child's current sequential development but is acquired as a result of outside pressure. Such skills are not an integral part of the orderly sequential skill development.

tactile perception　Perception obtained through the sense of touch via the fingers and skin surfaces.

visual discrimination　The ability to note visual differences or similarities between objects, including letters and words.

visual perception　The identification, organization, and interpretation of sensory data received by the individual through the eye.

Suggested Activities

1. Develop an informal motor test. Use it to test four children of different ages.

2. Test a child using the Informal Test of Auditory Perception Skills in Table 10.1.

3. Teach a child a motor activity.

4. Design an activity to teach auditory perception or visual perception.

5. Find a game, song, story, or nursery rhyme that helps children develop phonological awareness or rhyming ability. Try it out with a preschool child.

Pages for Making Transparencies

These pages can be transferred to transparencies for use with an overhead projector during class instruction.

1. Concepts about Motor Learning

2. Auditory Perception

3. Examples of Visual Perception Tasks (Figure 10.1)

4. Visual Perception

5. A Card for Segmenting Speech Sounds (Figure 10.2)

CONCEPTS ABOUT MOTOR LEARNING

- **Human learning begins with motor learning.**

- **There is a natural sequence of developmental motor stages.**

- **Many areas of academic and cognitive performance are based on successful motor experiences.**

AUDITORY PERCEPTION

- **Auditory perception — interpreting what is heard**

- **Phonological awareness**

- **Auditory discrimination**

- **Auditory memory**

- **Auditory sequencing**

- **Auditory blending**

Figure 10.1
Examples of Visual Perception Tasks

WHOLE AND PART PERCEPTION: VISUAL CLOSURE

If one sees the parts, there are no letters here — only straight and curved lines. By looking at the whole, the letters are perceived.

To perceive a square, one must see this form as a whole.

VISUAL-MOTOR PERCEPTION

Copy these patterns

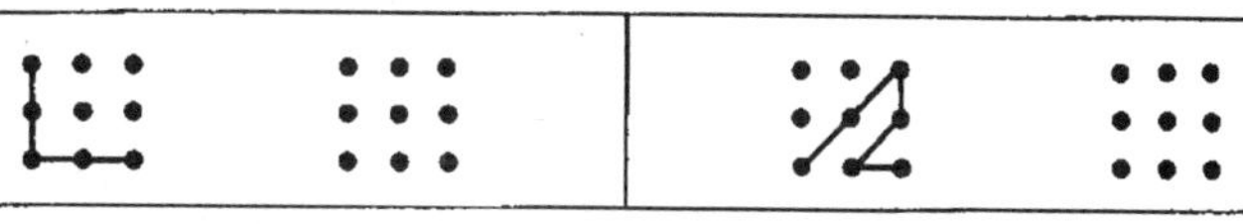

This task is a visual-motor task. The child must receive the information through the visual modality and then transfer to a motor movement.

FIGURE-GROUND PERCEPTION

Find the football.

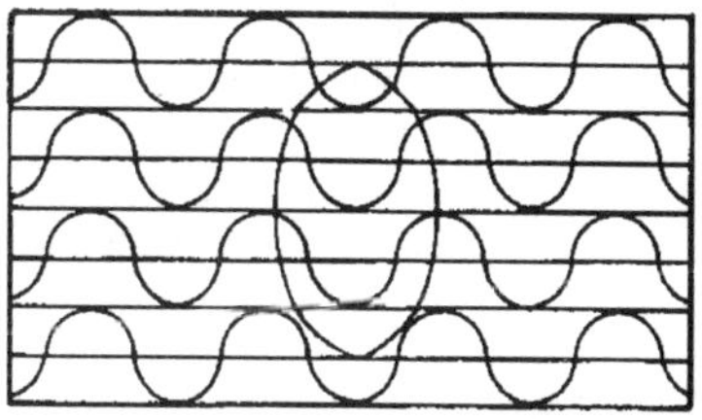

In this task the child is required to visually perceive a foreground figure against the background stimuli.

VISUAL FORM PERCEPTION: PERCEPTUAL CONSTANCY

Find the form like the first one.

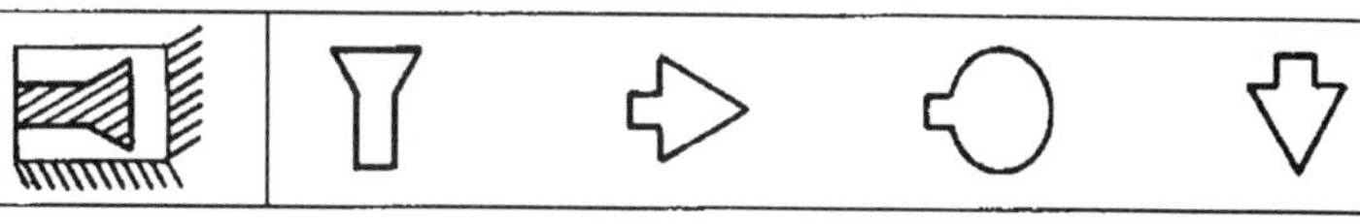

The child must maintain visual form constancy to find the shape when the position is changed.

VISUAL DISCRIMINATION: LETTERS

Find the form like the first one.

| D | F | D | M | P | L |

The child is required to visually discriminate and match identical letter shapes.

VISUAL DISCRIMINATION: WORDS

Find the form like the first one.

| horse | house | hose | horse | enough |

The child is required to visually discriminate and match identical words.

VISUAL PERCEPTION

- **Visual perception — interpreting what is seen**

- **Visual discrimination**

- **Figure-ground perception**

- **Visual closure**

- **Spatial relations**

- **Object-letter recognition**

- **Reversals**

- **Whole-part perception**

Figure 10.2
A Card for Segmenting Speech Sounds

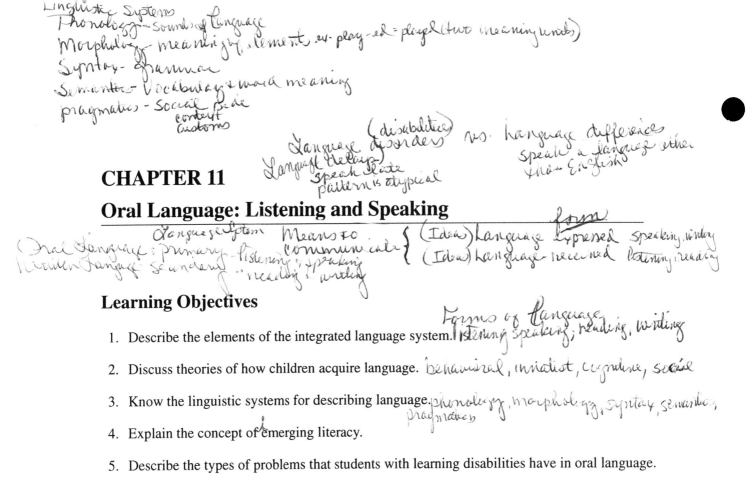

[Handwritten notes at top of page:]

Linguistic System
Phonology - Sounds of language
Morphology - meaning element ev. play-ed = played (two meaning units)
Syntax - grammar
Semantics - Vocabulary + word meaning
Pragmatics - Social side
context
customs

Language disorders (disability) vs. language difference
Language delay - speak late
pattern is atypical
Speak a language other than English

Oral Language: Primary - Listening + speaking   Language system   Means to communicate   (Idea) Language expressed   speaking, writing
Written language: Secondary - reading + writing   (Idea) Language received   listening, reading

CHAPTER 11

Oral Language: Listening and Speaking

Learning Objectives

1. Describe the elements of the integrated language system. *Forms of Language: Listening, speaking, reading, writing*

2. Discuss theories of how children acquire language. *behavioral, innatist, cognitive, social*

3. Know the linguistic systems for describing language. *phonology, morphology, syntax, semantics, pragmatics*

4. Explain the concept of emerging literacy.

5. Describe the types of problems that students with learning disabilities have in oral language.

6. Describe strategies for teaching listening skills.

7. Describe strategies for teaching speaking skills.

Focus

Theories

Language is unique to human beings and plays a vital role in learning. It enhances thinking and permits us to speak of things unseen, of the past, and of the future. Oral language has two forms, listening and speaking, which are part of an integrated language system that includes oral language, reading, and writing. As children gain competence in one form of language, they build an underlying language system that carries into learning another form of language.

Language also serves as a means for human beings to communicate. Ideas are expressed to others through speaking and writing, and ideas are received from others through listening and reading.

The close relationship between language deficits and learning can be seen in the examples of two groups of students—those with language disorders and those with language differences. Language disorders and language delays characterize children who learn to speak late or whose language pattern is atypical. Language differences are found in students who have a language system other than standard English. The limited English proficiency (LEP) category comprises bilingual students who speak a native language that is not English. Some bilingual students have both a language difference and a learning disability.

There are several theories about how children acquire language. They include behavioral, innatist, cognitive, and social theories.

Linguistics is the study of language itself. The linguistic systems include phonology (the sounds of language), morphology (the meaning elements), syntax (grammar), semantics (vocabulary and word meaning), and pragmatics (the social side of language).

The language problems of students with learning disabilities are the basis for many of their learning problems. Children with poor phonological awareness do not perceive the sounds in language. Children with slowness in word finding have difficulty in rapidly retrieving words. Children with language disorders have language delays, receptive language disorders, or expressive language disorders.

Children who use a nonstandard version of English have a language difference that interferes with school learning.

Many children in today's diverse society speak a language other than English and are described as having limited English proficiency (LEP). Some of these children also have learning disabilities.

Emergent literacy refers to the child's early entrance into the comprehensive world of words, language, books, poetry, and stories. Young children should be provided with a literary environment.

Both informal language measures and formal language tests are useful for assessing language.

Teaching Strategies

Oral language involves both listening and speaking. Listening has been neglected as an area of teaching. Listening skills can be improved through direct instruction. Learning disabilities may first be suspected when a child does not begin to talk at the normal age. The first stages of language acquisition are babbling, jargon, single words, and two- or three-word sentences.

Activities to help students develop the oral language skills of listening and speaking are described in this section.

Lecture-Discussion Outline

Theories

I. Oral language, reading, and writing: an integrated system. Language appears in several forms: oral language (listening and speaking), reading, and writing. All are linked and integrated through an underlying language core.

A. Forms of the language system

B. Language as a communication process
Problems)

II. Theories of how children acquire language. Several theories explain how children acquire language: the behavioral, innatist, cognitive, and social theories of human growth and development. Each has different implications for teaching language.

Provide a stimulating language environment

A. Behavioral theories   *modelling, imitation & reinforcement*

B. Innatist theories   *biologically predisposed*

C. Cognitive theories *link between language, thinking & experience*

D. Social theories *requires a reciprocal (give & take) relationship between the child & others*

III. Linguistic systems. Linguistics is the study of the pattern of language systems and the nature, development, function, and use of language. Linguistic concepts include the attitude toward language and the linguistic systems of phonology, morphology, syntax, semantics, and pragmatics.

A. Attitudes toward language

B. The language systems

IV. Language problems of students with learning disabilities. Language problems of one form or another underlie many learning disabilities. Problems include lack of phonological awareness, slowness in naming, receptive and expressive language disorders, nonstandard English, and limited English proficiency

Many children w/ LDs exhibit deviations & delays in language development.
Require additional time & teaching to internalize the language systems

A. Lack of phonological awareness

B. Slowness in naming: word-finding problems

C. Language disorders

1. Language delay

2. Receptive language disorders

3. Expressive language disorders *difficulty in using language*

D. Nonstandard English

E. Limited English proficiency (LEP). Children whose native language is not English are often called bilingual children. Some have language disorders in both their native language and in English.

1. English as a second language (ESL)

2. Bilingual education

3. Sheltered English

4. Immersion method

V. Emergent literacy

VI. Assessing oral language. A student's language proficiency can be assessed with both informal measures and formal tests.

A. Informal measures

B. Formal tests

Teaching Strategies

VII. Listening. Strategies for teaching listening are needed because listening is an element of the language system that is often neglected.

    A. Problems in listening

    B. Activities for teaching listening

VIII. Speaking. Talking is the output side of the oral language system. Oral language often does not receive as much emphasis as written language. Children with learning disabilities often need much experience with oral language development and many speaking activities.

    A. Development of oral language

    B. Natural language stimulation activities

    C. Activities for teaching oral language

    D. Improving the oral language of adolescents

Key Terms and Definitions

Students should take note of the following terms as they appear in this chapter. Students who have difficulty should refer to the glossary in Appendix E of the text or to the text page on which the term is discussed

apraxia   Difficulty in directing one's motor movements.

bilingual approach   A teaching method in which students use their native language for part of the instructional day and English for part of the instructional day.

developmental aphasia   The term used to describe a child who has severe difficulty in acquiring oral language. This term implies that the disorder is related to a central nervous system dysfunction.

dysnomia   A deficiency in remembering and expressing words. Children with dysnomia may substitute a word such as *thing* for many objects when they cannot remember the name of the object. They may attempt to use other expressions to talk around the subject.

emergent literacy   The child's early entrance into the world of words, language, and stories. Literacy emerges in children through the simultaneous experiences with oral language, reading, and writing.

ESL (English as a second language) approach   A method of teaching English to students whose native language is not English.

expressive language disorder   Difficulty in using language (or speaking).

immersion approach   An approach in which students receive extensive exposure to a second language.

language delay   Slowness in the acquisition of language. The child with a language delay may not be talking at all or may be using very little language at an age when language normally develops.

language difference   A language problem of students who use nonstandard English and whose native language is not English. A language difference can interfere with school learning.

language disorder   The term that refers to children with a language delay or a language disability.

limited English proficiency (LEP)   The term used to describe students whose native language is not English and who have difficulty understanding and using English.

linguistics   The scientific study of the patterns, nature, development, function, and use of human language.

morpheme   The smallest meaning unit of a language system.

morphology   The linguistic system of meaning units in any particular language. For example, the word *played* contains two meaning units (or morphemes): *play* + *ed* (past tense).

oral expressive language   The skills required to produce spoken language for communication with other individuals.

oral receptive language   Understanding of the language spoken by others. Listening is a receptive oral language skill.

phoneme   The smallest sound unit of a language system.

phonological awareness   A child's recognition of the sounds of language. The child must understand that speech can be segmented into syllables and phonemic units.

phonology   The linguistic system of speech sounds in a particular language. The word *cat,* for example, has three sounds (or phonemes): c-a-t.

pragmatics   The social side of language; the social context and social customs surrounding language.

primary language   The child's first language, usually oral language. In relation to bilingual students, the term can refer to the student's native language.

receptive language disorder   Difficulty in understanding oral language or in listening.

secondary language system   The student's second language, usually written language. In the case of bilingual students it may refer to their second language (English).

semantics   A linguistic term referring to the vocabulary system of language.

sheltered English   A method of teaching children who have some proficiency in English learn English more rapidly by having them use English written materials.

speech disorder   A disorder of articulation, fluency, or voice.

Standard English   The linguistic system of English recognized by the literate culture and used in school.

syntax   The grammar system of a language; the linguistic rules of word order; the function of words in a sentence.

Suggested Activities

1. Observe a young child or a class of young children. Pay particular attention to the language used by an individual child or the interactions among a group of children.

2. Develop a series of oral directions for a child to follow (example: "Draw a red line across the center of the sheet, put a green circle in the upper left-hand corner," and so on). Record the instructions on tape and have a child listen to and follow them.

3. Plan a lesson for an oral expression activity (telling a story, relating an incident, explaining how to do something).

4. Say words with one, two, or three syllables and have the child tap out the syllables.

5. Say some words with three phoneme sounds (for example, *cat* or *sack*) and have the child tap out the number of sounds.

6. Find an example of a rhyming or word-play game for young children.

Pages for Making Transparencies

These pages can be transferred to transparencies for use with an overhead projector during class instruction.

1. Language Forms and the Integrated Language Core (Figure 11.1)

2. A Model of the Communication Process (Figure 11.3)

3. Theories of How Children Acquire Language

4. Linguistic Systems

5. Emergent Literacy

Figure 11.1
Language Forms and the Integrated Language Core

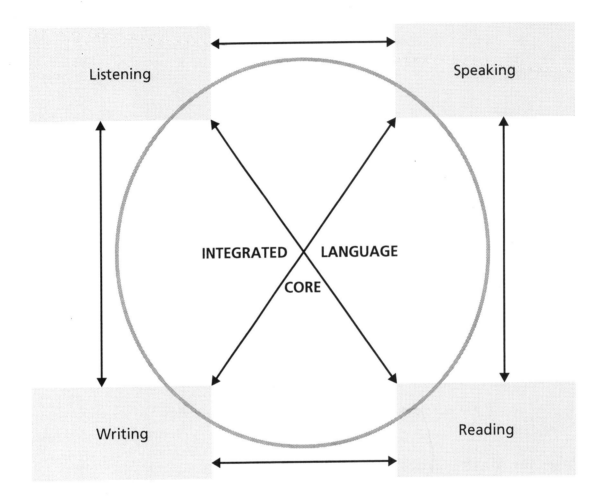

Figure 11.3
A Model of the Communication Process

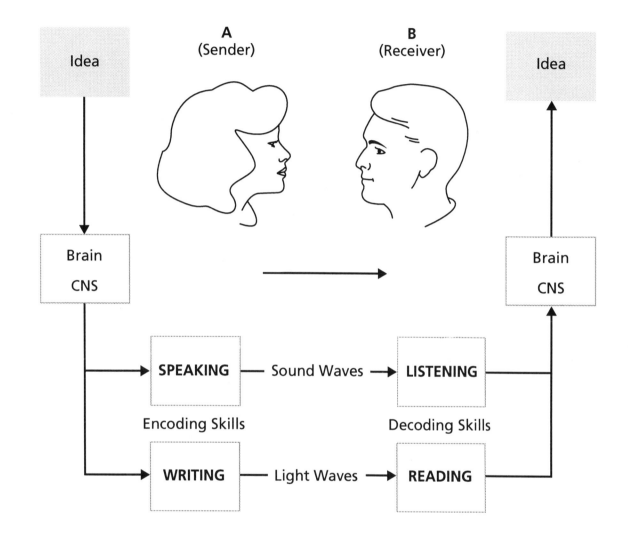

THEORIES OF HOW CHILDREN ACQUIRE LANGUAGE

- ## Behavioral theories

- ## Innatist theories

- ## Cognitive theories

- ## Social theories

LINGUISTIC SYSTEMS

- **Phonology: phonemes (sound units)**

- **Morphology: morphemes (meaning units)**

- **Syntax: grammar (sentence structure)**

- **Semantics: word meaning (vocabulary)**

- **Pragmatics: social side of language (intonation)**

EMERGENT LITERACY

- ## Oral language proficiency

- ## Concepts about print

- ## Alphabet knowledge

- ## Phonological awareness

- ## Letter-sound correspondence

- ## Beginning reading vocabulary

CHAPTER 12
Reading

Learning Objectives

1. Know the consequences that reading disabilities have for the individual, society, and the nation. *Academic achievement   success in life   employment*

2. Become familiar with the condition of dyslexia. *structural & functional differences in brain*

3. Know the philosophy of whole-language instruction and the implications for students with learning disabilities.

4. Describe the explicit code-emphasis approach to teaching reading.

5. Describe the two major components of reading: word recognition and reading comprehension.

6. Describe four clues to word recognition. *phonics sight words, context, structural analysis, combination*

7. Understand three interacting elements in reading comprehension. *reader, text, context*

8. Describe both informal and formal methods for assessing reading performance. *IRI, miscue analysis*

9. Know strategies for improving word recognition.

10. Describe methods for using the whole-language philosophy for teaching reading.

11. Know various methods for teaching reading comprehension.

12. Test yourself on phonics rules and generalizations (Part II of the Rapid Review Questions).

Focus

Theories

Reading is one form of the integrated language system and is linked to oral language and written language. It is one of the major academic difficulties for students with learning disabilities. Inability to read has detrimental consequences for society as well as for the poor reader.

Dyslexia is one form of learning disability in which the individual encounters extreme difficulty in learning to read. The problem is thought to be organic, related to abnormalities in brain structure or function.

The reading process is complex. Five generalizations about the reading process of effective readers are the following: (1) reading is a constructive process; (2) reading must be fluent; (3) reading must be strategic; (4) reading requires motivation; (5) reading is a lifelong pursuit.

There are two views about the teaching of reading: whole-language instruction and the explicit code-emphasis instruction. The best approach is to integrate these two instructional methods.

The philosophy of whole-language instruction includes the integration of reading and writing, the use of authentic literature, and the focus on meaning in reading.

The explicit code-emphasis instruction provides systematic, direct instruction of the elements of the alphabet code with an early emphasis on decoding skills.

Two major components should be considered in teaching reading: word recognition and reading comprehension. Word-recognition clues include phonics, sight words, context clues, and structural analysis. The ability to recognize words is a prerequisite to comprehension.

Reading comprehension involves three interactive elements: the reader, the text, and the context of the reading situation. Several concepts are important for reading comprehension: what the reader brings to the text, reading as a language process, reading as a thinking process, and the need for active intervention with the text. Other topics related to reading comprehension are fluency, reading of narrative materials, and reading of expository materials.

There are many ways to assess reading ability. Informal measures include the informal reading inventory, miscue analysis, and portfolio assessment. Formal tests include survey tests, diagnostic tests, and comprehensive batteries.

Teaching Strategies

Teaching strategies are organized into the following sections: (1) developing word recognition, (2) strategies for building fluency, (3) strategies for improving reading comprehension, (4) using special remedial methods, (5) dealing with special reading problems, and (6) using computers to teach reading.

A number of special methods are used with students with reading disabilities. Teachers of these students should have competencies in using the methods.

Lecture-Discussion Outline

Theories

I. The consequences of reading disabilities. The major problem of over 80 percent of the students with learning disabilities is in the area of reading. Poor reading can be debilitating to the individual and has disastrous repercussions for society and the nation.

II. Dyslexia. Dyslexia, a severe reading disorder, is a puzzling condition. People with this condition have extreme difficulty recognizing letters and words. There is growing evidence that dyslexia is related to a neurological dysfunction.

III. Two views about teaching reading are the whole-language approach and explicit code-emphasis instruction.

   A. Whole-language instruction. Whole language is a philosophy about teaching reading and the language arts that has revolutionized the teaching of reading in our schools. It integrates learning to read with learning to write and use oral language.

B. Explicit code-emphasis instruction. This approach emphasizes direct instruction of the elements of the alphabet code with an early emphasis on decoding skills.

IV. Major elements of reading. Both word recognition and reading comprehension are needed in reading.

V. Word recognition. To develop fluency in reading, the reader needs to develop dependable word-recognition skills.

A. Phonics

B. Sight words

C. Contextual clues

D. Structural analysis

E. Combining word-recognition strategies

VI. Reading comprehension. The purpose of reading is to gather meaning from the printed page. Every reading program should provide for the development of reading comprehension abilities.

A. Interactive elements in reading comprehension

B. Concepts of reading comprehension

C. Fluency in reading

D. Comprehension of narrative materials

E. Comprehension of expository materials

VII. Assessing reading. There are a wide variety of ways to assess reading performance. Reading can be evaluated through informal measures and through formal reading tests.

A. Informal measures

B. Formal tests

Teaching Strategies

VIII. Strategies for improving word recognition. To become fluent, readers need to recognize words quickly and easily. This section deals with the methods for doing so.

A. Building phonological awareness

B. Phonics methods

IX. Strategies for improving fluency

   A. Repeated reading

   B. Predictable books

   C. Neurological impress method

X. Strategies for improving reading comprehension. The strategies described in this section are designed to improve reading comprehension.

   A. Using basal readers

   B. Activating background knowledge

   C. The reading-writing connection

   D. Thinking strategies

   E. Learning strategies for reading

XI. Special remedial approaches to teaching reading. The methods described in this section are special methods, not usually used in regular reading classrooms.

   A. VAKT

   B. The Fernald method

   C. The Orton-Gillingham method

   D. Reading Recovery

   E. Direct instruction

XII. Methods for dealing with special reading problems. Students with reading and learning disabilities have unique problems that require specific methodology.

   A. Reversals

   B. Finger pointing and lip moving

   C. Disfluent oral reading

   D. Inability to read silently

   E. Tape-recorded textbooks

XIII. Computers and reading. Computer technology offers a motivating method of teaching reading. There are a number of different types of computer applications for teaching reading.

Key Terms and Definitions

Students should take note of the following terms as they appear in this chapter. Students who have difficulty should refer to the glossary in Appendix E of the text or to the text page on which the term is discussed.

background knowledge   Information and experiences that are gained about the topic of instruction or about a reading selection.

basal reading series   A graduated series of readers used to teach reading. The series begins with very simple stories using a few words and increases in difficulty until the sixth- or eighth-grade level. Teacher's manuals, children's activity books, and other auxiliary material often accompany the basal reading series.

cloze procedure   A technique that is useful in testing, in teaching reading comprehension, and in determining readability (or difficulty level of the material). The cloze procedure involves deleting words from the text and inserting underlined blank spaces. Measurement is made by counting the number of blanks that students can correctly fill.

context clues   Clues that help readers recognize words through the meaning or context of the sentence or paragraph in which the words appear.

directed reading-thinking activity   A guided method of teaching reading comprehension in which readers first read a section of text, then predict what will happen next, and then read to verify the accuracy of the predictions.

dyslexia   A severe reading disorder in which the individual cannot learn to read or does not acquire fluent and efficient reading skills. Research suggests that there is a connection between dyslexia and neurological dysfunction.

emergent literacy   The child's early entrance into the world of words, language, and stories. Literacy emerges in children through the simultaneous experiences with oral language, reading, and writing.

explicit code-emphasis instruction   Systematic and direct teaching of decoding and phonics skills.

fluent reading   The act of reading quickly and smoothly. Fluency requires the reader to recognize words easily. The word identification process must be automatic, not a conscious, deliberate effort.

grapheme   The written representation of a phoneme sound.

informal reading inventory   An informal method of assessing the reading level of a student by having the student orally read successively more difficult passages.

language experience method   A method of teaching reading based on the experiences and language of the reader. The method involves the generation of experience-based materials that are dictated by the student, written by the teacher, and then used as the material for teaching reading.

miscue analysis   An evaluation of the errors the student makes in oral reading.

neurological impress method   An approach for teaching reading to students with severe reading disabilities that consists of a system of rapid-unison reading by the student and the instructor.

phoneme   The smallest unit of sound in a language.

phonics   An application of phonetics to the teaching of reading in which the sound (or phoneme) of a language is related to the equivalent written symbol (or grapheme).

phonological awareness   A child's recognition of the sounds of language. The child must understand that speech can be segmented into syllables and phonemic units.

portfolio assessment   A method of evaluating student progress by analyzing samples of the student's classroom work.

reading comprehension   Understanding of the meaning of printed text.

Reading Recovery   A reading program first used in New Zealand in which first graders who rank very low in reading are selected for a period of intensive reading instruction.

sight words   Words that a student recognizes instantly, without hesitation or further analysis.

structural analysis   The recognition of words through the analysis of meaningful word units, such as prefixes, suffixes, root words, compound words, and syllables.

VAKT   The abbreviation for *v*isual, *a*uditory, *k*inesthetic, and *t*actile learning, a multisensory approach for teaching reading that stimulates all avenues of sensory input simultaneously.

whole language   A philosophy about reading that embraces the wholeness of the integrated language forms—oral language, reading, writing. It makes extensive use of literary materials.

word-recognition skills   Strategies for recognizing words, including phonics, sight words, context clues, structural analysis, and combinations of these strategies.

Suggested Activities

1. Use the Fernald method to teach reading to a child with a severe reading disorder. Refer to Grace Fernald, *Remedial Techniques in Basic School Subjects* (New York: McGraw-Hill, 1943; Austin, TX: Pro-Ed, 1988).

2. Analyze a basal reading series, examining the entire series from readiness to sixth-grade level. Consider its philosophy, phonics approach, vocabulary load, story content, and auxiliary materials (such as workbooks). Analyze its value for students with learning disabilities.

3. Select another approach to the teaching of reading. Examine the materials and analyze their value.

4. Give a child an informal reading test (see word lists in Chapter 3) or have the child read a page from a reader. Note what kinds of problems the child has.

Pages for Making Transparencies

These pages can be transferred to transparencies for use with an overhead projector during class instruction.

1. Whole-Language Views

2. Word-Recognition Strategies

3. Flow Chart of the Steps in the Informal Reading Inventory (Figure 12.2)

4. K-W-L Strategy Sheet

5. Cloze Passage

WHOLE-LANGUAGE VIEWS

- **Use integrated language system: oral language, reading, writing**

- **Both oral and written languages are acquired through natural usage**

- **Use only authentic literature**

- **Teach writing early**

- **Provide abundant opportunities for writing**

- **Avoid instruction on separate nonmeaningful parts of language or use of exercises and drills**

WORD-RECOGNITION STRATEGIES

- ## Sight words

- ## Phonics

- ## Context clues

- ## Structural analysis

- ## Combining word-recognition strategies

Figure 12.2
Flow Chart of the Steps in the Informal Reading Inventory

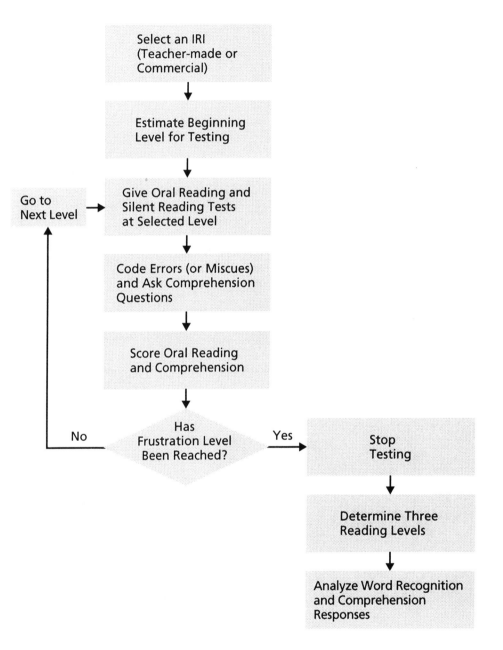

Source: Adapted from M. Richek, L. List and F. Lerner, *Reading Problems: Diagnostic and Remediation* (Englewood Cliffs, N.J.: Prentice Hall, Inc., 1989). Reprinted by permission.

K-W-L STRATEGY SHEET

K	W	L
What we <u>Know</u>	**What we <u>Want</u> to Find Out**	**What we <u>Learned</u>**

CLOZE PASSAGE

This is a book **1** learning disabilities, a problem **2** impedes learning for **3**, adolescents, and adults, affecting **4** schooling and adjustment to **5**. There is growing concern **6** children and youth with **7** disabilities who have extreme **8** in learning academic and **9** skills, despite their mental **10** for doing so.

The **11** of the youngster who **12** extreme difficulty in learning, **13**, is not new. Children from **14** walks of life have **15** such difficulties throughout the **16**.

CHAPTER 13

Written Language: Written Expression, Spelling, and Handwriting

Learning Objectives

1. Recognize the connections between writing and the language system.

2. Describe the stages of the writing process.

3. Compare the differences between instruction for the written *product* and the writing *process.*

4. Describe how word processing can help students with learning disabilities in writing.

5. Explain why students with learning disabilities often have problems in spelling.

6. Explain *invented spelling* and why it is encouraged in the early grades.

7. Describe three ways to produce writing taught in the schools—manuscript writing, cursive writing, and keyboarding—and how each affects students with learning disabilities.

Focus

Theories

Three areas of written language in which students with learning disabilities have difficulty are written expression, spelling, and handwriting. Writing is a part of the integrated language system, and experiences with writing and composing improve an individual's language system and facilitate improvement in reading and oral language. Written expression is the most difficult of the language skills to achieve and the most common communication disability.

The writing process consists of several stages: (1) prewriting, (2) writing (or drafting), (3) revising, and (4) sharing with an audience. Principles for teaching writing as a process include (1) providing sufficient prior experience in prewriting, (2) freeing students from overconcentration on the mechanics of writing in the early stages of the process, (3) encouraging students to revise their work, and (4) avoiding excessive correction of the student's written work. Word-processing applications on the computer are one of the most effective tools for teaching writing.

Spelling is particularly difficult in English because of the irregularity between spoken and written forms of the language. The stages of learning to spell are (1) developing prephonetic writing, (2) using letter names and beginning phonetic strategies, (3) using written word patterns, (4) using syllable junctures and multisyllabic words, and (5) developing a mature spelling perspective. Spelling requires many intact skills, such as reading, knowledge of phonics rules, visual memory, and the motor facility to write legibly. Invented spelling is the beginning writer's ability to write words by attending to their sound units and associating letters with them in a systematic, although unconventional, way. One theory for teaching writing is to encourage students to use invented spelling to increase the amount of writing that young children do. Two theories of selecting words for spelling study are the linguistic approach and the frequency-of-use approach. The linguistic approach bases spelling word selection on phonic patterns and underlying linguistic rules. The frequency-of-use approach selects spelling words for study based on words found most often in the students' reading materials.

Handwriting is a fine-motor skill, and so it is a difficult skill for students with learning disabilities and motor disorders. Teachers must give special consideration to the decision to teach either cursive or manuscript writing. Also, left-handed students need special techniques. Handwriting difficulties can be eased by the use of a computer.

Teaching Strategies

Teaching strategies are presented for each of the areas of the curriculum concerned with writing: strategies for written expression, strategies for word processing, strategies for spelling, and strategies for handwriting.

Lecture-Discussion Outline

Theories

I. Written expression. Written language is the third form of the integrated language system. For many students, writing is the most difficult form of language. Experiences in oral language and reading help strengthen written expression.

    A. The writing connection in the integrated language system

    B. Emergent literacy

    C. The writing process

    D. Strategies for writing

    E. Computers and word processing

    F. Assessment of written expression

II. Spelling. Spelling requires the ability to remember the sequence of the letters of a word. Unlike reading, spelling offers no clues. In English there is not a consistent one-to-one relationship between the sound and letter patterns, making spelling even more difficult.

    A. Development stages of learning to spell

    B. Problems related to spelling

C. Invented spelling

D. Self-questioning strategies for spelling

E. Multisensory approaches to spelling

F. Two theories of word selection for teaching spelling

G. Assessment of spelling

III. Handwriting. Handwriting is a necessary skill in school and adult life. Students who have fine-motor problems may find writing an extremely challenging task. Computers and word processing can help people with writing difficulties.

A. Manuscript writing

B. Cursive writing

C. The left-handed student

D. Keyboarding or typing skills

Teaching Strategies

IV. Strategies for teaching written expression. To learn to write, students need many opportunities to develop a written product. Learning to write requires time and experience with various types of writing.

V. Strategies for using word processing. Word processing is becoming an essential skill for all individuals. Several strategies for teaching word processing are provided.

VI. Strategies for teaching spelling. A number of specific methods for teaching spelling are described in this section.

VII. Strategies for teaching handwriting. Students need direct instruction in manuscript writing and in cursive writing. Some suggestions are provided.

Key Terms and Definitions

Students should take note of the following terms as they appear in this chapter. Students who have difficulty should refer to the glossary in Appendix E of the text or to the text page on which the term is discussed.

cursive writing The style of writing, sometimes called script, in which the individual letters are joined in writing a word. Children typically learn cursive writing in third grade.

drafting A stage in the writing process in which a preliminary version of the written product is developed.

dysgraphia   Extremely poor handwriting or the inability to perform the motor movements required for handwriting. The condition is associated with neurological dysfunction.

emergent literacy   The child's early entrance into the world of words, language, and stories. Literacy emerges in children through simultaneous experiences with oral language, reading, and writing.

graphic organizers   Visual displays that organize and structure ideas and concepts.

invented spelling   The beginning writer's attempt to write words. The young writer attends to the sound units and associates letters with them in a systematic, although unconventional, way.

keyboarding   The processing of typing on a computer keyboard.

linguistic approach to spelling   A theory of word selection and instruction in spelling. It is based on the belief that the spelling of English is sufficiently rule-covered to warrant a method of selection and instruction that stresses phonological, morphological, and syntactic rules or word patterns.

manuscript writing   The form of handwriting sometimes called printing. This form of writing, closer to the printed form, is easier to learn than cursive writing because it consists of only circles and straight lines.

prewriting   The first step of the writing process, in which writers evoke and gather ideas for writing.

revising   A stage of the writing process in which the writer reworks a draft of a written product.

sharing with an audience   The stage of the writing process in which the final written product is read by others.

word-frequency approach to spelling   A method of word selection and instruction for spelling. Words are selected for spelling instruction on the basis of how frequently they are used in writing.

word processing   Writing with a computer (as contrasted with writing by hand or on a conventional typewriter).

writing process   A series of stages writers go through during writing: (1) prewriting, (2) writing or drafting, (3) revising, and (4) sharing with an audience.

Suggested Activities

1. Have groups of children plan for writing with a graphic organizer. Have each group select a topic and make a graphic organizer on the topic. Have each group display and explain the graphic organizer to the entire class.

2. Learn to write the letters of the alphabet in both manuscript writing and cursive writing.

3. Analyze a child's errors in spelling in terms of (1) the student's stage of writing and (2) the strategies the child uses for spelling.

4. Learn to use a word-processing program with a computer. Teach a child to write with a word-processing program.

5. Give a child an informal spelling test, using the words in Table 13.4. Stop testing when the student misses three consecutive words. Estimate the student's spelling grade level.

6. Obtain a sample of a child's writing from a primary grade. Note any examples of invented spelling.

Pages for Making Transparencies

These pages can be transferred to transparencies for use with an overhead projector during class instruction.

1. Stages in the Writing Process

2. Emergent Literacy and Writing

3. Sample Manuscript and Cursive Alphabets

4. Multisensory Spelling Method

STAGES IN THE WRITING PROCESS

1. Prewriting

2. Writing (or drafting)

3. Revising

4. Sharing with an audience

EMERGENT LITERACY AND WRITING

- **Encourages early writing**

- **Children use invented spelling**

- **Children explore the alphabetic properties of writing**

- **Children develop concepts about print**

Sample Manuscript and Cursive Alphabets

MANUSCRIPT ALPHABET

A B C D E F G H I J K L M N O P Q R
S T U V W X Y Z a b c d e f g h i j k l m
n o p q r s t u v w x y z 1 2 3 4 5 6 7 8 9 10

CURSIVE ALPHABET

Aa Bb Cc Dd Ee Ff
Gg Hh Ii Jj Kk Ll
Mm Nn Oo Pp Qq Rr
Ss Tt Uu Vv Ww Xx
Yy Zz 1 2 3 4 5 6 7 8 9 10

Source: From the *Sample Manuscript Alphabet*, Grade 3, and the *Sample Cursive Alphabet*, Grade 3 (Columbus, OH: Zaner-Bloser, 1958).

MULTISENSORY SPELLING METHOD

1. Meaning and Pronunciation

2. Imagery

3. Recall

4. Writing the word

5. Mastery

CHAPTER 14
Mathematics

Learning Objectives

1. Describe the characteristics of students with mathematics disabilities.

2. Discuss the changing ideas about teaching mathematics over the years.

3. Know the recommendations of the National Council of Teachers of Mathematics.

4. Describe informal methods and formal instruments for assessing mathematics abilities.

5. Know the principles of mathematics instruction for students with learning disabilities.

6. Describe activities for teaching mathematics concepts, skills, and problem solving.

Focus

Theories

Some students with learning disabilities have severe difficulty in learning mathematics. Mathematics basal series used in general education classes have a number of deficiencies for students with learning disabilities.

Students with a mathematics disability display a number of characteristics. Precursors of mathematics learning disabilities include disturbances in spatial relationships, poor sense of body image, disturbances in visual-motor and visual-perception abilities, language and/or reading problems, poor concepts of direction and time, memory problems, deficiences in mathematics learning strategies, and math anxiety.

Notions about how to teach mathematics have changed over the years. We have seen a "modern math" movement and a back-to-basics movement. We are now in the midst of an education reform movement. The math problems of secondary students differ from those of elementary students.

Several learning theories provide the basis for mathematics instruction for students with learning disabilities. They include progression from concrete to abstract learning, constructive learning, direct instruction, learning strategies instruction, and problem solving.

Mathematics proficiency can be assessed with informal measures (such as informal inventories, individual clinical tests, analysis of errors) or formal tests (such as standardized survey tests).

Teaching Strategies

The teaching of mathematics follows a sequence through the grades. Principles of remediation in mathematics include prenumber concepts and a readiness for mathematics learning, progression from the concrete to the abstract, opportunity for practice and review, generalization of what has been learned, the building of a solid foundation of concepts and skills, and a balanced mathematics curriculum that includes concepts, skills, and problem solving.

Principles of instruction for students with mathematics disabilities include the following: teach precursors of mathematics learning, progress from the concrete to the abstract, provide opportunities for practice and review, teach students to generalize, teach mathematics vocabulary, consider the student's strengths and weaknesses, build a solid foundation of mathematics concepts and skills, and provide a balanced mathematics program.

Teachers need a variety of strategies for teaching each of the three components of the mathematics curriculum. The teaching strategies section offers methods for teaching concepts, skills, and problem solving.

Lecture-Discussion Outline

Theories

I. Mathematics disabilities. Many students with learning disabilities encounter major problems in learning mathematics. Students with mathematics disabilities are likely to have deficits or problems in one or more of several areas of learning.

II. Indicators of mathematics disabilities. *Dyscalculia* is the medical term for severe mathematics problems. *[handwritten: a specific disturbance in learning mathematical concepts & computation & associated with central nervous system dysfunction]*

   A. Precursors of mathematics learning *[handwritten: Insufficient experience w/ object manipulation Count, match, sort, one to one correspondence compare]* *[handwritten: one-to-one correspondence Classification Seriation conservation]*

   B. Disturbances of spatial relations *[handwritten: space time size distance order quantity up-down top-bottom near-far over-under high-low front-back beginning-end across]*

   C. Poor sense of body image *[handwritten: Draw a picture of a human being]*

   D. Disturbances of motor and visual-perception abilities *[handwritten: grasping instead of pointing / unable to see objects in groups / perceive geometric shapes as individual, no integrated lines]*

   E. Language and reading problems *[handwritten: Word problems]*

   F. Poor concepts of direction and time

   G. Memory problems *[handwritten: Automaticity of computational facts]*

   H. Deficiencies in mathematics learning strategies *[handwritten: no strategy or inappropriate strategy (Adolescent) / Provide instruction]*

   I. Math anxiety *[handwritten: Generalize to other areas / Scripture / Teacher Implications]*

III. Changing ideas about mathematics education. Mathematics instruction has been subject to outside pressures. Instruction has gone through the phases of modern math, back-to-basics, and education reform. Many of these instructional policies have adversely affected students with learning disabilities. *[handwritten: Modern Math - compounded math problems of individuals, but doesn't say how - CONFUSION]* *[handwritten: Back to Basics - stressed computation neglected instruction in math concepts, quantitative thinking, problem solving]*

[handwritten: Handout or Transparency]
[handwritten: Transparency]

A. Educational reform movement

[handwritten: higher standards / more testing in math / increase in math courses in HS curriculum]

B. Secondary students with mathematics disabilities

[handwritten: Students who have difficulties are faced with higher standards & expectations]

C. Math curriculum recommendations of the NCTM (National Council for Teachers of Mathematics)

IV. Perspectives and learning theories for mathematics education. Various theories of learning have implications for mathematics instruction.

A. Progression from concrete to abstract learning

B. Constructive learning

C. Direct instruction

D. Learning strategies

E. Problem solving

[handwritten: Secondary Curriculum & LD / more sophisticated / more abstract / based on presumption of learned basic skills / ie. Algebra Increased requirements for HS grad / more testing / BIG Question / How prepare Math LD students to succeed in algebra?]

V. Assessing mathematics. As with other areas of the curriculum, there are informal assessment methods and formal assessment methods.

A. Formal tests

B. Informal measures

Teaching Strategies

VI. The mathematics curriculum. Mathematics is a sequential area of the curriculum. Learning one skill provides the basis for learning the next. The skills taught at the various grade levels are described.

A. The sequence of mathematics through the grades

B. The secondary mathematics curriculum

[handwritten: Homemade Transparency]

VII. Principles of instruction for students with mathematics disabilities. There are a number of principles that guide instruction in mathematics for students with learning disabilities.

A. Teach precursors of mathematics learning

B. Progress from the concrete to the abstract

C. Provide opportunity for practice and review

D. Teach students to generalize to new situations

E. Teach mathematics vocabulary

F. Consider the student's strengths and weaknesses

G. Build a solid foundation of mathematics concepts and skills

H. Provide a balanced mathematics program

VIII. Activities for teaching mathematics. Activities for teaching mathematics are organized into teaching mathematics concepts, teaching skills, and teaching problem solving.

A. Teaching mathematics concepts

B. Teaching mathematics skills

C. Teaching mathematics problem solving

IX. Using technology for mathematics instruction

A. Calculators

B. Computers

Key Terms and Definitions

Students should take note of the following terms as they appear in this chapter. Students who have difficulty should refer to the glossary in Appendix E of the text or to the text page on which the term is discussed.

abstract-level instruction   At this level of mathematics instruction, students manipulate symbols without the help of concrete objects or representational pictures or tallies.

back-to-basics movement   Educational instruction that emphasizes intensive teaching of academic skills. In reading, the emphasis is on word-recognition skills; in mathematics, it is on computation facts.

computer literacy   General knowledge about computers and their varied uses.

concrete instruction   A method of teaching in which the child manipulates real objects for learning.

constructive learning   A theory of learning that is based on the idea that children can build their own mental structures. In mathematics, they create their own number ideas.

direct instruction   A method associated with behavioral theories of instruction. The focus is directly on the curriculum or task to be taught and the steps needed to learn that task.

dyscalculia   A medical term indicating lack of ability to perform mathematical functions. The condition is associated with neurological dysfunction or brain damage.

math anxiety   A debilitating emotional reaction to mathematics situations.

mathematics computation   The basic mathematical operations, consisting of addition, subtraction, multiplication, division, fractions, decimals, and percentages.

mathematics problem solving   The kind of thinking needed to solve mathematics problems. The individual must analyze and interpret information as the basis for making selections and decisions.

modern math   A widely used math curriculum of the 1970s, designed to teach the concepts underlying mathematics instead of the mechanics of arithmetic.

number line   A sequence of numbers forming a straight line that allows the student to manipulate computation directly. Number lines help students develop an understanding of number symbols and their relationship to each other.

one-to-one correspondence   A relationship in which one element of a set is paired with one and only one element of a second set.

place value   The aspect of the number system that assigns specific significance to the position a digit holds in a numeral.

representational-level instruction   Mathematics instruction that is between the concrete and abstract levels. It is semiconcrete in that students use pictures or tallies to represent concrete objects.

spatial relationships   Concepts such as *up-down, over-under, top-bottom, high-low, near-far, beginning-end,* and *across.* A disturbance in spatial relationship can interfere with the visualization of the entire number system.

time concepts   The sense of time, which is difficult for some students with learning disabilities, who may be poor at estimating the span of an hour, a minute, several hours, or a weekend and may have difficulty estimating how long a task will take. Trouble with time concepts characterizes students with mathematics disabilities.

Suggested Activities

1. Design a lesson to teach arithmetic computation (addition, subtraction, multiplication, division, or fractions) using manipulative materials (buttons, washers, blocks, Popsicle sticks, or the like).

2. Analyze a student's arithmetic test and work page to determine the types of errors made.

3. Design an informal arithmetic test.

4. Evaluate a computer program for teaching mathematics as to its suitability for students with learning disabilities.

Pages for Making Transparencies

These pages can be transferred to transparencies for use with an overhead projector during class instruction.

1. Progressing from Concrete to Abstract

2. Precursors of Mathematics Disabilities

3. Theories of Math Instruction

4. Common Math Errors

5. Math Vocabulary

PROGRESSING FROM CONCRETE TO ABSTRACT

1. Concrete level:

real objects

4 apples + 3 apples = 7 apples

+

2. Representational level:

graphic symbols

0 0 0 0 + 0 0 0 = 0 0 0 0 0 0 0 (7)

3. Abstract level:

numbers

3 + 4 = 7

PRECURSORS OF MATHEMATICS DISABILITIES

Problems with:

- **Spatial relations**
- **Direction**

- **Body image**
- **Time**

- **Visual-motor**
- **Memory**

- **Visual perception**
- **Learning strategies**

- **Language**
- **Math anxiety**

THEORIES OF MATH INSTRUCTION

- **Progression from concrete to abstract**

- **Constructive learning**

- **Direct instruction**

- **Learning strategies instruction**

- **Problem solving**

COMMON MATH ERRORS

Place value

$$\begin{array}{r} 72 \\ + 29 \\ \hline 91 \end{array}$$

Computation facts

$$\begin{array}{r} 5 \\ \times\ 9 \\ \hline 47 \end{array}$$

Wrong process

$$\begin{array}{r} 16 \\ -\ 2 \\ \hline 18 \end{array}$$

Working from left to right

$$\begin{array}{r} 42 \\ + 85 \\ \hline 28 \end{array}$$

MATH VOCABULARY

- **Addition**

$$
\begin{array}{r}
3 \\
+\ 5 \\
\hline
8
\end{array}
$$

  3 —> Addend
  + 5 —> Addend
  8 —> Sum

- **Subtraction**

  9 —> Minuend
  – 3 —> Subtrahend
  6 —> Difference

- **Multiplication**

  7 —> Multiplicand
  × 5 —> Multiplier
  35 —> Product

- **Division**

  7 —> Quotient
  Divisor <— 6)42 —> Dividend

CHAPTER 15
Social and Emotional Behavior

Learning Objectives

1. Describe the characteristics of social problems that affect some students with learning disabilities.

2. Describe the causes of emotional problems and their effects on students with learning disabilities.

3. Describe the quality of resiliency found in some individuals with learning disabilities.

4. Explain behavior management and the implications of this approach to students with learning disabilities.

5. Indicate methods of developing social competencies.

6. Indicate methods of building self-esteem.

7. Describe how behavior management strategies can be used with students with learning disabilities.

8. Know ways a teacher can make accommodations for students with learning disabilities in the general education classroom.

Focus

Theories

Many students with learning disabilities have problems with social skills and social perception. Often they behave differently from others in the classroom, do not do well in conversations with peers or in cooperative work, and are described as hostile. The characteristics of social disabilities include lack of judgment, difficulty in perceiving the feelings of others, problems in socializing and making friends, problems in family relationships, and poor self-concept.

Emotional difficulties pose another problem for some students with learning disabilities. The emotional consequences of failure undermine a student's ability to learn. Such students have little self-confidence, have poor ego development, and have few opportunities to develop feelings of self-worth.

Behavioral problems of students with attention deficit disorders (ADDs) also must be considered. ADD is characterized by persistent difficulty in attention span, poor impulse control, and sometimes hyperactivity.

Motivation is the force that energizes and directs one's drive to accomplish goals. Students must have a strong desire to learn, because much of academic learning requires persistence and hard work over a long period of time.

Behavior management strategies are used to systematically plan and structure environmental events to bring about changes in student behavior. The behavioral unit consists of the antecedent event or stimulus, the target behavior of the student, and the consequent event or reinforcement. Key concepts in behavior management include reinforcement, response cost, shaping behavior, contingency management, token reinforcements, and time out.

Assessment instruments for social and emotional factors include interviews, rating scales, checklists, inventories, and tests.

Teaching Strategies

Teaching strategies are presented for developing social competencies, for building self-esteem, for managing behavior, and for making accommodations for inclusive classrooms.

Children usually learn social perception and skills without direct instruction. However, students with learning disabilities often need direct instruction in how to act and respond in social situations.

This section provides suggestions to help students with learning disabilities build self-concept, self-esteem, and confidence so that they can learn.

Behavioral approaches are effective in changing the behavior of students with learning disabilities. It is important to determine what reinforcements will change the target behavior, to find workable reinforcers, and to monitor the behavior.

Lecture-Discussion Outline

Theories

I. Social skills disabilities. Some students with learning disabilities exhibit deficits in social skills. Inept social skills can affect almost every aspect of the student's life. They imply a lack of sensitivity to people and poor perception of social situations.

    A. Characteristics of a social disability

    B. Teaching social skills

II. Emotional problems. Repeated failure and the inability to achieve and develop a sense of competence and self-worth are indelible. Psychodynamic development and personality structure have important implications for understanding the emotional consequences of learning disabilities.

    A. Causes and effects of emotional problems

    B. Building concepts of self-worth

C. The quality of resiliency

D. Strengthening self-esteem

III. Behavioral considerations: behavior problems of children with attention deficit disorders. Students with learning disabilities may have attention deficit disorders.

A. Attention deficit hyperactivity disorders

B. Motivation

C. Behavior management

D. Cognitive behavior modification

IV. Assessing social and emotional behaviors. The assessment of social skills and emotional status is difficult to perform. Methods include observations, rating scales, interviews, student inventories, and sociometric techniques.

Teaching Strategies

V. Developing social competencies. Students with social deficits need conscious effort and specific teaching to learn about the social world, its nuances, and its silent language.

A. Body image and self-perception

B. Sensitivity to other people

C. Social maturity

D. Learning strategies for social skills

E. Social skills programs

VI. Building self-esteem. When emotional problems accompany learning failures, the student may be a victim of a continuous cycle of failure to learn and an emotional reaction to this failure. Teaching should be designed to reverse this cycle of failure.

VII. Behavior management strategies. Behavior management strategies can be used with students with learning disabilities, both for managing behavior and for teaching academic skills.

A. Reinforcement

B. Response cost

C. Punishment

D. Ignoring

        E. Shaping behavior

        F. Contingency management

        G. Token reinforcements

        H. Timeout

        I. Home-school coordination

VIII. Accommodations for the inclusive classroom. More children with learning disabilities are being placed in the general education classroom. Classroom teachers must make accommodations for these students.

Key Terms and Definitions

Students should note the following terms as they appear in this chapter. Students who have difficulty should refer to the glossary in Appendix E of the text or to the text page on which the term is discussed.

attention deficit hyperactivity disorder (ADHD)   Difficulty in concentrating and staying on task, accompanied by hyperactivity. The condition of ADHD is identified and defined by the American Psychiatric Association's *Diagnostic and Statistical Manual of Mental Disorders,* fourth edition.

attribution   A person's ideas concerning the causes of his or her successes and failures.

contingency contract   A behavioral management strategy that entails a written agreement between the student and the teacher stating that the student will be able to do something the student wants to do after first completing a specified task.

home-school coordination   A behavior management strategy for helping a child learn. Progress made at school is reinforced in the child's home.

modifications   Reasonable changes to accommodate needs of students with disabilities in general education classrooms.

negative reinforcement   An event following a behavior that decreases the likelihood that the behavior will occur again.

positive reinforcement   An event following a behavior that increases the likelihood that the person will make a similar response in similar situations in the future.

Premack principle   A behavioral method using preferred activities to reinforce less preferred activities. This concept is also referred to as "Grandma's Rule"—for example, "If you finish your vegetables, you can have dessert."

response cost   A punishment for a behavior or response, in which positive reinforcers are withdrawn.

self-esteem   Feelings of self-worth, self-confidence, and self-concept that provide an experience of success.

shaping behavior   See successive approximations.

social perception   The ability to understand social situations, as well as sensitivity to the feelings of others.

social skills   Skills necessary for meeting the basic social demands of everyday life.

successive approximations   A behavioral method that is also referred to as shaping behavior. Desired goals are broken down into a sequence of ordered steps or tasks, behavior that the child already emits is reinforced, and then requirements are gradually increased with appropriate reinforcement until the child reaches the desired goal.

token reinforcers   Reinforcements that are accumulated to be exchanged at a later time for a more meaningful "backup" reinforcer.

Suggested Activities

1. Develop a contingency contract with a child in your class.

2. Use the Premack principle to reward yourself with something you desire for performing a task you dislike. Write a report on your experience.

3. Develop a plan for making accommodations in a general education classroom for students with disabilities.

4. Read an article on one of the following topics and analyze its implications for students with learning disabilities: social perception, emotional problems, behavior management, motivation, self-esteem, attribution styles, hyperactive behavior.

Pages for Making Transparencies

These pages can be transferred to transparencies for use with an overhead projector during class instruction.

1. Indicators of Social Disabilities

2. Accommodations for Students with Attention Deficit Disorders in the Classroom

3. Behavior Management Strategies

4. ABC—Components of a Behavioral Unit

5. Contingency Contract (Figure 15.1)

6. Managing Behaviors in Inclusive Classrooms

INDICATORS OF SOCIAL DISABILITIES

- **Poor social perception**

- **Lack of judgment**

- **Lack of sensitivity to others**

- **Difficulty making friends**

- **Problems establishing family relationships**

- **Social problems in school**

- **Social disabilities of adolescents and adults**

ACCOMMODATIONS FOR STUDENTS WITH ATTENTION DEFICIT DISORDERS IN THE CLASSROOM

- Seat student to minimize disruptions

- Vary activities to allow student to move

- Provide structure and routine

- Require a daily assignment notebook

- Obtain student attention before teaching

- Make directions concise and clear

- Break assignments into workable chunks

- Give extra time as needed

- Provide feedback quickly

- Ask parents to set up study space at home

- Use learning aids (calculators, audiotapes, computers)

- Find something student does well

- Modify the testing situation

BEHAVIOR MANAGEMENT STRATEGIES

- ## Reinforcements
    - ✓ Positive
    - ✓ Negative

- ## Shaping behavior
    - ✓ Successive approximation
    - ✓ Catch them being good

- ## Contingency contracting

- ## Token reinforcements

- ## Response cost

- ## Time out

- ## Home-school coordination

A B C - COMPONENTS OF A BEHAVIORAL UNIT

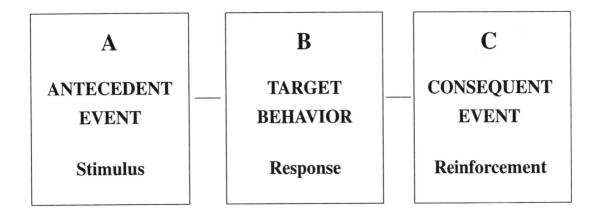

A	B	C
ANTECEDENT EVENT	**TARGET BEHAVIOR**	**CONSEQUENT EVENT**
Stimulus	Response	Reinforcement

Figure 15.1
Contingency Contract

CONTRACT

This contract is an agreement between _____
_____ (student)

and _____ .
_____ (teacher)

_____ will _____
(student)

_____

by _____ .
____ (date of completion)

If the work described above is completed on time,

_____ will _____
(teacher)

_____

_____

_____

by _____ .
____ (date of reward)

_____   _____
Signature of student   date

_____   _____
Signature of teacher   date

MANAGING BEHAVIORS IN INCLUSIVE CLASSROOMS

- ## Limiting distractions

- ## Increasing attention

- ## Improving organization

- ## Improving listening skills

- ## Managing time

- ## Providing opportunities for moving

PART TWO
Test Questions

Short-Answer Questions and Answers
Essay-Discussion Questions and Answers

This section contains short-answer and essay questions for each chapter, along with sample answer guides.

CHAPTER 1
Learning Disabilities: A Field in Transition

Short-Answer Questions and Answers

1. **What are the five common elements in most of the definitions of learning disabilities?**
   Answer: (1) Central nervous system dysfunction; (2) uneven growth pattern and psychological processing differences; (3) difficulty in academic and learning tasks; (4) discrepancy between potential and achievement; (5) exclusion of other causes.

2. **To determine a discrepancy between potential and achievement, it is necessary to measure which three areas?**
   Answer: (1) The individual's potential for learning (intelligence, IQ, aptitude); (2) the individual's current achievement level (academic performance level); (3) the degree of discrepancy between potential and achievement.

3. **Give several reasons why the number of students identified as having learning disabilities is increasing.**
   Answer: (1) More awareness of learning disabilities; (2) improvement in procedures for identifying and assessing learning disabilities; (3) social acceptance and preferences of the learning disabilities classification; (4) cutbacks in other programs and lack of general education alternatives for children who experience problems in the regular class; (5) court orders.

4. **The category of learning disabilities comprises what percentage of all students with disabilities in the schools?**
   Answer: 50.2 percent, or about half.

5. **List the four general age groups of individuals with learning disabilities and a characteristic of each age level.**
   Answer: Preschool (language and motor disorders); elementary (reading difficulties); secondary (academic and social/emotional difficulties); adult (employment, friendships, postsecondary education).

Essay-Discussion Questions and Answers

1. **What are the various definitions of learning disabilities that have been proposed, and how do they differ? Do you think it is important to formulate a single definition that all will agree upon? Why or why not?**
   Answer: (1) Federal definition derived from IDEA (disorder in basic psychological processes, difficulty in learning, not primarily due to other causes, severe discrepancy between potential and achievement); (2) Interagency Committee on Learning Disabilities (includes social disabilities, can occur concomitantly with other disabling conditions, intrinsic to the individual, presumed to be caused by central nervous system dysfunction); (3) National Joint Committee on Learning Disabilities (heterogeneous group of disorders, intrinsic to the individual, related to a central nervous system dysfunction, may occur with other disabilities).

2. **What are the five dimensions, or components, common to most definitions of learning disabilities? Discuss the nature of and the controversies surrounding each component.**
Answer: (1) Neurological dysfunction (controversy: difficult to diagnose); (2) uneven growth pattern (controversy: issues related to concept of psychological processing dysfunctions and underlying psychological deficits); (3) difficulty in academic and learning tasks (controversy: which learning areas should be considered in identifying a learning disability); (4) discrepancy between potential and achievement (controversies: this is an underachievement definition; use of discrepancy formulas for identification); (5) exclusion clause (controversy: existence of other disabilities, such as emotional disturbance, in many students with learning disabilities).

3. **The age range of individuals with learning disabilities has expanded over the years. There are four general age levels. Describe the characteristics of each age level.**
Answer: Preschool (language and motor disorders); elementary (reading difficulties); secondary (academic and social/emotional difficulties); adult (employment, friendships, postsecondary education).

4. **The number of students classified as having learning disabilities has increased substantially since the special education law (Public Law 94-142) was first implemented in 1977–78. Discuss the reasons for this increase.**
Answer: (1) More awareness of learning disabilities (the media, through television programs, articles, radio, and movies, publicize learning disabilities; parents, teachers, and individuals with learning disabilities are more aware of the problems); (2) improvement in procedures for identifying and assessing learning disabilities (there is an increase in assessment tests, screening for early childhood, and referral methods in the schools); (3) social acceptance and preferences of the learning disabilities classification (more students are identified as having learning disabilities, and fewer are identified in other categories of disability that are viewed as less acceptable labels); (4) cutbacks in other programs and lack of general education alternatives for children who experience problems in the regular class (there is a lack of remedial programs and other programs in the schools, such as Chapter 1 programs); (5) court orders (through class action suits brought by parents, it was determined that the classification of many children as mentally retarded was discriminatory).

5. **Learning disabilities is an interdisciplinary field. What are the various disciplines that contribute to the field of learning disabilities, and what is the nature of their contributions?**
Answer: Many disciplines contribute to the field of learning disabilities in research, assessment, and treatment. They include education (special, regular, and other types), psychology (developmental, behavioral, cognitive, school), language disciplines (speech and language pathology, linguistics, psycholinguistics), medicine (neurology, pediatrics, psychiatry, and others), and other professions (optometry, law and legal advocacy, guidance and counseling, occupational therapy, and others). Parents also contribute.

CHAPTER 2
Historical Perspectives and Emerging Directions

Short-Answer Questions and Answers

1. **Alfred Strauss, who identified children with severe learning problems as brain-injured, hypothesized that the brain could have been injured during any of what three periods in the child's life?**
   Answer: Before birth, during birth, after birth.

2. **In Strauss's terminology, the child who experiences a figure-ground distortion that causes confusion between the background and foreground, or the child who sees parts instead of wholes, has what kind of disorder?**
   Answer: Perceptual disorder.

3. **At a meeting of professionals and parents in 1963, Sam Kirk proposed that what term (now part of the federal law) be used to describe what these children were experiencing?**
   Answer: Learning disabilities.

4. **The special education law that had the greatest influence on serving students with disabilities was passed in 1975. The public law number and name of the law was Public Law _____. This law was reauthorized in 1990, as _____. The reauthorization of IDEA was passed in _____.**
   Answer: (1) Original law: PL 94-142, Education for All Handicapped Children Act; (2) reauthorized law: PL 101-476, Individuals with Disabilities Education Act (IDEA); (3) Reauthorized IDEA in 1996.

5. **According to the clarification memo issued by the U.S. Department of Education, children with attention deficit disorder (ADD) or attention deficit hyperactivity disorder (ADHD) can be identified or served under what categories?**
   Answer: Learning disabilities, emotional disturbance, other health-impaired. They also can be served under Section 504 of the Rehabilitation Act.

Essay-Discussion Questions and Answers

1. **Describe the four distinct historical phases in the development of the field of learning disabilities. Discuss how each phase contributed to the discipline of learning disabilities.**
   Answer: (1) Foundation phase: early brain research, 1800–1930 (basic scientific investigation of brain function and brain dysfunction; by conducting autopsy studies of adult patients with brain damage, scientists gained essential knowledge about the brain); (2) transition phase: clinical study of children, 1930–1960 (basic information about brain injury in adults was applied in studying children with severe learning problems; the term *brain-injured child* is ascribed to Alfred Strauss); (3) integration phase: rapid expansion of school programs, 1960–1980 (learning disabilities became an established program within schools throughout the United States; learning disabilities interest groups were organized, teachers were trained, and public school classes were formed; special education legislation, Public Law 94-142, was passed by Congress); (4) current phase: emerging directions, 1980 to present (current major trends include inclusion, cultural and linguistic diversity, educational reform, and computer technology).

2. **Discuss some of the terms that have been used over the years to describe individuals with learning disabilities. Why have many of these descriptive terms not received general acceptance?**

   Answer: Brain-injured child (hard to diagnose, too medical); Strauss syndrome (never received general acceptance); minimal brain dysfunction (MBD) (hard to diagnose, too medical, not behavioral); learning disabilities (has received general acceptance).

3. **What is inclusion, the philosophy underlying the full inclusion movement, and the impact on children with learning disabilities?**

   Answer: Inclusion is the policy of placing children with disabilities into general education classrooms in neighborhood schools for instruction. The term *full inclusion* is sometimes used to indicate that *all* children with disabilities, including all categories and severities of disabilities, are instructed in the general education classroom. The policy promotes social integration and the least restrictive environment, and does not have the stigma of special placement. The concern is that children with learning disabilities may not receive the individualized instruction they need.

4. **Discuss some of the emerging directions in the field of learning disabilities and how these directions will affect learning disabilities programs in our schools.**

   Answer: Children and youth with learning disabilities are increasingly being placed in inclusion classes. Collaboration is the process of special and regular educators working together for the child. Many culturally and linguistically diverse students are in our schools who have learning disabilities. Children with an attention deficit disorder (ADD) or attention deficit hyperactivity disorder (ADHD) are recognized by the Department of Education as being eligible for special education services, and many students with ADD will be served in learning disabilities programs. The education reform movements require more stringent criteria and thereby affect students with learning disabilities. Computers are increasingly being used by students with learning disabilities.

CHAPTER 3
Assessment

Short-Answer Questions and Answers

1. **Name five different uses of assessment information.**

   Answer: Screening, referral, classification, instructional planning, monitoring pupil progress.

2. **Procedural safeguards are regulations designed to protect the rights of students with disabilities and their families. Name three procedural safeguards.**

   Answer: (1) Parents must consent in writing to an evaluation; (2) assessment must be conducted in the student's native language; (3) tests must be free of racial or cultural bias; (4) parents have the right to see all information; (5) parents and students have the right to an impartial due-process hearing; (6) confidentiality of reports is protected.

3. **Name the three major phases of the individualized education program.**

   Answer: Referral, assessment, instruction.

4. **Mr. and Mrs. Jackson were told at the IEP meeting that their son does not have a learning disability and is not eligible for special education services. They disagree with that assessment and think their son does have learning disabilities. What are some of the steps that they can take?**
   Answer: Not sign the IEP; talk further with the school authorities, principal, director of special education, school psychologist, or teacher and ask for a due-process hearing; talk to a parent support group such as the Learning Disabilities Association, for help; seek an assessment from another psychoeducational evaluator.

5. **There are two models of assessment: traditional and alternative. Give an example and advantages and disadvantages of each method.**
   Answer: The students can choose from various examples given in the text.

6. **Standards used to determine whether the student's problem warrants placement in the school's learning disabilities program are referred to as _____.**
   Answer: Eligibility criteria.

7. **The quantitative difference, or gap, between a student's potential for learning and current achievement is called a _____ score.**
   Answer: Discrepancy.

Essay-Discussion Questions and Answers

1. **Compare and contrast two models of assessment: traditional and alternative.**
   Answer: (1) Traditional assessment (uses standardized tests and other information measures; identifies strengths and weaknesses; determines what characteristics impede learning for the student); (2) alternative assessment (evaluates how a student performs in a classroom setting or in the curriculum).

2. **Describe the six stages of the individualized education program (IEP) process. What is the purpose of each stage?**
   Answer: The stages of the IEP process include referral (prereferral, referral) to identify students with disabilities; assessment (multidisciplinary evaluation, the IEP meeting) to gather information and to develop and write the IEP; and instruction (implementing the teaching plan, monitoring progress) to teach the student and check on progress.

3. **The Individuals with Disabilities Education Act (IDEA) provides important procedural safeguards for students with learning disabilities and their families. Discuss four of the six procedural safeguards described in this chapter.**
   Answer: (1) Parents must consent in writing to an assessment; (2) assessment must be conducted in the student's native language; (3) tests must be free of racial or cultural bias; (4) parents have the right to see all information; (5) parents and students have the right to an impartial due-process hearing; (6) all reports are confidential.

4. **Legally, the content of the written IEP must contain five statements. Discuss each of the IEP content statements.**
   Answer: (1) Present level of educational performance (to determine the student's current achievement level); (2) statement of annual goals and short-term objectives (sets a goal of annual attainment and breaks the goal into several objectives); (3) special education and related services, and extent of participation in regular education (to specify placement and consider the

least restrictive environment); (4) projected date of beginning service and anticipated duration of service (to ensure that special instruction is begun in a timely manner); (5) criteria and evaluation to determine, at least annually, if short-term objectives are being met (to make plans for reassessment and monitoring).

5. **What are the four ways of obtaining data for an evaluation of a student with learning disabilities? Give examples of information that might be obtained in each way.**
   Answer: (1) Case history information (interview the parents); (2) observation (teacher observes the child in the classroom); (3) informal measures (teacher gives an informal reading inventory); (4) formal tests (assessing achievement with a standardized test).

6. **Discuss the meaning of the phrase "discrepancy between potential and achievement" and the implications for the assessment of students with learning disabilities.**
   Answer: The phrase refers to the difference, or gap, between what the student is actually achieving and what the student is thought to be capable of achieving. A formula or a discrepancy score is often used to quantify this discrepancy and may be used with other information as eligibility criteria.

7. **Use the learning quotient method to determine whether the following students have a learning disability. Determine their learning quotients (LQs), using both the verbal IQ and the performance IQ. The higher score is indicated with an asterisk (*).**

Jimmy	*Pam*
Age: 8 years, 6 months	**Age: 10 years, 0 months**
Present grade: 3.3	Present grade: 5.7
WISC-III: full IQ 105, verbal IQ 96, performance IQ 114*	WISC-III: full IQ 80, verbal IQ 85*, performance IQ 75
Reading achievement grade score: 1.8	Reading achievement grade score: 4.5

Answer: Formula: (1) EA (expectancy age) = (MA + CA + GA)/3; (2) LQ (learning quotient) = AA (achievement age): EA. Note: Convert all grade-level scores to grade age (add 5.2).

Jimmy: Using verbal IQ:

Verbal   MA = $(8.5 \times 96) \div 100 = 8.2$
           EA = $(8.2 + 8.5 + 8.5) \div 3 = 8.4$
           LQ = $7.0 \div 8.4 = .83$

Yes, Jimmy has a learning disability, using the verbal IQ.

Using performance IQ:

* Performance   MA = $(8.5 \times 114) \div 100 = 9.7$
                EA = $(9.7 + 8.6 + 8.5) \div 3 = 8.9$
                LQ = $7.0 \div 8.9 = .79$

Yes, Jimmy has a learning disability, using the performance IQ.

Pam: Using verbal IQ:

$$\text{* Verbal} \quad \text{MA} \quad = \quad (10.0 \times 85) \div 100 = 8.5$$
$$\text{EA} \quad = \quad (8.5 + 10.0 + 10.9) \div 3 = 9.8$$
$$\text{LQ} \quad = \quad 9.7 \div 9.8 = .99$$

No, Pam does not have a learning disability, using the verbal IQ.

Using performance IQ:

$$\text{Performance} \quad \text{MA} \quad = \quad (10.0 \times 75) \div 100 = 7.5$$
$$\text{EA} \quad = \quad (7.5 + 10.0 + 10.9) \div 3 = 9.5$$
$$\text{LQ} \quad = \quad 9.7 \div 9.5 = 1.02$$

No, Pam does not have a learning disability, using the performance IQ.

CHAPTER 4
Clinical Teaching

Short-Answer Questions and Answers

1. **It is important to consider the student's ecological system, or the different types of environments that influence the desire and ability to learn. Specify four types of environmental systems.**
   Answer: (1) Home; (2) school; (3) social; (4) cultural.

2. **There are many suggested methods of teaching students with learning disabilities. The model suggested in Figure 4.2 classifies teaching methods according to three types of analysis. They are:**
   Answer: (1) Analysis of the student; (2) analysis of the curriculum; (3) analysis of the environment.

3. **There are many variables over which teachers have little control. However, there are certain instructional variables that teachers can change in the learning setting. Name four of these controllable factors and give an example.**
   Answer: (1) Difficulty level (use easier material); (2) space (have fewer problems on a page); (3) time (give students a longer time to complete an assignment); (4) language (be careful of language used with the student; do not overload with language input); (5) interpersonal relationships (build a trusting relationship between teacher and students).

4. **The effective schools research found that high-achieving students come from schools with certain characteristics. Name three of these characteristics.**
   Answer: (1) Strong principals and administrative leadership; (2) orderly school climate; (3) high expectations for students; (4) high level of engaged time spent in learning; (5) continuous monitoring of student performance; (6) immediate and academically oriented feedback; (7) teaching activities that focus on academic matters.

5. **List the steps for a task analysis of a curriculum area and give an example for each step.**
    Answer: (1) Clearly state the task (learning objective); (2) list all the subskills needed to meet the objective; (3) test informally to determine the subskills that the student already possesses; (4) begin teaching, in sequential order, the next skills in the task analysis hierarchy. (Example of task analysis of making a cheese sandwich: take two slices of bread; butter the bread slices; unwrap a slice of cheese; put cheese on bread; put lettuce on cheese; put tomato on lettuce; put on top slice of bread.)

Essay-Discussion Questions and Answers

1. **Discuss the importance of considering the student's ecological system and the various environments in which students live that can affect their learning.**
    Answer: The various environments in which a student lives make up the student's ecological system. The *home* is the student's first environment and lays the foundation for later school learning. A substantial part of the student's day is spent in the *school* environment. Teachers must be sensitive to negative factors in the school that can discourage learning. The *social* environment should provide the student with friendships and satisfying social experiences. For students with learning disabilities, the social realm is another world of failure. In today's pluralistic society, the *cultural* environment is another important consideration. Effective teachers should promote multicultural understanding.

2. **Discuss three different approaches to teaching students with learning disabilities.**
    Answer: (1) Analysis of the student (cognitive processing, developmental, and learning strategies approaches); (2) analysis of the curriculum (mastery learning, special techniques, and materials approaches); (3) analysis of the environment (behavioral, psychotherapeutic, and pedagogical approaches).

3. **Teachers can do little about many of the factors related to learning disabilities. Some instructional variables, however, can be controlled or adjusted by the teacher. Describe and gave an example of three instructional variables that teachers can control.**
    Answer: (1) Difficulty level (giving students reading material at an easier level); (2) space (making the work area large enough and free from distracting material); (3) time (giving students more time to complete a task or less work to be completed within a given time frame); (4) language (being careful of the words and language used; if necessary, simplify the language); (5) interpersonal relationship (building rapport between the teacher and student by providing successful experiences and appreciating accomplishments).

4. **Compare and contrast the direct instruction approach and the active learning approach.**
    Answer: Direct instruction sets goals and objectives, sequences learning activities, provides drill and practice, provides feedback and correction, and uses continuous assessment. Active learning encourages interactive learning, recognizes the importance of prior experience, prepares the student for the lesson, encourages active involvement, structures lessons for success, and teaches students to "learn how to learn."

5. **Describe task analysis. Give an example of an instructional sequence (or the steps to learning a specific skill).**
    Answer: There are two ways to look at task analysis. One is the analysis of what is to be learned (the curriculum); the other is the analysis of the abilities the learner must have to accomplish the task. Example: Steps of task analysis of a curriculum area of long division include estimating, dividing, multiplying, subtracting, checking, bringing down the next digit, and repeating the process.

CHAPTER 5
Systems for Delivering Educational Services

Short-Answer Questions and Answers

1. **Name two important concepts related to placement of students with disabilities.**
   Answer: (1) Continuum of alternative placements; (2) least restrictive environment.

2. **About 78 percent of students with learning disabilities are in what two types of placements?**
   Answer: (1) Resource room; (2) general education classroom.

3. **Name three relatively recent administrative arrangements that tend to integrate regular and special education.**
   Answer: (1) Mainstreaming; (2) regular education initiative; (3) full inclusion.

4. **List three principles to promote effective collaboration between general education teachers and special education teachers.**
   Answer: (1) Establish common goals; (2) participation should be voluntary; (3) recognize equality among participants; (4) share responsibility for participation and decision making; (5) share responsibility for outcomes; (6) share resources.

5. **What activities can the school undertake to provide support for parents?**
   Answer: Parent support groups, family counseling, parent-teacher conferences, helping parents with home management.

Essay-Discussion Questions and Answers

1. **Discuss the key concepts concerning the delivery of education services that are features of the special education law.**
   Answer: As part of the student's individualized education program (IEP), the case conference team recommends specific educational placements for services. To abide by the IDEA, the team must consider two features written into the law: the continuum of alternative placements (the school must have a range of services to meet the student's needs) and the least restrictive environment (to the greatest extent possible, the team must place the student with students who do not have disabilities).

2. **Discuss some of the recent trends in providing services to students with learning disabilities.**
   Answer: There is a recent trend toward integrating regular and special education. The placements that meet this objective include the following: (1) full inclusion, which has the goal of placing all students with all types of disabilities and levels of severity into the neighborhood school and in the general education class; (2) mainstreaming, the policy of putting students with learning disabilities in the general education class, thereby providing experiences in the mainstream of the school; (3) the regular education initiative, a concept of education that students with a variety of learning and behavior problems can be taught more effectively in the general education classroom than in special education placements. These integrated systems need sufficient support services if they are to succeed.

3. **What are some of the ways to promote partnerships between general and special educators?**
   Answer: As students with learning disabilities are increasingly placed in general education classrooms, partnerships are needed by special and general educators. Peer tutoring is an effective way for two children to work together in the learning situation. In collaboration classroom teachers and learning disabilities teachers interact to find creative solutions. In co-teaching, two professionals deliver instruction to a diverse group of students in a single space. In cooperative learning, students in the general education classroom seek solutions to problems together instead of working competitively.

4. **What are the responsibilities of the learning disabilities teacher?**
   Answer: The responsibilities of the learning disabilities teacher are expanding. They include assessment, instruction, collaboration with other professionals, in-service education, and working with parents.

5. **Compare and contrast the types of placement that serve the majority of students with learning disabilities in the schools.**
   Answer: The data show that about 44 percent of the students with learning disabilities are served through resource rooms. About 34 percent are in general education classes only. Because resource room students are also in general education classes, this means that 78 percent are in general education classes for much of their education. About 21 percent are served in separate classes, and most of these students have more severe learning disabilities.

6. **Discuss the family system approach.**
   Answer: This view is that what happens to one member of the family affects all other members of the family. It also suggests that it is important to consider the entire family in the treatment process. Parents go through stages of acceptance as they come to accept that their child has learning disabilities. The stages include shock, disbelief, denial, anger, bargaining, and finally acceptance. Parents can be helped through parent support groups, family counseling, and parent-teacher conferences.

CHAPTER 6
Theories of Learning: Implications for Learning Disabilities

Short-Answer Questions and Answers

1. **What three branches of psychology have implications for teaching students with learning disabilities?**
   Answer: (1) Developmental psychology; (2) behavioral psychology; (3) cognitive psychology.

2. **Name the developmental psychologist who formulated the theory that the cognitive abilities of children change and mature as they grow.**
   Answer: Jean Piaget.

3. **The application of behavioral psychology to teaching is called:**
   Answer: Direct instruction; behavior analysis.

4. **The information-processing model includes what three types of memory?**
Answer: (1) Sensory register; (2) short-term (working) memory; (3) long-term memory.

5. **The ability to facilitate learning by taking control and directing one's own thinking and learning is called:**
Answer: Metacognition; executive function.

6. **What are the three parts of the behavioral unit?**
Answer: A—antecdent event (or stimulus); B—target behavior; C—consequent event or reinforcement.

Essay-Discussion Questions and Answers

1. **Discuss the concept of stages of maturation. How can lags in maturation lead to learning disabilities?**
Answer: There is a sequential progression in the maturation of cognitive skills. An individual student's ability to learn will depend upon the student's stage of maturation. Piaget envisioned four stages: sensorimotor (ages birth–2), preoperational (ages 5–7), concrete operations (ages 7–11), and formal operations (above age 11). Schools may create learning disabilities by making intellectual demands for which the student is not ready.

2. **What approaches to instruction are based on theories of behavioral psychology?**
Answer: The behavioral unit consists of three parts: A—antecedent event or stimulus; B—target behavior; and C—consequent event or reinforcement. Behavioral approaches include direct instruction, mastery learning, directed teaching, explicit instruction, and sequential skills teaching. These approaches emphasize structuring the environment to ensure the learning of skills, sequencing the subskills, providing sufficient drill and practice, and providing continuous monitoring.

3. **What is meant by the phrase "disorders of psychological processing"? Discuss the implication of this concept for instruction in the field of learning disabilities.**
Answer: "Disorders of psychological processing" is a phrase used in the federal definition of learning disabilities in the Individuals with Disabilities Education Act (IDEA). It refers to underlying intrinsic deficits in certain developmental preacademic areas of learning. It includes disorders in perceptual, motor, linguistic, and memory functions. The implication is that disorders in these psychological processes are intrinsic human limitations that interfere with human learning.

4. **Name the three memory systems of the information-processing model. Discuss the relationships among these three memory systems.**
Answer: The multistore memory system conceptualizes a flow of information among three types of memory: sensory register, short-term (working) memory, and long-term memory. Memory is quickly lost if the individual does not invoke active attention and interest to move memory from one system to another. Specific instructional practices and strategies can help students retain memory for learning.

5. **Describe three of the principles underlying cognitive learning theories. Give an illustration of each principle.**
Answer: (1) Learning is constructive, and each person must build his or her own knowledge (the concept of a chair is gradually built as the child has experiences with different kinds of

chairs); (2) learning is linking new information to prior knowledge (learning to add is built upon knowledge of counting); (3) learning occurs within a guided social environment (the teacher provides guidance and support in learning until the student can do it on his or her own); (4) learning is strategic (students must develop strategies or plans to direct their own learning); (5) some skills must be automatic (some skills must be subconscious, requiring little effort to be efficient, such as sight word recognition and knowledge of number computation facts); (6) learning requires motivation (learning is hard work, and students must have interest, drive, and motivation).

6. **Define metacognition. Discuss the problems of students with learning disabilities with regard to metacognitive strategies.**
   Answer: Metacognition is the ability to take control and direct one's learning. Often students with learning disabilities are passive learners and do not have the strategies for directing their own learning. Students with learning disabilities can be taught metacognitive strategies to improve their approach to learning.

CHAPTER 7
Medical Aspects of Learning Disabilities

Short-Answer Questions and Answers

1. **Name the two halves of the brain and describe a function of each half.**
   Answer: (1) Left hemisphere (location of language); (2) right hemisphere (location of spatial perception, music, directional orientation, body awareness, emotion).

2. **Name two major parts of the neurological examination.**
   Answer: (1) Conventional exam; (2) examination for soft neurological signs.

3. **Name three characteristics of attention deficit disorders.**
   Answer: Difficulty in focusing attention, impulsivity, and hyperactivity.

4. **Name three commonly used medications for attention deficit disorders.**
   Answer: Ritalin, Dexedrine, Cylert.

5. **Describe the roles of three medical specialties involved with learning disabilities.**
   Answer: (1) Pediatrics and family practice: general child care; (2) pediatric neurologist: disorders of the central nervous system; (3) ophthalmology and optometry: assessment and treatment of visual problems; (4) otology and audiology: assessment and treatment of auditory problems; (5) psychiatry: emotional factors and family therapy.

Essay-Discussion Questions and Answers

1. **Discuss the relevance of medical information for teachers of students with learning disabilities in terms of assessment, treatment, and research.**
   Answer: Medical information has value for teachers for several reasons: learning is a neurological process that occurs within the brain; medical specialists are often part of the assess-

ment and treatment of students with learning disabilities; teachers must often understand medical reports and provide feedback about the effects of medication; new technological advances and research have implications for learning disabilities; and the neuroscientific research helps to explain learning disabilities.

2. **Discuss some of the new methods for studying the brain. What are the implications of this research for learning disabilities?**
   Answer: Postmortem studies that have analyzed the brain structures of a small number of individuals who had dyslexia show differences in brain structure from the normal brain. New studies of the living brain are being conducted through magnetic resonance imaging (MRI), brain electrical activity mapping (BEAM), and positron emission tomography (PET). These studies show differences between the normal brain and that of the individual with learning disabilities. Familial and twin studies suggest that there is a genetic basis for learning disabilities.

3. **Name the three characteristics of attention deficit disorders (ADD). Must individuals display all three to have attention deficit disorders?**
   Answer: The characteristics of attention deficit disorders include inattention, impulsivity, and hyperactivity. According the DSM-IV, an individual could manifest (a) primarily inattention, (b) primarily impulsivity-hyperactivity, or (c) both a and b.

4. **Discuss the contributions of three medical specialists to the field of learning disabilities.**
   Answer: Various medical specialties are involved in the research, assessment, and treatment of individuals with learning disabilities: (1) pediatricians and family-care physicians are often the first to see the child's problem and to work with the family; (2) pediatric neurologists are specialists in the dysfunctions of the central nervous system; (3) ophthalmologists and optometrists become involved in the visual aspects of learning, particularly reading; (4) otologists and audiologists diagnose and treat hearing problems; (5) child psychiatrists are particularly involved with the emotional factors that accompany learning disabilities, and work with the parents and families.

CHAPTER 8
Young Children with Disabilities

Short-Answer Questions and Answers

1. **For early childhood, the reauthorized IDEA addresses the problems of what three groups of children?**
   Answer: (1) Preschool children with disabilities, ages 3–5; (2) infants and toddlers with disabilities, ages birth–2; (3) young children at risk for disabilities.

2. **What are the precursors of learning disabilities?**
   Answer: Deficits in phonological awareness, ability to analyze and synthesize language sounds, rapid naming skills, knowledge of letter names and the sounds of letters, visual-perceptual matching, visual-motor integration.

3. **Name the four phases of assessment of young children with disabilities.**
   Answer: (1) Locating young children with disabilities in the community (Child Find); (2) screening many children in the community through a cursory assessment; (3) diagnosing children thought to have problems through a comprehensive team assessment and study; (4) evaluating to make judgments about the child's progress and to determine a future course of action.

4. **Name five different types of curriculum models for early childhood special education.**
   Answer: (1) Developmentally appropriate practice (DAP); (2) enrichment; (3) direct instruction; (4) cognitive emphasis; (5) combination.

5. **Name four activities that are part of a comprehensive early childhood curriculum for children with special needs.**
   Answer: (1) Self-help and self-concept activities; (2) gross-motor activities; (3) fine-motor activities; (4) communication activities; (5) visual activities; (6) auditory activities; (7) cognitive activities; (8) social activities.

6. **List three benefits of early childhood programs for young children with disabilities or at risk for having disabilities.**
   Answer: (1) Enhance intelligence; (2) promote gains in all developmental areas; (3) inhibit secondary problems; (4) reduce family stress; (5) reduce institutionalization; (6) reduce need for special education at school age; (7) save society health-care and education costs.

Essay-Discussion Questions and Answers

1. **Define the two age groups covered in IDEA for early childhood. Compare and contrast the effect of the law for these two age groups.**
   Answer: (1) Part B covers preschoolers, ages 3–5 (extends rights of IDEA; team can designate category of disability or use noncategorical label such as developmental delay; team develops either individualized education program [IEP] or individual family service plan [IFSP]; lead agency is the state education agency; the early childhood special education teacher; services are mandated by federal law); (2) Part H covers infants and toddlers, ages birth–2 years (states are assisted to develop plans for this age group; team must develop IFSP for each child; can use developmental delay category; services are permissive; lead agency appointed by governor; personnel—service coordinator or case manager).

2. **Discuss learning disabilities in young children.**
   Answer: Even though preschoolers may not yet have failed in academic subjects, preschool children with learning disabilities can be identified. They display many precursors of learning problems, such as problems in language, motor, cognitive, attention, memory, visual, and auditory perception. Providing these children with help before they encounter school difficulty can prevent later academic problems.

3. **Discuss the importance of transition decisions during the preschool years and what such decisions involve for children in both age groups.**
   Answer: Transition involves going from one placement or organized program to another and can be traumatic for the child and the family. The transition should be carefully planned with opportunities for bridging the two placements. Infants and toddlers in Part H programs will be moving from a very personal program to one with a larger group of children in the Part B program. For preschoolers in the Part B program, the transition involves going to the next placement, which could be a regular class, transition class, resource room, special class, or residential facility.

4. **Discuss the research findings of the early childhood education programs for preschoolers with disabilities and children at risk for disabilities. What are the policy implications of these findings?**

Answer: The research of children at risk for disabilities, such as the Head Start research, and that stemming from the compensatory programs, such as the High/Scope research, show the significant benefits of early intervention for the individual and for society. Early intervention helps the child by accelerating cognitive and social development, it helps the family, and it benefits society. Society is slowly beginning to recognize that there is a tremendous payoff to offering early intervention to children with disabilities and children who are at risk for disabilities. Legislative bodies are beginning to support early intervention programs.

5. **Describe four curriculum models for early childhood special education.**

Answer: (1) Developmentally appropriate practice (DAP) (emphasizes exploratory play, child-initiated learning, and the child's interests); (2) enrichment model (based on the developmental "whole-child" theory, which encompasses the child's physical, emotional, language, social, and cognitive development; offers a variety of experiences and encourages the child's natural growth sequence); (3) direct teaching model (based on behavioral psychology and concentrates on straightforward and structured teaching of specific skills; materials and activities carefully structured to develop the specific skills); (4) cognitive emphasis curriculum (based on theories of Piaget and promotes development of thinking skills; emphasizes building problem solving, verbal learning, and comprehension); (5) combination (many early childhood special education programs contain elements of all of the curriculum models).

CHAPTER 9
Adolescents and Adults with Learning Disabilities

Short-Answer Questions and Answers

1. **Name three characteristics of adolescents with learning disabilities.**

Answer: Passive learning, poor self-concept, inept social skills, attention deficits, lack of motivation.

2. **The secondary level presents a number of special problems for adolescents with learning disabilities. List three of them.**

Answer: Increasing high school requirements, minimum competency tests, heavy curriculum demands, secondary teachers.

3. **The passage from school to the adult world is known as:**

Answer: Transition.

4. **The transition IEP should include several features. Name them:**

Answer: Current levels of performance, interests and aptitude, postschool goals, transition activities, responsible persons, plan for review.

5. **Name three curriculum models used in high school with adolescents with learning disabilities.**

Answer: Basic skills instruction, tutorial instruction, functional skills instruction, work-study programs, collaboration programs, learning strategies instruction.

6. **A learning strategies instruction program developed at the University of Kansas Center for Research on Learning is known as SIM. What do these letters stand for?**
   Answer: Strategies intervention model.

7. **There are eight steps in the SIM model. Name three of them.**
   Answer: (1) Pretest; (2) describe learning strategy; (3) model the strategy; (4) use verbal rehearsal; (5) practice with controlled materials; (6) practice with classroom materials; (7) posttest; (8) generalize.

Essay-Discussion Questions and Answers

1. **Describe three characteristics of adolescents with learning disabilities. Discuss how these characteristics affect high school achievement.**
   Answer: Adolescents with learning disabilities have both the normal problems of adolescence and the learning disabilities. All adolescents have conflicts between independence and security, experience rapid physical changes from developing sexuality, have conflicts between peer and family pressures, and have self-consciousness. In addition, adolescents with learning disabilities tend to be passive learners; have a poor self-concept, inept social skills, and attention deficits; and lack motivation. All of these problems add to the learning problems experienced by students with learning disabilities in high school.

2. **Describe three special problems that occur at the secondary level, and discuss how these problems affect adolescents with learning disabilities.**
   Answer: Secondary schools are very different from elementary schools in the following ways: (1) there are increasing high school academic requirements; (2) states are passing minimum competency test requirements; (3) students are required to take four courses with heavy curriculum demands; (4) secondary teachers are more content-oriented. Facing all of these pressures makes school a discouraging place for many adolescents with learning disabilities.

3. **What are transition plans, and what is the importance of making transition plans for adolescents with learning disabilities?**
   Answer: *Transition* refers to the movement from school to adult life and the world of work. The process of going into the adult world is very difficult for many adolescents with learning disabilities, and transition plans are required as part of the IEP to help them. Post-high school goals for secondary students with learning disabilities include competitive employment, vocational training, college attendance, and supported employment. The transition team should consider the following: where the student is going, what is needed to help the student reach identified goals, and who needs to be involved.

4. **Discuss alternative models or methods for teaching adolescents with learning disabilities.**
   Answer: There are several ways to approach secondary school instruction for students with learning disabilities. Some programs emphasize basic skills in reading and mathematics; others provide students with tutorial instruction to pass academic courses; others emphasize functional skills to help students survive in the world outside of school; still others provide a work-study program for adolescents with learning disabilities. Many schools use a collaboration model with regular and special educators team-teaching. Many programs offer instruction in learning strategies.

5. **Discuss the nature of learning strategies instruction for adolescents with learning disabilities.**

   Answer: The goal of instruction in learning strategies is to help students learn how to learn. The instruction helps adolescents take control and direct their own learning instead of being passive receivers of instruction. The strategies intervention model (SIM) was developed at the University of Kansas Center for Research on Learning. The eight steps in this learning strategies model include pretesting, describing the strategy, modeling the strategy, verbally rehearsing the strategy, practicing the strategy with controlled materials, using the strategy with classroom materials, posttesting, and generalizing to new situations.

6. **Discuss some of the problems that adults with learning disabilities encounter in postsecondary education and in meeting the challenges of life.**

   Answer: For many individuals, learning disabilities continue to affect their lives into adulthood. These adults may have trouble finding and keeping a job, developing a satisfying social life, and coping with daily living. Life skills they may have trouble mastering include social skills, good work habits, independent living skills, and the ability to cope with money management.

CHAPTER 10
Developmental and Preacademic Learning

Short-Answer Questions and Answers

1. **Academic learning disabilities include problems in reading, mathematics, writing, and spelling. Name three areas of developmental learning disabilities.**

   Answer: Developmental learning disabilities include precursors in areas of learning, such as motor, perceptual, language, and thinking skills.

2. **Name three underlying beliefs of motor theories and learning.**

   Answer: (1) Human learning begins with motor learning; (2) there is a natural sequence of motor learning, and each stage provides the foundation for the next stage; (3) many kinds of academic and cognitive performance are based upon successful acquisition of motor learning.

3. **What are the four senses that are important for school learning?**

   Answer: Visual, auditory, tactile, and kinesthetic.

4. **There are two types of motor skills. *Jumping* is (a) _____ motor skill. *Buttoning* is a (b)_____ motor skill.**

   Answers: (a) Gross-motor skill; (b) fine-motor skill.

5. **One theory of motor development and learning disabilities suggests that many children with learning disabilities have atypical motor development and must contend with a perceptual-motor world that is still unstable and unreliable. Give (a) the name of this theory and (b) the person who is associated with the theory.**

   Answers: (a) Perceptual-motor theory; (b) Newell Kephart.

6. **Three systems of sensory integration are:**
   Answer: (1) Tactile system; (2) vestibular system; (3) proprioceptive system.

7. **The auditory perception ability to recognize that words are composed of the individual sounds within the words is called:**
   Answer: Phonological awareness.

8. **Name some of the other auditory perception skills.**
   Answer: Auditory discrimination, auditory memory, auditory sequencing, auditory blending.

9. **Name some of the visual perception skills.**
   Answer: Visual discrimination, visual closure, spatial relations, object recognition.

Essay-Discussion Questions and Answers

1. **Compare and contrast developmental learning disabilities and academic learning disabilities.**
   Answer: Developmental learning disabilities include deficits in the prerequisite skills (such as motor, perceptual, language, and thinking skills) that a child needs in order to learn academic subjects. Children with learning disabilities often need to be taught these essential skills. Academic learning disabilities include deficits in school subjects, such as reading, writing, spelling, and mathematics.

2. **Describe and illustrate the sensitivity systems through which human beings obtain information about the world.**
   Answer: Human beings have six perceptual systems for receiving information about the world: visual (sight), auditory (sound), tactile (touch), kinesthetic (muscle feeling), olfactory (smell), and gustatory (taste). Educational instruction emphasizes the visual, auditory, kinesthetic, and tactile systems as the most practical approaches for learning.

3. **List the basic concepts underlying theories of motor learning and learning disabilities.**
   Answer: The basic concepts of motor learning are (1) human learning begins with motor learning; (2) there is a normal sequence of motor learning, and acquisition of skills at one stage provides the foundation for learning at the next stage; and (3) many areas of academic and cognitive performance are based on successful motor experiences.

4. **Discuss how problems in perception relate to learning disabilities.**
   Answer: Perception is the process of recognizing and interpreting sensory information. Deficits in perception can fall into the visual, auditory, tactile, or kinesthetic realm. Perceptual skills provide the foundation for many kinds of academic learning, and when a child has difficulty in visual or auditory perception, this problem can interfere with reading and or mathematics learning.

5. **What is meant by the perceptual modality concept?**
   Answer: This theory suggests that people learn in different ways. Some learn best by seeing (visual), others by listening (auditory), and some by doing (kinesthetic). Knowing a student's learning style provides the teacher with information for instructing that student.

6. **Explain phonological awareness and the role it plays in learning to read.**
   Answer: Phonological awareness refers to the realization that language is made up of individual sounds, syllables, and words. This recognition is a necessary precursor to learning to

read. Some children are not aware of the sounds in language and need direct instruction in the awareness of language sounds. Instruction in phonological awareness helps children who are having difficulty learning to read.

CHAPTER 11
Oral Language: Listening and Speaking

Short-Answer Questions and Answers

1. **Several different forms of language are integrated in the language system. Name the four forms.**
   Answer: Listening, speaking, reading, writing.

2. **Name the four different theories of how children acquire language.**
   Answer: Behavioral, innatist, cognitive, social.

3. **Linguistics is the study of languages through the analysis of linguistic systems within each language. Name the five linguistic systems of language.**
   Answer: Phonology, morphology, syntax, semantics, pragmatics.

4. **Children who do recognize that words are made up of sound elements and are not sensitive to the phoneme sounds of language are poor in what area?**
   Answer: Phonological awareness.

5. **The initials LEP are often used to describe children who speak a language other than English in their homes and have difficulty with English. What do the initials LEP stand for?**
   Answer: Limited English proficiency.

Essay-Discussion Questions and Answers

1. **What are the forms of language, and how are they related to each other?**
   Answer: The forms of language include oral language (listening and speaking), reading, and writing. They are all integrated through the underlying language system. Learning in one form strengthens the language system, thereby strengthening ability in the other forms.

2. **Describe language as a communication process. Discuss the kinds of problems that a student may encounter in the communication process.**
   Answer: Language is a communication process. Listening and reading are receptive language modes; talking and writing are expressive language modes. One person sends a message or communicates with another through language. The sender of the message must convert the idea in language symbols (speaking or writing) to send it. The receiver of the message must convert the oral or written symbols (through listening or reading) back into the idea. Problems can occur anywhere along this communication process—in coding the idea into symbols, in the mechanics of sending it, in decoding the message, in translating the message into the idea.

3. **What are the major linguistic systems? Give an example of each.**
   Answer: (1) *Phonology* refers to the phonemes or sound elements (the word *pan* has three phonemes: p-a-n); (2) *morphology* refers to the morphemes, or meaning system of the language (the word *books* has two morphemes: book and plural); (3) *syntax* refers to the grammar system of language, the order of words in a sentence (a common sentence order in English is subject-verb-object: the boy hits a ball); (4) *semantics* refers to the vocabulary, or word meanings, of language (students with learning disabilities may have difficulty understanding word meanings); (5) *pragmatics* refers to the social use of language (students with social disabilities often have pragmatic language problems).

4. **Discuss the problems of a student whose native language is not English and who also has a learning disability.**
   Answer: An increasing number of students in U.S. schools come from homes where a language other than English is spoken. Because they are not proficient in two languages, these children are not actually bilingual. They are better described as having limited English proficiency (LEP). Some students with LEP have two problems: the LEP problem and learning disabilities. They need instruction that treats both of these problems—special education and bilingual education.

5. **What types of language disabilities do students with learning disabilities have?**
   Answer: Students with learning disabilities can have many different types of language problems: lack of phonological awareness, delayed speech, disorders of grammar or syntax, limited vocabulary, and poor understanding of oral language. These students can also have difficulty in the written mode of language, including reading, writing, and spelling. Some students display language differences such as nonstandard English or limited English proficiency.

6. **What is *emergent literacy* and how does it apply to teaching children with learning disabilities?**
   Answer: *Emergent literacy* refers to the child's early entrance into the world of language, which includes words, books, poetry, and stories. It is important that children with learning disabilities be given an abundant and rich literature environment. Activities that foster emergent literacy include oral language activities, activities that build concepts about print, and activities that teach alphabet knowledge, phonological awareness, letter-sound correspondence, and beginning reading vocabulary.

CHAPTER 12
Reading

Short-Answer Questions and Answers

1. **Whole-language instruction is considered a philosophy of reading instruction. List three characteristics of whole-language teaching.**
   Answer: (1) Builds upon whole-language situations; (2) assumes respect for language, learner, and teacher; (3) focuses on meaning; (4) uses authentic speech and literacy; (5) integrates reading and writing.

2. **What are the characteristics of "explicit code-emphasis instruction"?**
   Answer: This method of teaching reading is structured and sequenced and uses direct instruction to teach the alphabet code and phonics.

3. **In the cognitive view of language, reading is the process of constructing a dynamic interaction of three elements. What are they?**
   Answer: (1) Reader; (2) text; (3) context of the reading situation.

4. **The teaching of reading can be divided into what two elements?**
   Answer: Word recognition and reading comprehension.

5. **Name the four word-recognition strategies.**
   Answer: Phonics, sight words, contextual clues, structural analysis.

6. **Name four special remedial methods that are not usually used in the regular classroom.**
   Answer: (1) VAKT; (2) Fernald method; (3) Orton-Gillingham method; (4) Reading Recovery; (5) neurological impress method.

7. **What is meant by the K-W-L method?**
   Answer: Activating the reading situation through these three questions: K—What I know; W—What I want to find; L—What I learned.

Essay-Discussion Questions and Answers

1. **What is whole language? Discuss the assumptions of the whole-language philosophy and its implications for learning disabilities.**
   Answer: Whole language is both a philosophy about learning to read and use language and an approach for teaching reading. The method encourages the integration of reading and writing, and writing is considered an integral element of the reading program. Whole language is based on the belief that learning to read is similar to learning to talk; both are acquired through natural language usage. It provides many opportunities for literacy, including writing and reading. It avoids undue emphasis on separate nonmeaningful parts of language, such as phonics drills.

2. **It is essential that readers develop skill in recognizing words. Describe the different methods of word recognition they use.**
   Answer: (1) Phonics (readers match the sound of a phoneme to a printed written symbol, or letter[s]; phonological awareness, part of phonics, is the ability to recognize that spoken words consist of sounds of speech); (2) sight words (the ability to recognize words instantly, without hesitation; at least 90 percent of the written passage should be recognized as sight words for fluent reading); (3) context clues (the recognition of a word through the meaning or context of the sentence or paragraph in which it appears; students should be encouraged to use context clues for words they do not know); (4) structural analysis (the recognition of words through the analysis of meaningful word units, such as prefixes, suffixes, root words, compound words, and syllables). Most readers combine these strategies, using as many as necessary until the word is recognized.

3. **Describe three strategies for improving fluency.**
   Answer: (1) Repeating reading (students improve fluency by reading a passage several times); (2) predictable books (contain patterns or refrains that are repeated over and over, such as folk

tales and fairy tales; children begin to learn the language of the story by hearing it repeatedly); (3) neurological impress method or the read-along method (gives students experiences with connected reading).

4. **Compare and contrast narrative reading materials and expository reading materials.**
   Answer: Narrative materials are stories, usually fiction, and they have characters, a plot, and a sequence of events. Expository materials are informational materials, such as textbooks, and become more important in the later grades in content-area courses.

5. **Describe two special remedial approaches for teaching reading to students with severe reading disabilities.**
   Answer: (1) VAKT (stands for visual, auditory, kinesthetic, and tactile; all of these sensory avenues are used simultaneously to reinforce the learning); (2) Fernald method (also a multi-sensory approach, using the visual, auditory, kinesthetic, and tactile to teach the student whole words); (3) Orton-Gillingham method (uses multisensory instruction to teach single letters and their sound equivalents, which are then combined into words); (4) Reading Recovery (a reading program for at-risk first graders that provides individual instruction to children who are the lowest rank of the class).

6. **Contemporary cognitive psychology has had an impact on the teaching of reading. Discuss the theoretical applications of cognitive psychology to the teaching of reading.**
   Answer: The cognitive view of reading applies contemporary cognitive psychology to the teaching of reading. Reading is viewed as the process of constructing meaning through the dynamic interaction of the reader, the text, and the context of the reading situation. The view includes several generalizations: (1) reading success depends upon prior experiences and background knowledge; (2) reading is a language process; (3) reading is a thinking process; (4) reading requires active interaction with the text.

7. **Describe two strategies for helping students with reading comprehension.**
   Answer: (1) Building meaning and reading vocabulary (teaching multiple word meanings, providing concrete experiences with words, using a variety of sources for vocabulary words, teaching classification of words); (2) cloze procedure (rewrite a passage using a blank for a deleted word; students must fill in and complete the passage, (3) word webs (used to enrich associations and deepen the understanding of the word; (4) advance organizers (a technique to establish a mindset for the reading and to develop linkages to known material); (5) questioning strategies (to help students think about what they are reading; self-questioning strategies help students ask themselves questions about the reading passage).

CHAPTER 13
Written Language: Written Expression, Spelling, and Handwriting

Short-Answer Questions and Answers

1. **List the stages of the writing process.**
   Answer: (1) Prewriting; (2) writing (or drafting); (3) revising; (4) sharing with an audience.

2. **What is meant by the term *emergent literacy?***
Answer: This term refers to the child's early entrance into the world of words, language, and stories. It includes early writing, listening to stories, telling stories, and the beginnings of recognizing letters and words in print.

3. **Explain invented spelling.**
Answer: This term refers to the beginning writer's attempt to write words. Children are encouraged to write words any way they wish, from scribbling to trying to use some letter-sound relationships. No corrections are made, and all invented spellings are accepted as the child's written communication.

4. **What are the two different theories for selecting words to use in the teaching of spelling?**
Answer: (1) Linguistic approach; (2) word frequency approach.

5. **List the two major styles of writing taught in the schools and the approximate grade levels at which they are taught.**
Answer: (1) Manuscript writing, which more closely resembles print (primary grades—kindergarten to third grade); (2) cursive writing, or connected script writing (third grade and up).

Essay-Discussion Questions and Answers

1. **Explain the differences between instruction that focuses on the written product and instruction that focuses on the writing process.**
Answer: Traditional instruction focuses on the finished product of writing, and teachers judge that product on the basis of expectations of perfection. In the writing process, the emphasis is on the entire process of writing, including thinking, selecting, organizing, and rewriting.

2. **Describe, in sequence, the stages of the writing process.**
Answer: (1) Prewriting (the writer gathers ideas); (2) writing, or drafting (the writer records ideas on paper and develops a first version of the final product); (3) revising (the writer refines: makes changes, additions, deletions, etc.); (4) sharing with an audience (the writer shares the product with someone else).

3. **Discuss the advantages of computer word processing for writing.**
Answer: Using a word processor, the writer can write without worrying about handwriting and can revise without making a mess of the written document. The process can be motivating for the student, allows for collaboration, provides ease of revision, and overcomes fine-motor problems that are displayed in writing. Word-processing programs also have features such as a spell checker and a thesaurus, which can be very helpful in writing.

4. **Discuss the concepts underlying two views on selecting words for spelling instruction.**
Answer: (1) Linguistic approach (word selection is based on the phonological properties of words, so that word families are selected and phonics is part of the spelling lesson); (2) word frequency approach (words are selected on the basis of how frequently children use certain words in writing).

5. **Identify the two major forms of handwriting taught in schools. Discuss the advantages and disadvantages of each.**
Answer: (1) Manuscript writing (easier to learn, consisting of circles and straight lines; more similar to print; and usually the writing of kindergarten to third grade); (2) cursive writing (the

adult form of writing, in which letters are connected; during third grade, it is typical to shift from manuscript to cursive writing; but many students with learning disabilities find making the shift difficult).

6. **Discuss how LD characteristics affect the writing of students with learning disabilities in written expression, spelling, and handwriting.**
   Answer: Many students find all three areas of written language difficult. Because the underlying language system of many students with learning disabilities is not strong, this problem is evidenced in *written expression*. These students need many more input experiences so that they have something to write about. *Spelling* is difficult for many students because they have poor reading skills and also because they cannot visually remember the spelling words. Phonics instruction may be helpful for these students. *Handwriting* will be troublesome for students who have poor fine-motor skills. They can be helped to improve handwriting; also, they will find computer word processing a welcome alternative.

CHAPTER 14
Mathematics

Short-Answer Questions and Answers

1. **Name three characteristics of mathematics disabilities.**
   Answer: (1) Lack of readiness; (2) problems in spatial relations; (3) poor sense of body image; (4) visual-motor and visual–perception disorders; (5) language problems; (6) reading problems; (7) poor concept of direction and time; (8) memory problems; (9) lack of mathematics learning strategies; (10) math anxiety.

2. **Ideas about teaching mathematics have changed over the years. Name the major trends of the last forty years.**
   Answer: (1) Modern math; (2) back-to-basics; (3) education reform.

3. **What four different theories of teaching mathematics were discussed?**
   Answer: (1) Developmental learning; (2) direct instruction; (3) learning strategies; (4) problem solving.

4. **Describe three perspectives or theories for mathematics instruction.**
   Answer: (1) Teach precursor skills; (2) go from concrete to abstract; (3) use constructive learning; (4) use direct instruction; (5) teach learning strategies; (6) teach problem solving.

5. **A balanced mathematics program provides instruction in what three areas?**
   Answer: (1) Mathematics concepts; (2) mathematics skills; (3) problem solving.

Essay-Discussion Questions and Answers

1. **Discuss how the teaching of mathematics has changed over the years and what effect these changes have had on students with learning disabilities.**
   Answer: The way mathematics is taught in the schools has been subject to international events and national political pressures. When the former Soviet Union appeared to be a threat after it

launched *Sputnick,* there was a national call for changes in mathematics education. The "modern math" curriculum was placed in schools throughout the nation. In general, modern math was not effective for students with learning disabilities. This phase was followed by the back-to-basics movement, which stressed drill with computation skills. Math concepts and problem-solving instruction were neglected. More recently, the demand for accountability has brought the education reform movement, with more high-level mathematics requirements and more testing of students. This movement also has an adverse effect on students with learning disabilities.

2. **The Individuals with Disabilities Education Act (IDEA) recognizes two areas in which students can have mathematics disabilities. Describe these two areas and discuss the implications for services.**
   Answer: The two areas are mathematics calculation and mathematics reasoning. Students with learning disabilities can be identified with deficits in either of these areas. Many students with learning disabilities need specific instruction in computation skills; many more need instruction in mathematics reasoning.

3. **Discuss four characteristics of students with mathematics disabilities and their implications for instruction.**
   Answer: Students with mathematics difficulties display many different characteristics. (It is important to note that some students with learning disabilities have strengths in the area of mathematics.) Among the characteristics noted are lack of mathematics readiness, disturbances in spatial relationships, poor sense of body image, visual-motor and visual-perception disorders, language problems, reading problems, poor concepts of direction and time, memory problems, lack of strategies for learning mathematics, and math anxiety. These characteristics interfere with quantitative thinking and with mathematics performance.

4. **Discuss the use of calculators in mathematics instruction.**
   Answer: Calculators have revolutionized functional arithmetic for many people. There is a place for the use of calculators in mathematics instruction, as noted by the National Council of Teachers of Mathematics. It is critical that students learn computation skills and develop them until they become automatic. However, in certain situations, when the goal is problem solving, calculators can help students with learning disabilities avoid becoming bogged down with calculation errors.

5. **Discuss three principles that guide teaching mathematics to students with learning disabilities.**
   Answer: (1) Establishing the readiness or precursor skills of mathematics learning; (2) progressing from the concrete to the semiconcrete to abstract learning; (3) providing ample opportunities for practice and review; (4) offering specific instruction on generalizing what has been learned to new situations; (5) making certain that students understand the mathematics vocabulary; (6) considering the student's strengths and weaknesses in planning instruction; (7) providing a balanced mathematics curriculum that includes the elements of mathematics concepts, skills, and problem solving. These commonsense principles can be incorporated into lessons for students with learning disabilities.

CHAPTER 15
Social and Emotional Behavior

Short-Answer Questions and Answers

1. **Name three characteristics of social disabilities.**
   Answer: (1) Lack of judgment; (2) difficulties in perceiving how others feel; (3) problems in socializing and making friends; (4) problems in establishing family relations; (5) social disabilities in school; (6) poor self-concept.

2. **Name three accommodations that can be made in the general education classroom for students with learning disabilities.**
   Answer: (1) Limit distractions; (2) increase attention; (3) improve organization; (4) improve listening skills; (5) manage time; (6) provide opportunities for moving. See Table 15.4 for specific accommodations for each of these.

3. **What are the three components of the behavior unit in behavior management?**
   Answer: ABC—antecedent event or stimulus, target behavior, consequent event or reinforcement.

4. **Name three strategies for behavior management.**
   Answer: Reinforcement, response cost, punishment, ignoring, shaping behavior, contingency management, token reinforcements, time out, home-school coordination.

5. **What is the primary difference between extrinsic reinforcement and intrinsic reinforcement?**
   Answer: Extrinsic reinforcers are external, such as food or toys. Intrinsic reinforcers are internal, such as the pleasure of mastering a task.

Essay-Discussion Questions and Answers

1. **Discuss the characteristics of disabilities in social skills.**
   Answer: Some, but not all, students with learning disabilities exhibit social perception problems. Such disabilities can keep these individuals from meeting the basic social demands of everyday life. They make judgments about social situations, have trouble empathizing with others and perceiving how they feel, or have problems in socializing and making friends. In addition, these students may have difficulty establishing relationships with their families or have social disabilities in school. Usually they have a poor self-concept. Social problems often continue into adolescence and adult life.

2. **Analyze the relationship between learning failure and emotional problems.**
   Answer: Students may be caught in a cycle of failure leading to a poor sense of self-worth, which in turn leads to more failure, and so on. With many years of continual failure, it is not surprising that many students with learning disabilities develop emotional problems. A constructive approach for such students is to help them accomplish an educational task, which may bring a sense of accomplishment and strengthen their emotional outlook.

3. **Students with learning disabilities are often characterized as lacking motivation. Discuss motivation and its impact on students with learning disabilities.**

   Answer: Motivation is the force that energizes and directs one's drive to accomplish goals. In school, students need a strong desire to learn, because much of academic learning requires persistence and hard work over a long period of time. Attribution theory refers to the way people explain their successes and failures to themselves. Some individuals with learning disabilities achieve despite the hurdles because of high motivation and resiliency.

4. **Discuss behavior management procedures for managing the behavior of students with learning disabilities.**

   Answer: Behavior management procedures are methods for changing the observable behavior of students and for making systematic changes in the academic and social learning of students with learning disabilities by modifying environmental events. The behavioral unit involves three components: an antecedent event (stimulus), a response (target behavior), and a consequent event (reinforcement). The target behavior to be changed is sandwiched between two sets of environmental influences, those that precede the behavior and those that follow the behavior.

5. **Analyze the importance of self-esteem and self-confidence and how these qualities affect the behavior and learning of students with learning disabilities.**

   Answer: For students with learning disabilities, a consequence of failing to learn is the emotional reaction to the failure. It leads to feelings of self-derision, to loss of confidence in one's self, and to lower self-esteem. This cycle of failure and poor self-esteem will continue unless some intervention is undertaken. Teachers must find a way to reverse this cycle—to build feelings of self-worth, to increase self-confidence and self-concept, and to provide experiences of success.

PART THREE
Multiple-Choice Questions

This section contains two alternative multiple-choice tests for each chapter, Test A and Test B. Instructors can select questions from each test or use the different sets for different groups. Answers appear at the end of the section.

CHAPTER 1

Learning Disabilities: A Field in Transition

Test 1A

SMT 1. A definition of learning disabilities that is used in the schools is incorporated into national legislation known as
   a. the Americans with Disabilities Act.
   b. Chapter I.
   c. Head Start.
   d. the Individuals with Disabilities Education Act.
   e. the Bilingual Education Act.

2. Which dimension of the definition of learning disabilities requires an estimate of the student's capacity to learn?
   a. Neurological dysfunction
   b. Uneven growth pattern
   c. Difficulty in academic learning
   d. Discrepancy between achievement and potential
   e. The exclusion clause

SMT 3. The current definition of learning disabilities in IDEA does *not* include
   a. psychological processing disorders.
   b. language disabilities.
   c. the exclusion clause.
   d. mathematics disabilities.
   e. social disabilities.

4. What is the approximate percentage of children in the general population identified under the category of learning disabilities?
   a. 2 percent
   b. 5 percent
   c. 10 percent
   d. 15 percent
   e. 20 percent

5. The operational portion of the definition of learning disabilities states that a child with learning disabilities has a severe discrepancy between achievement and intellectual ability in one or more of seven areas of learning. Which of the following is *not* included among those seven areas?
   a. Listening comprehension
   b. Written expression
   c. Spelling
   d. Mathematics reasoning
   e. Oral expression

6. The portion of the definition that refers to the discrepancy between achievement and potential emphasizes
   a. underachievement.
   b. overachievement.
   c. lack of motivation.
   d. poor teaching.
   e. lack of interest.

7. What are the initials of the special education law?
   a. LDA
   b. ADA
   c. ADD
   d. IDEA
   e. EHA

8. Learning disabilities are found among
   a. youngsters from poor families.
   b. youngsters with superior intelligence.
   c. juvenile delinquents.
   d. youngsters from the middle socioeconomic class.
   e. all of the above.

9. The Individuals with Disabilities Education Act
   a. gives every child with disabilities the right to a free and appropriate public education.
   b. mandates that every child with disabilities be taught in a regular classroom.
   c. does not include children with very severe disabilities.
   d. includes children who are gifted and talented.
   e. advocates certain techniques to be used with children with disabilities.

10. The term *learning disabilities* has been used since the first national organization meeting of parent groups and professionals in
    a. 1947.
    b. 1963.
    c. 1969.
    d. 1975.
    e. 1982.

11. All individuals with learning disabilities have
    a. motor problems.
    b. reading problems.
    c. mathematics problems.
    d. attention problems.
    e. problems in some aspect of learning.

12. The concept of *a disorder in one or more of the basic psychological processes* is an element of which definition of learning disabilities?
    a. Federal (IDEA)
    b. Interagency Committee on Learning Disabilities
    c. National Joint Committee on Learning Disabilities
    d. Learning Disabilities Association
    e. None of the above

13. The concept of *social disabilities* is an element of which definition of learning disabilities?
    a. Federal (IDEA)
    b. Interagency Committee on Learning Disabilities
    c. National Joint Committee on Learning Disabilities
    d. Learning Disabilities Association
    e. None of the above

14. The concept of *learning disability that is intrinsic to the individual* is an element of which definition of learning disabilities?
    a. Federal (IDEA)
    b. Interagency Committee on Learning Disabilities
    c. Americans with Disabilities Act
    d. National Joint Committee on Learning Disabilities
    e. None of the above

15. Since the special education law was first passed in 1975, the number of students identified as having learning disabilities
    a. has remained stable.
    b. has been decreasing.
    c. has been increasing.
    d. is unknown.
    e. is erratic, sometimes increasing and sometimes decreasing.

16. Approximately what percentage of all students with disabilities are identified as having learning disabilities?
    a. 10 percent
    b. 30 percent
    c. 50 percent
    d. 70 percent
    e. 90 percent

17. The largest number of students with learning disabilities served by the schools are ages
    a. 3–5.
    b. 7–9.
    c. 10–14.
    d. 15–17.
    e. 18–22.

18. The term *learning disabilities* reflects the perspective of which discipline?
    a. Medicine
    b. Speech pathology
    c. Occupational therapy
    d. Linguistics
    e. Education

19. Of the students in schools and clinics who are identified as having learning disabilities,
    a. there are more boys than girls.
    b. there are more girls than boys.
    c. there are an equal number of boys and girls.
    d. gender differences have never been studied.
    e. All of the above.

20. Learning disabilities have been noted among individuals who speak
    a. English.
    b. Spanish.
    c. Chinese.
    d. Hebrew.
    e. all of the above.

21. According to Howard Gardner's theory of "multiple intelligences," a person with an aptitude in engineering and mechanics has which kind of intelligence?
    a. verbal/linguistic
    b. musical/rhythmical
    c. interpersonal
    d. body kinesthetic
    e. visual/spatial

22. A growing trend in terms of placement for students with learning disabilities is
    a. separate schools.
    b. separate classes.
    c. inclusion.
    d. exclusion.
    e. resource rooms.

Test 1B

1. The federal law indicates that a student with learning disabilities is identified when he or she has a "discrepancy" between achievement and potential. This view emphasizes
    a. overachievement.
    b. lack of motivation.
    c. lack of interest.
    d. underachievement.
    e. poor teaching.

2. The acronym for the special education law is
    a. IDEA.
    b. ADA.
    c. EHA.
    d. LDA.
    e. ADD.

3. Learning disabilities are found among
    a. youngsters from the middle socioeconomic classes.
    b. youngsters from poor families.
    c. youngsters with superior intelligence.
    d. juvenile delinquents.
    e. all of the above.

4. Which of the following is true of the Individuals with Disabilities Education Act?
    a. It mandates that every child with disabilities be taught in a regular classroom.
    b. It does not include children with very severe disabilities.
    c. It advocates certain techniques to be used with children with disabilities.
    d. It includes children who are gifted and talented.
    e. It gives every child with disabilities the right to a free and appropriate public education.

5. The category name of "learning disabilities" has been used since the first national organization meeting of parent groups and professionals in
    a. 1930.
    b. 1947.
    c. 1963.
    d. 1975.
    e. 1991.

6. Which of the following laws contains a definition of learning disabilities?
    a. Chapter I
    b. Individuals with Disabilities Education Act
    c. Americans with Disabilities Act
    d. The Bilingual Education Act
    e. Head Start

7. Which of the common elements of the definition of learning disabilities requires an estimate of the student's capacity to learn?
   a. Neurological dysfunction
   b. The exclusion clause
   c. Difficulty in academic learning
   d. Discrepancy between achievement and potential
   e. Uneven growth pattern

8. The definition of learning disabilities in the Individuals with Disabilities Education Act does *not* include
   a. language disabilities.
   b. the exclusion clause.
   c. psychological processing disorders.
   d. social disabilities.
   e. mathematics disabilities.

9. What percentage of students in the general population is identified under the category of learning disabilities?
   a. 2 percent
   b. 5 percent
   c. 12 percent
   d. 18 percent
   e. 25 percent

10. Which of the following is *not* included among those areas in which a child can be identified as having a learning disability, according to IDEA?
    a. Spelling
    b. Written expression
    c. Mathematics reasoning
    d. Oral expression
    e. Listening comprehension

11. Of students in all categories of special education disabilities, what percentage is under the category of learning disabilities?
    a. 5 percent
    b. 15 percent
    c. 30 percent
    d. 50 percent
    e. 70 percent

12. The largest number of students with learning disabilities served by the schools are ages
    a. 3–5.
    b. 7–9.
    c. 10–14.
    d. 15–17.
    e. 18–22.

13. Many different disciplines, each with a specialized vocabulary, contribute to the field of learning disabilities. The term *learning disabilities* reflects the perspective of which discipline?
    a. Speech pathology
    b. Education
    c. Occupational therapy
    d. Linguistics
    e. Medicine

14. Which of the following is true of students *identified* with learning disabilities in the schools?
    a. There are an equal number of boys and girls.
    b. Gender differences have never been studied.
    c. There are more boys than girls.
    d. There are more girls than boys.
    e. None of the above.

15. Learning disabilities have been reported among children in the schools in
    a. England.
    b. Denmark.
    c. Israel.
    d. Canada.
    e. all of the above.

16. Which of the following is *not* a regulation in the Individuals with Disabilities Education Act?
    a. No single test may be used to make the assessment.
    b. The evaluation team must include at least one teacher or other specialist in the area of suspected disability.
    c. Tests must be given in clear and understandable English.
    d. Parents have the right to see all of their child's educational records.
    e. The evaluation team must be multidisciplinary.

17. "A disorder in one or more of the basic psychological processes" is a key element in which definition of learning disabilities?
    a. Interagency Committee on Learning Disabilities
    b. National Joint Committee on Learning Disabilities (NJCLD)
    c. Individuals with Disabilities Act (IDEA)
    d. Learning Disabilities Association
    e. Section 504 of the Rehabilitation Act

18. The concept of social disabilities is an element of which definition of learning disabilities?
    a. Interagency Committee on Learning Disabilities
    b. Section 504 of the Rehabilitation Act
    c. Federal definition (IDEA)
    d. Learning Disabilities Association
    e. Bilingual legislation

19. The concept that learning disabilities is a problem that is intrinsic to the individual is an element of which definition of learning disabilities?
    a. Interagency Committee on Learning Disabilities
    b. Americans with Disabilities Act
    c. National Joint Committee on Learning Disabilities
    d. Federal definition (IDEA)
    e. Section 504 of the Rehabilitation Act

20. The special education law mandating services for students with learning disabilities was first passed in 1975. Since that time, what has happened to the number of students identified as having learning disabilities?
    a. It is unknown.
    b. It has remained stable.
    c. It has been decreasing.
    d. It has been increasing.
    e. It is erratic, sometimes increasing and sometimes decreasing.

21. The theory of Howard Gardner's "multiple intelligences" suggests that in school the major kind of intelligence expected of students is
    a. visual/spatial.
    b. intrapersonal.
    c. body/kinesthetic.
    d. musical/rhythmical.
    e. verbal/linguistic.

22. Which of the following placements is the growing trend for delivering instruction to students with learning disabilities?
    a. One-to-one instruction
    b. Separate classes
    c. Inclusion
    d. Exclusion
    e. Resource rooms

CHAPTER 2

Historical Perspectives and Emerging Directions

Test 2A

1. Special education law, Public Law 94-142, which mandated special education for handicapped students, was first passed by Congress in
   a. 1963.
   b. 1968.
   c. 1975.
   d. 1986.
   e. 1991.

2. The current phase in the history of learning disabilities includes all the following *except*
   a. use of computer technology.
   b. awareness of cultural and linguistic diversity.
   c. discovery of Broca's aphasia.
   d. inclusion as a placement setting.
   e. collaboration between regular and special education teachers.

3. The term *learning disabilities* has been used since the first national organization meeting of a parent group in
   a. 1947.
   b. 1959.
   c. 1963.
   d. 1969.
   e. 1971.

4. The term *brain-injured child* was first used by
   a. Clements.
   b. Kirk.
   c. Birch.
   d. Strauss.
   e. Cruickshank.

5. In the historical development of the field of learning disabilities, scientists in the early foundation phase concentrated on studying
   a. learning strategies that children use.
   b. the impact of medication.
   c. functions and dysfunctions of the human brain.
   d. methods of teaching reading.
   e. the merging of regular and special education.

6. Which of the following is an "organic," or cause-related, term?
   a. Minimal brain dysfunction
   b. Perceptually handicapped
   c. Learning disabilities
   d. Distractibility
   e. Impulsivity

7. Which of the following is a "consequence-related," or behavior-related, term?
   a. Brain injury
   b. Central nervous system damage
   c. Neurological impairment
   d. Hyperactivity
   e. Minimal brain dysfunction

8. Alfred Strauss, in writing about brain-injured children, hypothesized that an injury to the brain affecting learning could occur
   a. before birth.
   b. during birth.
   c. after birth.
   d. at none of the above times.
   e. at any of the above times.

9. The Individuals with Disabilities Education Act describes individuals as having
   a. handicaps.
   b. disabilities.
   c. impairments.
   d. disorders.
   e. difficulties.

10. What is the age range in IDEA for which students with disabilities are eligible for a free appropriate public education?
    a. 3–18
    b. 0–18
    c. 3–21
    d. 0–21
    e. 5–18

11. The pioneering book in the field of learning disabilities *Psychopathology and Education of the Brain-Injured Child,* published in 1974, reports the work of
    a. Sam Kirk.
    b. Newell Kephart.
    c. Alfred Strauss.
    d. Marianne Frostig.
    e. Sam Clements.

12. Strauss noted all of the following as characteristics of brain-injured children *except*
    a. perceptual disorders.
    b. perseverance.
    c. withdrawn behavior.
    d. conceptual disorders.
    e. behavioral disorders.

13. What term was suggested by Sam Clements to distinguish between major and minor neuro-
    logical conditions?
    a. Learning disabilities
    b. Brain-injured child
    c. Strauss syndrome
    d. Strephosymbolia
    e. Minimal brain dysfunction

14. According to a memo written by the U.S. Department of Education in 1991, children with
    attention deficit disorders can be eligible for services under
    a. other health-impaired.
    b. learning disabilities.
    c. emotional or behavioral disturbance.
    d. Section 504 of the Rehabilitation Act.
    e. all of the above.

15. The Individuals with Disabilities Education Act (IDEA)
    a. uses the term *disabilities* instead of *handicaps*.
    b. uses the term *individuals* instead of *children*.
    c. includes the condition of autism as a separate category.
    d. includes the condition of traumatic brain injury as a separate category.
    e. includes all of the above.

16. Attention deficit disorder
    a. is synonymous with hyperactivity.
    b. is a separate category in the Individuals with Disabilities Education Act (IDEA).
    c. is synonymous with the term *learning disabilities*.
    d. often co-exists with learning disabilities.
    e. is not recognized as a disability requiring special services.

17. The education reform movement
    a. increases the amount of testing of student achievement.
    b. increases curriculum requirements for students.
    c. will probably make graduation harder for students with learning disabilities.
    d. has a goal of raising the standards in the schools.
    e. does all of the above.

18. Broca's work examined the location of brain damage in adults who had lost language function
    and subsequently died. Broca's work occurred during which historical phase in learning dis-
    abilities?
    a. Foundation phase
    b. Transition phase
    c. Integration phase
    d. Contemporary phase
    e. None of the above

19. The most recent trend for integrating regular and special education students is called
    a. the regular education initiative.
    b. mainstreaming.
    c. pull-programs.
    d. the education reform movement.
    e. inclusion.

20. The term that is used in federal law on disabilities is
    a. brain-injured child.
    b. learning disabilities.
    c. minimal brain dysfunction.
    d. Strauss syndrome.
    e. strephosymbolia.

21. The rapid growth of public school programs for learning disabilities occurred during which historical phase?
    a. Foundation phase
    b. Transition phase
    c. Integration phase
    d. Current phase
    e. None of the above

22. The American Psychiatric Association describes the criteria for attention deficit hyperactivity disorder (ADHD) in their *Diagnostic and Statistical Manual of Mental Disorders (DSM)*. Which edition of the DSM series describes three subtypes of ADHD?
    a. DSM-II
    b. DSM-III
    c. DSM-III-R
    d. DSM-IV
    e. DSM-V

Test 2B

1. The condition of *attention deficit disorder*
   a. is a separate category in the Individuals with Disabilities Education Act (IDEA).
   b. often co-exists with learning disabilities.
   c. is synonymous with hyperactivity.
   d. is not recognized as a disability requiring special services under the law.
   e. always occurs in individuals with learning disabilities.

2. A likely consequence of the education reform movement is
   a. decreased curriculum requirements for students.
   b. easier graduation for students with learning disabilities.
   c. increased testing of student achievement.
   d. lower standards in the schools.
   e. reduced test anxiety.

3. The part of the brain called Broca's area is named after the physician who studied the location of brain damage in adults who had lost language function. In which historical phase of learning disabilities did Broca conduct his research?
   a. Current phase
   b. Transition phase
   c. Integration phase
   d. Foundation phase
   e. None of the above

4. Which of the following historically was the first administrative arrangement for serving students with learning disabilities?
   a. Mainstreaming
   b. Separate special education classrooms
   c. Collaboration
   d. Integration of regular and special education
   e. Regular education initiative

5. Different terms have been used historically to refer to the type of student who is the subject of this book. The term used in federal law on disabilities is
   a. minimal brain dysfunction.
   b. brain-injured child.
   c. Strauss syndrome.
   d. strephosymbolia.
   e. learning disabilities.

6. Which of the following is an organic, or cause-related, term (as opposed to a consequent, or behavior-related, term)?
   a. Learning disabilities
   b. Distractibility
   c. Impulsivity
   d. Minimal brain dysfunction
   e. Perceptual disorders

7. In 1974, the book *Psychopathology and Education of the Brain-Injured Child* was published. It was authored by and reports the work of
   a. Sam Clements.
   b. Newell Kephart.
   c. Alfred Strauss.
   d. Marianne Frostig.
   e. Sam Kirk.

8. What was the term recommended by Sam Clements to distinguish between major and minor neurological conditions?
   a. Strauss syndrome
   b. Strephosymbolia
   c. Minimal brain dysfunction
   d. Learning disabilities
   e. Brain-injured child

9. The condition of *attention deficit disorders* can be identified under
   a. emotional disturbance.
   b. other health-impaired.
   c. Section 504 of the Rehabilitation Act.
   d. learning disabilities.
   e. all of the above.

10. The Individuals with Disabilities Education Act (IDEA)
    a. uses the term *disabilities* instead of *handicaps*.
    b. uses the term *children* instead of *individuals*.
    c. does *not* include the condition of autism as a separate category.
    d. does *not* include the condition of traumatic brain injury as a separate category.
    e. is permissive legislation.

11. Which of the following is a consequence (behavior-related) term, as opposed to an organic (cause-related) term?
    a. Neurological impairment
    b. Hyperactivity
    c. Minimal brain dysfunction
    d. Brain injury
    e. Central nervous system damage

12. In his writings, Strauss hypothesized that brain-injured children had suffered an injury to their brain
    a. before birth.
    b. during birth.
    c. after birth.
    d. At none of the above times.
    e. at any of the above times.

13. Which of the following is *not* among the characteristics of brain injury observed and described by Strauss?
    a. Withdrawn behavior
    b. Conceptual disorders
    c. Behavioral disorders
    d. Perceptual disorders
    e. Perseveration

14. Which of the following terms is used in IDEA to refer to individuals with problems?
    a. Disorders
    b. Disabilities
    c. Handicaps
    d. Impairments
    e. Difficulties

15. In what age range are individuals with disabilities entitled to educational services, according to the special education law?
    a. 5–18 years
    b. 3–18 years
    c. 0–21 years
    d. 0–18 years
    e. 3–21 years

16. In what year was the special education law (Public Law 94-142) first passed by Congress?
    a. 1963
    b. 1968
    c. 1975
    d. 1987
    e. 1996

17. The current phase in the history of learning disabilities includes all of the following *except*
    a. the recognition of brain-injured children.
    b. the educational reform movement.
    c. the use of computer technology.
    d. collaboration between regular and special education teachers.
    e. inclusion placements.

18. In what year did a group of parents and professionals first meet to establish an organization for children they identified as having learning disabilities?
    a. 1947
    b. 1963
    c. 1971
    d. 1980
    e. 1990

19. The term *learning disabilities* was first suggested by
    a. Clements.
    b. Kirk.
    c. Birch.
    d. Strauss.
    e. Cruickshank.

20. In the historical development of the field of learning disabilities, scientists in the early foundation phase concentrated on studying
    a. the functions and dysfunctions of the human brain.
    b. methods of teaching reading.
    c. the merging of regular and special education.
    d. the learning strategies that children use.
    e. the impact of medication.

21. Criteria for three subtypes of attention deficit hyperactivity disorder are provided by the American Psychiatric Association in which edition of their *Diagnostic and Statistical Manual of Mental Disorders (DSM)?*
    a. DSM-II
    b. DSM-III
    c. DSM-III-revised
    d. DSM-IV
    e. DSM-V

22. The clinical implications of brain injury were studied in which historical phase?
    a. Foundation phase
    b. Transition phase
    c. Integration phase
    d. Current phase
    e. None of the above

CHAPTER 3

Assessment

Test 3A

SMT 1. The IEP is
   a. an oral agreement.
   b. a class curriculum.
   c. a written plan for a student.
   d. collaboration between regular and special education teachers.
   e. an informal reading test.

2. Assessment is not useful for
   a. helping to plan a teaching program for a student.
   b. determining if schools have the legal responsibility for educating students with disabilities.
   c. making decisions about placement for special services for students.
   d. monitoring the progress of a student.
   e. screening to detect pupils who may be eligible for learning disabilities services.

3. Participants at the IEP meeting must include all of the following *except*
   a. a representative of the school.
   b. the child's teacher.
   c. one or both of the child's parents.
   d. a person with a legal background, such as an attorney.
   e. the child, if appropriate.

SMT 4. The content of the IEP does *not* have to include
   a. a lesson plan.
   b. present levels of educational performance.
   c. services to be provided.
   d. annual goals and short-term objectives.
   e. a date for initiation of services.

SMT 5. All of the following are alternative types of assessment methods *except*
   a. formal standardized tests.
   b. authentic assessment.
   c. dynamic assessment.
   d. portfolio assessment.
   e. performance assessment.

6. Which of the following steps is *not* required in determining whether a child has a learning disability?
   a. Assess the child's potential for learning.
   b. Assess present levels of achievement in various areas.
   c. Measure any discrepancy between potential and achievement.
   d. Assess the child through a neurological examination.
   e. Observe the child in the classroom.

7. The major purpose for using a discrepancy formula is
   a. to detect social disabilities.
   b. to determine if a child is eligible for learning disabilities services.
   c. to determine the child's ecological background.
   d. to determine emotional problems.
   e. to determine how a child reacts to failure.

8. Which of the following is generally used to determine a child's present level of performance?
   a. Intelligence test
   b. Behavior checklist
   c. Observation
   d. Adaptive behavior scales
   e. Achievement tests

9. Data for assessment can best be obtained through
   a. the interview with parents.
   b. observation of the child.
   c. informal testing.
   d. standardized testing.
   e. all of the above.

10. All of the following data are generally obtained in the interview with the parents *except*
    a. the conditions surrounding the child's birth.
    b. the age at which the child began to walk.
    c. the age at which the child began to talk.
    d. the child's IQ.
    e. illnesses the child has had.

11. Which of the following assessment methods compares a child's performance to that of children in a normed sample?
    a. Observation
    b. Standardized test
    c. Criterion-referenced test
    d. Case history
    e. Informal test

12. To be classified as having learning disabilities, a student must
    a. not currently be taking medication.
    b. have a medical diagnosis.
    c. be observed by some member of the team.
    d. be interviewed by the social worker.
    e. have failed a grade.

13. Which of the following describes standardized tests?
    a. They can be quickly and easily developed by teachers.
    b. They require teachers to follow a prescribed procedure in administration.
    c. They can be devised by teachers to cover many areas of the curriculum.
    d. They can be modified so that the child does well on the test.
    e. Information on reliability and validity is not provided.

14. Which of the following describes informal tests?
    a. Administrative procedures set out in the test manual must be followed strictly.
    b. Test scores have been normed on large representative populations.
    c. Teachers can modify test procedures to make sure children do their best.
    d. Reliability and validity information is generally provided.
    e. Scoring directions must be precisely followed.

15. What kind of measure is generally used to assess potential for learning?
    a. Achievement test
    b. Behavior test
    c. Motor test
    d. Personality test
    e. Intelligence test

16. The assessment procedure that requires direct and repeated charting of performance is
    a. the criterion-referenced test.
    b. curriculum-based assessment.
    c. portfolio assessment.
    d. standardized testing.
    e. diagnostic teaching.

17. Which of the following is a procedural safeguard to protect the rights of students and parents?
    a. Tests must be in clear and understandable English.
    b. Parents cannot see all of the information about their child.
    c. Reports must be given to parents in English.
    d. Once the IEP meeting is completed, decisions are final.
    e. Tests must be free of cultural or racial bias.

18. The IEP team decided that Louanne has learning disabilities, based on a discrepancy score derived by comparing her standard score on an intelligence test with her standard score on an achievement test. Which method did they use?
    a. Deviation from present grade level
    b. Discrepancy based on age scores or grade scores
    c. Standard-score comparison
    d. Regression analysis measures
    e. Team clinical judgment

19. Discrepancy formulas for determining whether students have learning disabilities have been criticized for not considering
    a. qualitative information.
    b. quantitative data.
    c. intelligence.
    d. achievement.
    e. standardized test scores.

20. Mr. Alvarez is interactively teaching a group of five students. As he works with them, he is assessing their ability to learn in a healthy social environment. Which model of assessment is Mr. Alvarez using?
    a. Screening assessment
    b. Traditional assessment
    c. Dynamic assessment
    d. Curriculum-based assessment
    e. None of the above

21. Why are some authorities in the field of learning disabilities criticizing the use of the IQ-discrepancy formula to determine learning disabilities?
    a. The IQ score may not assess a child's potential.
    b. The discrepancy score varies from state to state.
    c. The method is not effective in identifying young children with learning disabilities.
    d. Children must fail before being identified.
    e. All of the above.

22. Which type of test measures mastery of specific skills?
    a. Norm-referenced test
    b. Formal survey test
    c. Diagnostic teaching
    d. Standardized test
    e. Criterion-referenced test

Test 3B

1. The content of the IEP does *not* have to include
    a. a lesson plan.
    b. present levels of educational performance.
    c. services to be provided.
    d. annual goals and short-term objectives.
    e. a date for initiation of services.

2. An IEP is
    a. an informal reading test.
    b. a rating scale.
    c. a written plan for a student.
    d. an oral agreement between parent and teacher.
    e. a lesson plan.

3. Which of the following is used to determine a student's potential for learning?
    a. Informal tests
    b. Diagnostic teaching
    c. Observation
    d. Teachers' reports and school records
    e. An intelligence test

4. In which kind of assessment does the teacher assess the student within a teaching situation?
    a. Dynamic
    b. Traditional
    c. Standardized testing
    d. Medical
    e. Formal

5. Curriculum-based assessment
    a. requires student performance to be charted on a graph.
    b. uses standardized instruments.
    c. is a test for classifying students.
    d. is normed on a large population.
    e. is an annual assessment method.

6. All of the following are *alternative* types of assessment *except*
    a. performance assessment.
    b. portfolio assessment.
    c. dynamic assessment.
    d. norm-referenced tests.
    e. authentic assessment.

7. The major purpose for using a discrepancy formula is to determine
    a. if a student is eligible for learning disabilities services.
    b. the student's background and environment.
    c. the student's social skills.
    d. the student's attitude toward school.
    e. the relationship between the student and teacher.

8. Procedural safeguards
   a. protect the rights of students.
   b. require that parents must consent in writing to an evaluation.
   c. require the assessment in the student's native language.
   d. require that tests be free of cultural bias.
   e. include all of the above.

9. Why are some authorities in the field of learning disabilities critical of the use of the IQ-discrepancy formula to determine if the child has learning disabilities?
   a. Children must fail before they are identified.
   b. The discrepancy formula is not effective in identifying young children with learning disabilities.
   c. The IQ score may not effectively assess a child's potential for learning.
   d. Children will have discrepancy scores that vary from state to state.
   e. All of the above.

10. Which type of assessment demonstrates growth through work samples over a period of time?
    a. Norm-referenced test
    b. Survey test
    c. Diagnostic teaching
    d. Portfolio assessment
    e. Criterion-referenced test

11. Observation of a student with learning disabilities
    a. is required in the law.
    b. is a sufficient method for obtaining data for the IEP.
    c. must be done by a social worker.
    d. should not be done in the child's classroom.
    e. All of the above.

12. Which of the following assessment procedures requires direct and repeated charting of performance?
    a. Portfolio assessment
    b. Standardized testing
    c. Diagnostic teaching
    d. Criterion-referenced testing
    e. Curriculum-based assessment

13. All of the following types of information are generally obtained during the interview with the parents *except*
    a. the child's birth history.
    b. developmental milestones.
    c. the child's IQ.
    d. the child's health history.
    e. the age at which the child said his or her first word.

14. The IEP team has decided that Angela has learning disabilities. In making this decision, the team had to override the determination of the discrepancy score formula. Which method did the team use?
    a. Deviation from present grade level
    b. Discrepancy based on age scores or grade scores
    c. Standard-score comparison
    d. Regression analysis measures
    e. Team clinical judgment

15. Participants at the IEP meeting must include all of the following *except*
    a. a medical professional.
    b. the child, if appropriate.
    c. a representative of the school.
    d. the child's teacher.
    e. one or both of the child's parents.

16. The IEP
    a. is written by the multidisciplinary assessment professionals.
    b. is not required for students to receive special education services.
    c. should not be of concern to the general education classroom teacher.
    d. is an oral agreement.
    e. is written at the case study conference, which includes the parents.

17. In which stage of the assessment-teaching process do general education classroom teachers try preventive intervention measures?
    a. Referral and initial planning
    b. Case study conference
    c. Prereferral
    d. Monitoring progress
    e. Multidisciplinary evaluation

18. In which method of assessment is a student's performance compared to that of many other students who have taken that test?
    a. Criterion-referenced test
    b. Case history
    c. Informal test
    d. Observation
    e. Standardized test

19. A standardized test
    a. can be modified so that the student does well on the test.
    b. does not provide information on validity.
    c. can be quickly and easily developed by teachers.
    d. requires teachers to follow a prescribed procedure in administration.
    e. can be devised by teachers to cover many areas of the curriculum.

20. In an informal test, which of the following applies?
    a. Teachers must strictly follow the procedures outlined in the test manual in administering the test.
    b. Test scores are normed on a large representative population.
    c. Teachers can modify test procedures to make sure students do their best.
    d. Reliability information and validity information are generally provided.
    e. The scoring directions must be precisely followed.

21. The WISC-III
    a. is an intelligence test.
    b. is an achievement test.
    c. is an informal test.
    d. is usually given by the classroom teacher.
    e. is a group test.

CHAPTER 4
Clinical Teaching

Test 4A

1. Teachers can make modifications to help the child learn. All of the following are examples of modifications that teachers can make *except*
   a. reducing or enlarging the space in which the child works.
   b. changing the difficulty level of material to be learned.
   c. modifying the time available for the child to perform the task.
   d. making minor adjustments in the physiological makeup of the child.
   e. simplifying the language used with the child.

2. Mr. Cain cuts a page of arithmetic computation problems into strips and attaches only one strip to a single sheet of paper. He has changed
   a. the task's content.
   b. the language factors.
   c. space factors.
   d. interpersonal relations.
   e. none of the above.

3. The interaction between an individual and the various environments in which he or she lives and learns is referred to as the
   a. biological system.
   b. neurological system.
   c. psychological system.
   d. ecological system.
   e. management system.

4. Research shows that the most important factor for successful learning is the
   a. material.
   b. method.
   c. diagnosis.
   d. class size.
   e. teacher.

5. All of the following are characteristics of teaching designed to promote active learning *except*
   a. encouraging student involvement.
   b. building on the student's prior experience.
   c. emphasizing drill and practice.
   d. integrating the student's background with the teaching.
   e. encouraging constructive learning.

6. Ms. Simmons is a seventh-grade social studies teacher. She obtained a fifth-grade reading level book covering the same social studies content for Jeremiah, a student with learning disabilities in her class. What variable did Ms. Simmons modify?
    a. The task's content
    b. Interpersonal factors
    c. Spatial factors
    d. Difficulty level
    e. All of the above

7. What is the first procedure of task analysis?
    a. Break the goal into a series of smaller steps.
    b. Teach the first step of the task.
    c. Put the steps of the task into a sequence.
    d. Set a learning goal.
    e. None of the above.

8. Subdividing the goal of tying shoelaces into an orderly sequence of steps is an example of
    a. task analysis.
    b. constructive learning.
    c. the learning strategies approach.
    d. the materials approach.
    e. the specialized techniques approach.

9. Instruction in learning *how to learn* is the objective of which approach?
    a. Materials
    b. Behavioral
    c. Psychotherapeutic
    d. Specialized techniques
    e. Learning strategies

10. Determining that Joey is having difficulty in learning because of poor visual perception abilities is an example of
    a. a psychological processing disorder.
    b. mastery learning.
    c. the specialized techniques approach.
    d. the psychotherapeutic approach.
    e. the materials approach to teaching.

11. The psychotherapeutic approach to teaching emphasizes
    a. the student's relationship with the teacher.
    b. the student's emotions and feelings.
    c. building the child's self-esteem.
    d. supplying experiences of success.
    e. all of the above.

12. The effective schools research studies show that effective schools
    a. are in rural communities.
    b. have a twelve-month calendar.
    c. have a winning football team.
    d. are in large cities.
    e. have an orderly school climate.

13. All of the following are ways of building self-esteem and motivation *except*
    a. finding an area of interest to the student.
    b. comparing the student's progress with the progress of a high-achieving sibling.
    c. encouraging the student to collaborate in planning the lesson.
    d. giving the student experiences of success.
    e. demonstrating the student's progress in concrete terms, such as a graph.

14. Juan's school is using a criterion-referenced testing system for mathematics. Juan passed the test for arithmetic skill number 10 at the 95 percent criterion level. This is an example of the
    a. mastery learning approach.
    b. cognitive processing approach.
    c. specialized techniques approach.
    d. child development approach.
    e. psychotherapeutic approach.

15. Ms. LeRoy uses the teaching method of an interactive dialogue in which the students and the teacher take turns leading discussions. This is an example of which teaching method?
    a. Direct instruction
    b. Mastery learning
    c. Reciprocal teaching
    d. Direct instruction
    e. Task analysis

16. Which of the following types of teaching emphasizes the sequence and structure of learning activities?
    a. Reciprocal teaching
    b. Direct instruction
    c. Learning strategies instruction
    d. Building self-esteem
    e. Discovery learning

17. The clinical teaching cycle
    a. clearly separates assessment and teaching.
    b. requires teachers to be continuous decision makers.
    c. depends upon materials that have been built into decision making.
    d. is designed for teaching an entire class.
    e. can only be used in a one-to-one setting.

18. Which of the following will *not* build self-esteem and motivation?
    a. Find an area of the student's interest.
    b. Give a student many experiences with success.
    c. Fail a student who does not meet minimum competency test standards.
    d. Establish rapport between student and teacher.
    e. Have the student share responsibility for planning the lesson and selecting material.

19. Clinical teaching
    a. is tailored to the unique needs of a particular student.
    b. can only be accomplished in a one-to-one setting.
    c. requires materials that are different from those used in the regular class.
    d. is not linked to assessment.
    e. is all of the above.

20. Subdividing the job of writing a research paper into a series of small steps is an example of
    a. cognitive processing.
    b. the psychotherapeutic approach to teaching.
    c. reciprocal teaching.
    d. task analysis.
    e. the materials approach to teaching.

21. Section 504 of the Rehabilitation Act
    a. serves students identified as having disabilities under IDEA.
    b. requires that students have an IEP.
    c. provides instruction in special schools.
    d. may serve students who are not eligible under IDEA in the regular classroom.
    e. does all of the above.

Test 4B

1. The clinical teacher can modify the learning environment by
   a. changing the difficulty level of the material.
   b. changing the amount of time the child is given to complete a task.
   c. changing the language used by the teacher.
   d. changing the space in which the child works.
   e. doing all of the above.

2. Teaching students to develop their own systematic way of learning, based on their learning strengths, uses what approach?
   a. Learning strategies
   b. Specialized techniques
   c. Materials
   d. Pedagogical
   e. Learning styles

3. Determining that Willie is not learning the "5's table" in arithmetic because he has a poor visual memory and visual perception deficits is an example of
   a. analysis of cognitive processing.
   b. task analysis of the curriculum.
   c. the specialized techniques approach.
   d. the materials approach.
   e. direct instruction.

4. In analyzing Joanne's learning disabilities, the multidisciplinary team discussed the interaction of the environments of her school, home, social, and cultural life. Together these environments are referred to as
   a. the management system.
   b. the biological system.
   c. the information-processing system.
   d. the ecological system.
   e. all of the above.

5. The assessment of Mavin shows that she learns well through the visual channel but has difficulty with learning through the auditory channel. The team suggested using a language experience method to tap her visual abilities. This is an example of what approach?
   a. Learning strategies
   b. Materials
   c. Psychological processing
   d. Psychotherapeutic
   e. Behavioral

6. Ms. Simon always uses the XYZ materials with all of her students. This is an example of what approach?
   a. Psychological processing
   b. Learning strategies
   c. Cognitive processing
   d. Mastery learning
   e. Materials approach

7. The research on effective schools shows that good schools have all of the following *except*
   a. a twelve-month calendar.
   b. an orderly school climate.
   c. principals who are strong leaders.
   d. high student expectations.
   e. a high degree of engaged time for students.

8. The eighth-grade science teacher obtained a fourth-grade reading level book covering similar science content. She gave this book to Allie, a student with learning disabilities in her class. What variable did the teacher modify?
   a. Interpersonal factors
   b. Task content
   c. Spatial factors
   d. Difficulty level
   e. All of the above

9. Which of the following is the most important element in clinical teaching?
   a. Finding *the* best teaching method
   b. Tailoring instruction for a unique student
   c. Making a thorough and complete diagnosis
   d. Finding the best teaching material
   e. Having appropriate furniture in the room

10. Promoting active learning is the purpose of all of the following methods *except*
    a. getting students involved in the lesson.
    b. integrating the student's background with the teaching.
    c. encouraging constructive learning.
    d. using the student's prior experience.
    e. emphasizing drill and practice.

11. Mr. Zee has retyped a social studies test for his students. He has not changed the questions, but he has placed them on two pages instead of one, with more space to make it easier to read the questions. He has changed
    a. the time factor.
    b. spatial factors.
    c. the task content.
    d. language factors.
    e. none of the above.

12. Instruction in learning how to learn is the goal of which approach?
    a. Psychotherapeutic
    b. Specialized techniques
    c. Learning strategies
    d. Materials
    e. Behavioral

13. The psychotherapeutic approach to teaching emphasizes
    a. analysis of underlying disabilities.
    b. the sequence of skills.
    c. the student's relationship with the teacher.
    d. schedules of reinforcement.
    e. specific materials for teaching.

14. Determining that Dan cannot write his letters because of poor visual perception is an example of
    a. psychological processing analysis.
    b. the specialized techniques approach.
    c. task analysis of the curriculum.
    d. psychotherapeutic teaching.
    e. the materials approach to teaching.

15. In which method of teaching does the teacher use an interactive dialogue in which teachers and students take turns leading discussions?
    a. Reciprocal teaching
    b. Materials approach
    c. Peer instruction
    d. Direct instruction
    e. Mastery learning

16. The objective set by Mr. Carter is to have students in his social studies class learn about the U.S. Constitution. Mr. Carter has subdivided this subject into a series of small, sequential steps and plans to have each step thoroughly mastered before continuing to the next step. This is an example of
    a. the psychotherapeutic approach to teaching.
    b. cognitive processing.
    c. reciprocal teaching.
    d. task analysis of the curriculum.
    e. the materials approach to teaching.

17. Which of the following is *not* controllable by the clinical teacher?
    a. The time available to the student to perform the task
    b. The physiological makeup of the child
    c. The language the teacher uses
    d. The space in which the child works
    e. The difficulty level of the material to be learned

18. Which of the following would *not* be a good method for building a student's self-esteem?
    a. Plan lessons that will give the student experiences with success.
    b. Use techniques to demonstrate the student's progress in concrete terms, such as a graph.
    c. Find an area in which the student expresses a keen interest.
    d. Compare the student's progress with the progress of a high-achieving sibling.
    e. Encourage the student to share the responsibility of planning the lessons.

19. Which method of teaching is based on the sequencing and structuring of learning activities?
    a. Direct instruction
    b. Building self-esteem
    c. Discovery learning
    d. Reciprocal teaching
    e. Learning strategies instruction

20. Ms. Smith has been giving her group five-minute timed reading tests. In five minutes the students must read a selection and answer four questions. One student, Ted, works very slowly and never passes these tests. Ms. Smith is allowing Ted to start the test two minutes before the rest of the group, thereby giving Ted seven minutes for this exercise. What has Ms. Smith changed?
    a. Difficulty level
    b. Space
    c. Time
    d. Language
    e. Interpersonal factors

21. Section 504 of the Rehabilitation Act
    a. requires students to have an IEP.
    b. may serve students who are not eligible under IDEA through accommodations in the regular classroom.
    c. serves students identified as having disabilities under IDEA.
    d. requires that students have a continuum of placements.
    e. does none of the above.

CHAPTER 5

Systems for Delivering Educational Services

Test 5A

1. Which of the following terms related to placement or delivery service systems are mentioned in the legislation of IDEA?
   a. Full inclusion
   b. Mainstreaming
   c. Least restrictive environment
   d. Regular education initiative
   e. Inclusion

2. Which of the following is considered a human relationship competency, as opposed to a knowledge/skills competency, of the learning disabilities teacher?
   a. Administering assessment tests
   b. Interpersonal problem solving with general education teachers
   c. Interpreting assessment information
   d. Awareness of theories of learning disabilities
   e. Information about special education law

3. The legal requirement that placement must take into account the extent to which a student with a disability is placed with students who do not have disabilities is called
   a. mainstreaming.
   b. the delivery service system.
   c. the least restrictive environment.
   d. the cascade model.
   e. the continuum of alternative placements.

4. The requirement in IDEA that schools have an array of educational placements to meet the varied needs of students with disabilities is referred to as
   a. mainstreaming.
   b. a continuum of alternative placements.
   c. the delivery service system.
   d. the least restrictive environment.
   e. noncategorical placement.

5. Mainstreaming is a placement practice that
   a. eliminates special education.
   b. is required by federal law.
   c. gradually includes a child in regular education as that child is ready.
   d. requires that all children with disabilities be placed in regular education classes.
   e. does none of the above.

6. In the term *least restrictive environment*, the word *restrictive* refers to restrictions in terms of
   a. curriculum content.
   b. freedom to move about the classroom.
   c. being with people who do not have disabilities.
   d. classroom behavior.
   e. certification of the teacher.

7. The regular education initiative (REI)
   a. was proposed by the Department of Education in the 1960s.
   b. places children with disabilities in general education classes.
   c. includes children who are considered at risk.
   d. has a purpose of social integration of children with disabilities.
   e. does all of the above.

8. What educational setting provides services to students with disabilities for a portion of the day?
   a. Resource room
   b. Hospital setting
   c. General education class
   d. Separate class
   e. Separate school

9. Who should be involved in collaboration about a child with learning disabilities?
   a. Paraprofessionals
   b. Classroom teachers
   c. Administrators
   d. Other specialists
   e. All participants in the system

10. The percentage of students with learning disabilities who are served through both the regular classroom and the combination of the resource room and the classroom is about
    a. 10 percent.
    b. 28 percent.
    c. 50 percent.
    d. 62 percent.
    e. 78 percent.

11. The intent of the Individuals with Disabilities Education Act is to
    a. increase the role of parents.
    b. decrease the role of parents.
    c. avoid interfering with the role of parents.
    d. remove the responsibility from parents.
    e. do none of the above.

MT 12. Historically, the first administrative arrangement for educating children with learning disabilities in the public schools assigned them to a
a. separate class.
b. hospital room.
c. general education classroom.
d. resource room.
e. separate school.

13. All of the following promote the concept of integrating special and regular education *except*
a. full inclusion.
b. mainstreaming.
c. the regular education initiative.
d. the separate class.
e. integrated programs.

14. The model in which students work together, as opposed to competitive learning, is
a. cooperative learning.
b. the resource room.
c. integrated programs.
d. the regular education initiative.
e. co-teaching.

15. The delivery system with the goal of teaching children with all types of disabilities and all levels of severity in the neighborhood school is
a. full inclusion.
b. mainstreaming.
c. the regular education initiative.
d. the separate class.
e. integrated programs.

16. Which of the following best describes the spirit of collaboration?
a. Regular classroom teachers are experts.
b. Special education teachers are the experts.
c. Both special and regular education teachers are experts.
d. Special education teachers tell classroom teachers what to do.
e. A person from outside the school system is called in to collaborate.

17. Most students with learning disabilities are served through
a. separate classes.
b. separate schools.
c. residential schools.
d. resource rooms.
e. one-to-one instruction.

18. What is a typical early reaction of parents to being told that their child has learning disabilities?
a. Overcompensation to make up for the disabilities
b. Acceptance of the child and the learning disabilities
c. Overprotection of the child
d. Disbelief or denial of the problem
e. None of the above

19. An instructional system in which a student with learning disabilities is taught by a classmate is
    a. co-teaching.
    b. the regular education initiative.
    c. collaboration.
    d. cooperative learning.
    e. peer tutoring.

20. The number of students with learning disabilities who are placed in general education classes
    a. is decreasing.
    b. is increasing.
    c. is remaining stable.
    d. is changing from year to year, up and down.
    e. is unknown; no data are available.

Test 5B

1. IDEA requires the team to consider the extent to which it is appropriate for a student with disabilities to be placed with students who do not have disabilities. This consideration is known as
   a. the regular education initiative.
   b. the least restrictive environment.
   c. collaboration.
   d. the continuum of alternative placements.
   e. none of the above.

2. A variety of educational placements is required under IDEA to match the many different needs of students with disabilities. This is known as
   a. the continuum of alternative placements.
   b. the regular education initiative.
   c. the least restrictive environment.
   d. mainstreaming.
   e. integration.

3. Which delivery system has the goal of teaching students with all types of disabilities and all levels of severity in the neighborhood school?
   a. Regular education initiative
   b. Mainstreaming
   c. Full inclusion
   d. Special classroom
   e. Integrated programs

4. In collaboration, who is considered the expert?
   a. The classroom teacher
   b. The learning disabilities teacher
   c. Both teachers
   d. Neither teacher
   e. Another professional who is called in

5. Which educational placement provides special education services for a portion of the day?
   a. Separate class
   b. Integrated placement
   c. General education class
   d. Separate school
   e. Resource room

6. The resource room placement
   a. provides students with special education services for a portion of the day.
   b. provides education for the students in the general education classroom for part of the day.
   c. meets the requirements of IDEA.
   d. allows students to remain with friends in the general education classroom for a portion of the day.
   e. does all of the above.

7. Which delivery system is designed to gradually place students with disabilities into regular education as they are ready?
   a. Mainstreaming
   b. Full inclusion
   c. Regular education initiative
   d. Cooperative learning
   e. Co-teaching

8. About what percentage of students with learning disabilities is in the regular classroom for at least a portion of the day? (These students are served through both the regular classroom and the combination of resource room and regular classroom.)
   a. 25 percent
   b. 50 percent
   c. 62 percent
   d. 78 percent
   e. 96 percent

9. The policy of teaching all students with disabilities, with all degrees of severity, in the neighborhood school is
   a. the regular education initiative.
   b. the individual education plan.
   c. the continuum of alternative placements.
   d. mainstreaming.
   e. full inclusion.

10. Most students with learning disabilities are served through
    a. the resource room.
    b. the separate class.
    c. separate schools.
    d. hospital programs.
    e. one-to-one instruction.

11. Parents of a child with learning disabilities may
    a. have a sense of shame.
    b. feel guilty.
    c. be overprotective.
    d. be aggressive in getting their child help.
    e. be all of the above.

12. Historically, the *first* organized system in the public schools to teach children with learning disabilities was
    a. the separate school.
    b. the resource room.
    c. the separate class.
    d. hospital instruction.
    e. the general education class.

13. The number of students with learning disabilities being placed in the general education classes
    a. is relatively stable.
    b. is unknown because there are no data.
    c. is increasing.
    d. is decreasing.
    e. is fluctuating, going up and down.

14. The setting in which an individual child is taught alone by a teacher is
    a. itinerant teaching.
    b. consultation.
    c. one-to-one instruction.
    d. peer tutoring.
    e. collaboration.

15. The Individuals with Disabilities Education Act mentions which of the following terms?
    a. Least restrictive environment
    b. Regular education initiative
    c. Merging of regular and special education
    d. Full inclusion
    e. Mainstreaming

16. In one system of instruction, a classmate teaches a student with learning disabilities. This is called
    a. peer tutoring.
    b. regular education initiative.
    c. collaboration.
    d. cooperative learning.
    e. co-teaching.

17. Learning disabilities teachers must have both human relations competencies and knowledge/ skill competencies. Which of the following activities reflects a human relations competency?
    a. Interpreting assessment information
    b. Administering assessment tests
    c. Knowing theories of learning disabilities
    d. Understanding the law
    e. Interpersonal problem solving with the regular teacher

18. In reference to parents, the intent of the Individuals with Disabilities Education Act is to
    a. avoid interfering with the role of parents.
    b. remove the responsibility from parents.
    c. increase the role of parents.
    d. decrease the role of parents.
    e. eliminate choices for parents.

19. The term *restrictive* in the phrase "least restrictive environment" means restrictive in
    a. opportunities for learning.
    b. being with students who do not have disabilities.
    c. freedom to move.
    d. learning opportunities.
    e. opportunities to talk.

20. About what percentage of students with learning disabilities is placed in separate classes?
    a. 10 percent
    b. 20 percent
    c. 30 percent
    d. 40 percent
    e. 50 percent

CHAPTER 6

Theories of Learning: Implications for Learning Disabilities

Test 6A

1. Being able to direct one's thinking strategies for learning is referred to as
   a. direct instruction.
   b. information processing.
   c. maturational lag.
   d. conservation.
   e. metacognition.

2. *Learned helplessness* describes students who approach learning tasks in what manner?
   a. Actively
   b. Passively
   c. Reflectively
   d. Inquisitively
   e. Independently

3. Name the psychologist who is credited with describing the developmental stages of children's cognitive development and who formulated the theory that the thinking of children is different from that of adults.
   a. Bloom
   b. Skinner
   c. Feuerstein
   d. Piaget
   e. Gagné

4. According to Piaget, the average child is capable of abstract thinking by what year of age?
   a. 5
   b. 7
   c. 9
   d. 12
   e. 17

5. The explanation that many children fail because they have not yet attained the readiness for learning is related to which psychological theory?
   a. Developmental
   b. Behavioral
   c. Psychological processing
   d. Direct instruction

6. All of the following connote a similar theory in learning disabilities *except*
   a. direct instruction.
   b. academic skills mastery.
   c. psychological processing.
   d. mastery learning.
   e. sequential skills teaching.

7. Tom learned a subtraction fact because he was able to relate it to an addition fact he already knew. This is an example of
   a. mnemonic strategy.
   b. review.
   c. repetition.
   d. drill.
   e. constructive knowledge.

8. Which model traces the flow of knowledge and memory in the person's mind as the individual learns and thinks?
   a. Behavioral
   b. Developmental
   c. Effective teaching
   d. Information processing
   e. Reinforcement theory

9. The definition of learning disabilities in the Individuals with Disabilities Education Act contains the concept of
   a. maturational lag.
   b. metacognition.
   c. behavior analysis.
   d. disorders of psychological processing.
   e. none of the above.

10. The process by which someone has learned so well that performance becomes subconscious and requires little processing effort is referred to as
    a. decoding.
    b. problem solving.
    c. metacognition.
    d. information processing.
    e. automaticity.

11. The psychologist who is considered the father of behavioral psychology and credited with reinforcement theory is
    a. Skinner.
    b. Feuerstein.
    c. Vygotsky.
    d. Piaget.
    e. Kirk.

12. For information to be remembered for an extended period of time it must be placed in
    a. the sensory register.
    b. departmentalized memory.
    c. long-term memory.
    d. short-term memory.
    e. working memory.

13. People who are efficient learners
    a. ask themselves questions.
    b. practice and rehearse the material to be learned.
    c. organize the material to help themselves remember.
    d. try to connect what they are learning to what they already know.
    e. do all of the above.

14. The stages of learning theory state that it takes a period of time to "know" and there are several stages of learning. In the "stages of learning" theory, which is the first stage?
    a. Proficiency
    b. Acquisition
    c. Maintenance
    d. Generalization
    e. Transfer of knowledge

15. In the "ABC" behavioral unit in behavioral psychology, the "reinforcement" is the
    a. antecedent event.
    b. target behavior.
    c. consequent event.
    d. stimulus.
    e. cognitive event.

16. According to Piaget, children learn mainly through their sense and motor movements at ages
    a. birth –2 years.
    b. 2–4.
    c. 5–8.
    d. 8–11.
    e. over age 12.

17. The concept that for successful student learning teachers must determine the appropriate level of difficulty for teaching a student is called
    a. the zone of proximal development (ZPD) theory.
    b. reinforcement theory.
    c. behavior analysis.
    d. psychodynamic theory.
    e. mastery learning theory.

18. All of the following are steps in behavior analysis *except*
    a. setting goals and objectives.
    b. providing carefully sequenced materials.
    c. providing many opportunities to practice the skill.
    d. giving students immediate feedback and correction.
    e. determining the child's underlying deficit processing skills.

19. The idea that learning occurs in a social context and that the relationship between an adult and the student is an important element is contained in the learning theory of
    a. Jean Piaget.
    b. Len Vygotsky.
    c. B. F. Skinner.
    d. Benjamin Bloom.
    e. John Dewey.

20. The terms *scaffolding, prior knowledge,* and *constructing* one's own knowledge are part of which theory of learning?
    a. Behavioral
    b. Developmental
    c. Cognitive
    d. Information processing
    e. Behavior analysis

Test 6B

1. Whose theory proposes that the child's schema develops through the processes of assimilation and accommodation?
   a. Feuerstein
   b. Bloom
   c. Dewey
   d. Strauss
   e. Piaget

2. Being able to direct and plan one's thinking strategies for efficient learning is referred to as
   a. metacognition.
   b. automaticity.
   c. learned helplessness.
   d. passive learning.
   e. maturational lag.

3. All of the following connote a similar theory of learning disabilities *except*
   a. directed teaching.
   b. psychological processing.
   c. academic skills mastery.
   d. sequential skills teaching.
   e. mastery learning.

4. All of the following connote a similar theory of learning disabilities *except*
   a. academic skills mastery.
   b. psychological processing.
   c. perceptual processing.
   d. learning style.
   e. cognitive processing.

5. Willie was not paying attention while his teacher first explained the homework assignment. Therefore he has problems with the *first* phase of the memory system, which is
   a. long-term memory.
   b. the sensory register.
   c. working memory.
   d. short-term memory.
   e. retrieval.

6. Allan learned a subtraction fact because he was able to build upon an addition fact he already knew. This is an example of learning through
   a. a mnemonic device.
   b. drill and practice.
   c. positive reinforcements.
   d. contingency contracting.
   e. a constructive process.

7. When Juan completed 10 arithmetic problems, he received 5 points. In terms of the behavioral unit, the points are
   a. the antecedent event.
   b. the target behavior.
   c. the consequent event.
   d. the stimulus event.
   e. none of the above.

8. A model that traces the flow of information and integrates the various cognitive processing elements is
   a. decoding.
   b. problem solving.
   c. metacognition.
   d. information processing.
   e. automaticity.

9. Betsy has learned the 5's tables through several of the stages of learning. She can now apply them to other situations. What stage is this?
   a. Acquisition
   b. Proficiency
   c. Maintenance
   d. Generalization
   e. Sensorimotor

10. The definition of learning disabilities that includes disorders in basic psychological processes comes from
    a. IDEA.
    b. Section 504 of the Rehabilitation Act.
    c. the National Joint Committee on Learning Disabilities.
    d. the Interagency Committee on Learning Disabilities.
    e. DSM-IV.

11. Mr. Roberts relates the ideas in his social studies class through a diagram he draws with his students on the chalkboard. This diagram helps students see the relationship among the ideas. This technique is
    a. a graphic organizer.
    b. drill and practice.
    c. verbal rehearsal.
    d. automaticity.
    e. cognitive behavior modification.

12. Many students with learning disabilities have characteristics of passive and dependent learners. This is referred to as
    a. metacognitive learning.
    b. discovery learning.
    c. learned helplessness.
    d. active learning.
    e. maturational lag.

13. Piaget's theory suggests that the average child is capable of abstract thinking by age
    a. 6 years.
    b. 8 years.
    c. 12 years.
    d. 15 years.
    e. 18 years.

14. Which theory of learning examines the normal stages of learning in typical children?
    a. Effective teaching
    b. Information processing
    c. Metacognitive
    d. Behavioral
    e. Developmental

15. Whose theory emphasizes the social context of learning and the importance of the relationship between an adult and the student?
    a. Bloom
    b. Dewey
    c. Piaget
    d. Vygotsky
    e. Skinner

16. Which learning theory highlights the importance of prior knowledge and the need to construct one's own knowledge?
    a. Cognitive
    b. Information processing
    c. Behavior analysis
    d. Maturational lag
    e. Developmental

17. Which theory suggests that learning failure occurs because students are expected to perform in skills for which they have not developed readiness?
    a. Behavioral
    b. Psychological processing
    c. Direct instruction
    d. Developmental
    e. Cognitive behavior modification

18. The early development of behavioral psychology is attributed to
    a. Skinner.
    b. Piaget.
    c. Vygotsky.
    d. Dewey.
    e. Bloom.

19. In the information-processing model, executive control is also called
    a. the sensory register.
    b. working memory.
    c. metacognition.
    d. episodic memory.
    e. long-term memory.

20. For some tasks, knowledge must be habitual and subconscious, requiring little processing effort. This type of knowledge is called
    a. problem solving.
    b. constructive knowledge.
    c. automaticity.
    d. metacognitive thinking.
    e. active thinking.

CHAPTER 7

Medical Aspects of Learning Disabilities

Test 7A

1. For most adults, language function is located in the
   a. left hemisphere.
   b. right hemisphere.
   c. center of the brain.
   d. frontal lobe.
   e. occipital lobe.

2. Each hemisphere of the brain consists of all the following areas *except* the
   a. motor strip area.
   b. occipital lobe.
   c. cognitive lobe.
   d. frontal lobe.
   e. temporal lobe.

3. The theory of lack of cerebral dominance as a cause of language problems was first proposed by
   a. Geschwind.
   b. Orton.
   c. Strauss.
   d. Galaburda.
   e. Piaget.

4. All of the following are neurological tests for soft signs *except*
   a. copying designs.
   b. observations of a child's walking.
   c. the test for finger agnosia.
   d. the MRI examination.
   e. the nose-ear test.

5. Medication to treat learning disabilities
   a. improves children's memories.
   b. makes children smarter.
   c. improves concentration and attention.
   d. leads to drug addiction in children.
   e. is helpful in only a small number of cases.

6. Which of the following is the most commonly prescribed medical treatment for individuals with learning disabilities?
   a. Cylert
   b. Dexedrine
   c. Valium
   d. Dextroamphetamine
   e. Ritalin

7. The medical condition known as *otitis media* can affect the student's
   a. vision.
   b. ability to concentrate.
   c. hyperactivity.
   d. sense of touch.
   e. hearing.

8. The treatment that consists of a diet free of food additives was proposed by
   a. Geschwind.
   b. Feingold.
   c. Orton.
   d. Conners.
   e. Strauss.

9. Students diagnosed with attention deficit disorders
   a. may be eligible for special education services.
   b. are not eligible for special education services.
   c. are only eligible for services if they also have learning disabilities.
   d. are only eligible for services if they also have behavior disorders.
   e. are not eligible for Section 504 services.

10. What term is used in the 1994 DSM-IV by the American Psychiatric Association?
    a. Attention deficit hyperactivity disorder
    b. Minimal brain dysfunction
    c. Childhood hyperkinetic syndrome
    d. Attention deficit disorders with hyperactivity
    e. Central processing dysfunctions

11. All of the following medications are psychostimulants commonly prescribed for youngsters with attention deficit disorders *except*
    a. Cylert.
    b. Ritalin.
    c. Dexedrine.
    d. dextroamphetamine.
    e. Tylenol.

12. Learning disabilities are most likely to be discovered in a neurological examination via
    a. reflexes.
    b. soft signs.
    c. cranial nerves.
    d. x-rays.
    e. an electroencephalogram.

13. Malnutrition is most damaging to the brain and is permanent during the
    a. first six months of life.
    b. second six months of life.
    c. second year of life.
    d. third year of life.
    e. fourth year of life.

14. According to the clarification memo on attention deficit disorders issued by the U.S. Office of Education, students with ADD can be identified for service under
    a. other health-impaired.
    b. emotional disturbance.
    c. learning disabilities.
    d. Section 504 of the Rehabilitation Act.
    e. all of the above.

15. Three types of ADHD are described in DSM-IV. Which identifies children who have attentional problems but not hyperactivity?
    a. ADHD-IA
    b. ADHD-HI
    c. ADHD-C
    d. None of the above
    e. All of the above

16. The measurement of *decibels* is used to assess
    a. the loudness of sounds that a person can hear.
    b. awareness of phonological sounds.
    c. how high a sound a person can hear.
    d. how low a sound a person can hear.
    e. auditory memory.

17. A visual score of 20/20 is a measure of
    a. astigmatism.
    b. near-point visual acuity.
    c. far-point visual acuity.
    d. binocular vision.
    e. visual discrimination.

18. The medical specialist whose area of expertise is the child's mental health and emotional status is the
    a. family practice physician.
    b. ophthalmologist.
    c. neurologist.
    d. pediatrician.
    e. psychiatrist.

19. The medical specialist whose area of expertise is the central nervous system is the
    a. pediatrician.
    b. ophthalmologist.
    c. neurologist.
    d. otologist.
    e. psychiatrist.

20. Assessment of a child's ability to hop on one foot is a
    a. fine-motor test.
    b. gross-motor test.
    c. visual-motor test.
    d. tactile perception test.
    e. auditory-visual test.

Test 7B

1. In which area of most people's brains is language located?
   a. Right hemisphere
   b. Frontal lobe
   c. Left hemisphere
   d. Occipital lobe
   e. Motor strip

2. The most commonly prescribed medication for students with learning disabilities is
   a. Valium.
   b. dextroamphetamine.
   c. Ritalin.
   d. Cylert.
   e. Dexedrine.

3. According to authorities, the use of medication to treat individuals with learning disabilities
   a. improves the individual's memory.
   b. is helpful in only a small number of cases.
   c. can make children drug addicts.
   d. makes people smarter.
   e. may help improve concentration.

4. During a neurological assessment, learning disabilities are most likely to be detected through the examination of
   a. cranial nerves.
   b. x-rays.
   c. an MRI.
   d. reflexes.
   e. soft signs.

5. Ben Feingold's theory is that learning disabilities are caused by
   a. the type of lighting in the room.
   b. food additives
   c. pollens in the air.
   d. inherited disorders.
   e. allergies.

6. Otitis media is related to disorders in
   a. attending.
   b. feeling (touch).
   c. hearing.
   d. seeing.
   e. thinking.

7. When a child with attention deficit disorders with hyperactivity is on medication, the teacher
   a. does not need to be informed.
   b. should provide feedback to the doctor on the medication's effectiveness in school.
   c. should suggest medications to the doctor that have been effective with other children.
   d. should suggest the dosage to the parents.
   e. should do all of the above.

8. Attention deficit hyperactivity disorder is defined in which document?
   a. Individuals with Disabilities Education Act
   b. Head Start legislation
   c. Section 504 of the Rehabilitation Act
   d. Americans with Disabilities Act
   e. *Diagnostic and Statistical Manual of Mental Disorders-IV*

9. Three types of ADHD are described in DSM-IV. Which type describes children who have both activity and attention problems?
   a. ADHD-IA
   b. ADHD-HI
   c. ADHD-C
   d. None of the above
   e. All of the above

10. In what stage of life is malnutrition most damaging to the brain and most likely permanent?
    a. First six months
    b. Second six months
    c. Second year
    d. Third year
    e. Fourth year

11. In a hearing test, the measurement of decibels is used to assess
    a. how low a sound a person can hear.
    b. the perception of phonemes.
    c. the loudness of sounds that a person can hear.
    d. ability in auditory blending.
    e. how high a sound a person can hear.

12. In a vision test, a score of 20/20 is a measure of
    a. astigmatism.
    b. near-point visual acuity.
    c. far-point visual acuity.
    d. binocular vision.
    e. visual discrimination.

13. Who proposed the theory that the cause of language problems in children was the lack of cerebral dominance within the brain?
    a. Orton
    b. Piaget
    c. Geschwind
    d. Strauss
    e. Galaburda

14. According to the U.S. Department of Education Clarification Memorandum of 1991, students with ADD
    a. are not eligible for special education services if they have co-existing learning disabilities.
    b. are not eligible for special education services if they have a co-existing emotional disturbance.
    c. do not need an IEP to receive accommodations in the general education classroom.
    d. cannot receive services under Section 504 of the Rehabilitation Act.
    e. are not eligible for special education services and related services.

15. The clarification memo on attention deficit disorders issued by the U.S. Office of Education indicates that students with ADD can be identified for service under
    a. other health-impaired.
    b. Section 504 of the Rehabilitation Act.
    c. learning disabilities.
    d. emotional disturbance.
    e. all of the above.

16. Dyslexia is
    a. a mathematics disability.
    b. a motor disability.
    c. a social disability.
    d. a reading disability.
    e. all of the above.

17. Which of the following is a neurological test for soft signs?
    a. Copying designs
    b. Cranial nerves
    c. BEAM test
    d. MRI examination
    e. Reflex test

18. Studies of the active brain are from
    a. family studies.
    b. magnetic resonance imaging studies.
    c. twin studies.
    d. postmortem anatomical studies.
    e. all of the above.

19. Which medical specialty investigates and treats hearing problems?
    a. Ophthalmology
    b. Psychiatry
    c. Otology
    d. Neurology
    e. Pediatrics

20. Which specialty focuses on the relationship between brain function and human behavior?
    a. Ophthalmology
    b. Dermatology
    c. Otology
    d. Neuropsychology
    e. Pediatrics

CHAPTER 8

Young Children with Disabilities

Test 8A

1. Preschool children with learning disabilities often exhibit problems in
   a. phonological awareness.
   b. rapid naming.
   c. language and communication.
   d. recognition of the alphabet letters.
   e. all of the above.

2. In regard to young children with disabilities, special education legislation *fully* protects the rights of young children, for ages
   a. 3–6 years.
   b. birth–6 years.
   c. 3–9 years.
   d. birth–9 years.
   e. 2–6 years.

3. Early childhood special education programs use intervention to improve all of the following *except*
   a. language skills.
   b. reading skills.
   c. cognitive skills.
   d. motor skills.
   e. preacademic skills.

4. Follow-up research indicates that participants in Head Start are
   a. more likely to finish high school without failing a grade.
   b. less likely to be referred for special education services.
   c. more likely to be taxpayers.
   d. less likely to be on welfare programs.
   e. all of the above.

5. The curriculum of the traditional nursery school is based on the
   a. enrichment curriculum.
   b. cognitive emphasis curriculum.
   c. directed instruction curriculum.
   d. behavioral curriculum.
   e. learning strategies curriculum.

6. The teaching of reading and arithmetic skills to preschool children is likely to be part of the
   a. enrichment curriculum.
   b. cognitive emphasis curriculum.
   c. Montessori curriculum.
   d. Piagetian curriculum.
   e. direct teaching curriculum.

7. In the early childhood special education programs, transition occurs at the end of
   a. the age birth–3 program.
   b. the age 3–5 program.
   c. the Part H program.
   d. the Part B program.
   e. all of the above.

8. The Piaget-based early childhood program follows
   a. the enrichment curriculum.
   b. the direct teaching curriculum.
   c. the cognitive emphasis curriculum.
   d. the Montessori curriculum.
   e. none of the above.

9. Part B of the special education law protects the rights of young children, ages
   a. 3–22 years.
   b. 3–6 years.
   c. birth–3 years.
   d. birth–6 years.
   e. 3–11 years.

10. Part H programs are for children ages
    a. birth–3 years.
    b. 3–6 years.
    c. birth–6 years.
    d. 3–19 years.
    e. 3–22 years.

11. A noncategorical classification for identifying young children with disabilities is
    a. language impairment.
    b. emotional disturbance.
    c. developmental delay.
    d. learning disabilities.
    e. mental retardation.

12. The percentage of 3- through 5-year-olds in the general population identified as needing special education services is
    a. 1–2 percent.
    b. 3–5 percent.
    c. 8–10 percent.
    d. 10–12 percent.
    e. 12–14 percent.

13. Research from the High/Scope program shows that it is an effective program for young children who are environmentally at risk. High/Scope is based on which curriculum approach?
    a. Cognitive emphasis
    b. Direct instruction
    c. Enrichment
    d. Montessori
    e. None of the above

14. The case study plan that emphasizes the needs of the families of young children with disabilities is the
    a. REI.
    b. IEP.
    c. LOGO.
    d. IFSP.
    e. EEPCD.

15. Legislation that supports compensatory programs for young children from low socioeconomic homes is
    a. the Individuals with Disabilities Act.
    b. the Rehabilitation Act.
    c. Section 504.
    d. the Americans with Disabilities Act.
    e. Head Start legislation.

16. Developmentally Appropriate Practice (DAP) refers to a set of guidelines for a curriculum for young children. These guidelines include which of the following?
    a. Direct instruction
    b. Teaching reading
    c. Teaching arithmetic
    d. Exploratory play
    e. All of the above

17. Children who lack cognitive stimulation at home are under which of the following risk categories?
    a. Established risk
    b. Biological risk
    c. Environmental risk
    d. No risk
    e. None of the above

18. Head Start programs must reserve what percentage of their enrollment for handicapped children?
    a. 5 percent
    b. 10 percent
    c. 15 percent
    d. 20 percent
    e. 25 percent

MT 19. Identifying those children who need a closer look through a short survey-type testing process occurs in which phase of assessment in early childhood special education?
   a. Locating
   b. Screening
   c. Diagnosing
   d. Evaluating
   e. None of the above

20. The delivery service system in which a child-care specialist goes to the child's house to train the parent(s) to work with the child is
   a. a center-based program.
   b. a home-based program.
   c. a combination program.
   d. a school-based program.
   e. none of the above.

MT 21. Most programs for young children with disabilities follow which curriculum model?
   a. Enrichment
   b. Cognitive emphasis
   c. Directed teaching
   d. Montessori
   e. A combination of several early childhood models

Test 8B

1. In the legislation for early childhood, Part H programs are for children ages
   a. birth–6 years.
   b. 3–18 years.
   c. 3–22 years.
   d. birth–3 years.
   e. 3–6 years.

2. For children ages birth–5 years, the case study team can develop a plan for young children with disabilities. What is the acronym for this plan?
   a. IFSP
   b. EEPCD
   c. REI
   d. IEP
   e. LOGO

3. Precursors of learning disabilities include all of the following problems *except*
   a. prealgebra skills.
   b. language and communication.
   c. phonological awareness.
   d. rapid naming.
   e. knowledge of the alphabet.

4. Which program is for young children from low-income homes?
   a. Individuals with Disabilities Education Act
   b. Head Start
   c. Americans with Disabilities Act
   d. Section 504 of the Rehabilitation Act
   e. Early childhood amendments

5. All of the following statements are true of early childhood assessment procedures for infants and toddlers *except* which one?
   a. The procedures cover children with disabilities from birth through age 2.
   b. Children are identified by the general label of "developmental delay."
   c. Planning must include the family.
   d. The evaluation team must write an IFSP.
   e. The evaluation teams must develop an individualized education plan (IEP) for each child.

6. Which of the following identifies children who lack cognitive stimulation at home?
   a. Environmental risk
   b. Established risk
   c. Biological risk
   d. All of the above
   e. None of the above

7. According to Head Start legislation, Head Start classes must reserve what percentage of their enrollment for handicapped children?
   a. 1 percent
   b. 5 percent
   c. 10 percent
   d. 20 percent
   e. 25 percent

8. The process known as Child Find occurs in what phase of the assessment in early childhood special education?
   a. Locating
   b. Screening
   c. Diagnosing
   d. Evaluating
   e. None of the above

9. Under the law, full rights of the IDEA are extended to preschool children beginning at
   a. birth.
   b. 1 year.
   c. 2 years.
   d. 3 years.
   e. 4 years.

10. In assessing preschool children, all of the following areas are tested *except*
    a. concept development.
    b. language skills.
    c. motor development.
    d. word-recognition skills.
    e. sensory acuity.

11. In the early childhood special education programs, transition involves going
    a. from an age 3–5 program to kindergarten.
    b. from an age 3–5 program to a special class.
    c. from one organized program to another.
    d. from a birth–2 program to an age 3–5 program.
    e. through all of the above.

12. In which delivery service system does the child-care specialist train the parent(s) to teach the child in his or her own household?
    a. Combination program
    b. Center-based program
    c. Home-based program
    d. School-based program
    e. None of the above

13. The computer should be used to help young children with disabilities learn all of the following *except*
    a. recognizing colors.
    b. reading multisyllable words.
    c. recognizing numbers of objects.
    d. cause and effect.
    e. using language.

14. Most programs for young children with disabilities follow which curriculum model?
    a. Direct teaching
    b. Enrichment
    c. Cognitive emphasis
    d. A combination of several early childhood models
    e. None of the above

15. In research that followed children in Head Start or other compensatory programs, the data show that children enrolled in these programs are
    a. more likely to be taxpayers.
    b. more likely to finish high school without failing a grade.
    c. less likely to be referred for special education services.
    d. less likely to be on welfare programs.
    e. all of the above.

16. In the traditional nursery school, the early childhood curriculum is based on what curriculum method?
    a. Direct instruction
    b. Behavioral
    c. Learning strategies
    d. Enrichment
    e. Cognitive emphasis

17. In which type of early childhood curriculum are children most likely to be taught reading skills?
    a. Piagetian
    b. Direct teaching
    c. Enrichment
    d. Cognitive emphasis
    e. Montessori

18. Which of the following is a noncategorical classification for identifying young children with disabilities?
    a. Developmental delay
    b. Learning disabilities
    c. Mental retardation
    d. Language impairment
    e. Attention deficit disorders

19. What percentage of 3–5-year-olds in the general population is identified as needing special education services?
    a. 1 percent
    b. 4 percent
    c. 6 percent
    d. 8 percent
    e. 10 percent

20. Early childhood educators suggested a set of curriculum guidelines known as *developmentally appropriate practice* (DAP) for typical young children. Which of the following is included in these guidelines?
    a. Teach reading skills
    b. Teach mathematics skills
    c. Use child-initiated interests
    d. Use direct instruction methods
    e. Use explicit teaching of academic skills

21. The Washington School District invites all parents in the neighborhood to bring their pre-school child in for a brief assessment. What phase of the assessment process is this brief cursory assessment?
    a. Locating
    b. Screening
    c. Diagnosing
    d. Evaluating
    e. Monitoring

CHAPTER 9

Adolescents and Adults with Learning Disabilities

Test 9A

1. Students in this secondary program receive daily instruction in essential reading and mathematics skills. This is an example of what kind of curriculum?
   a. Basic skills remediation
   b. Functional
   c. Tutorial
   d. Work-study
   e. Learning strategies

2. Students in this secondary program receive individual instruction directly designed to help them fulfill requirements and pass tests in their content subject courses. This is an example of what kind of curriculum?
   a. Basic skills remediation
   b. Functional
   c. Tutorial
   d. Work-study
   e. Learning strategies

3. Students in this secondary program receive instruction in filling out employment applications and comparing prices for items they might purchase. This is an example of what kind of curriculum?
   a. Basic skills remediation
   b. Functional
   c. Tutorial
   d. Work-study
   e. Learning strategies

4. Students in this secondary program go to school mornings and work on a job in the afternoon. This is an example of what kind of curriculum?
   a. Basic skills remediation
   b. Functional
   c. Tutorial
   d. Work-study
   e. Learning strategies

5. Students in this secondary program learn how to direct and control their own learning. This is an example of what kind of curriculum?
   a. Basic skills remediation
   b. Functional
   c. Tutorial
   d. Work-study
   e. Learning strategies

6. The transition goal of most students with learning disabilities is
   a. competitive employment.
   b. vocational training.
   c. college attendance.
   d. supported employment.
   e. sheltered workshop.

7. Transition plans are
   a. suggested under the law for some secondary students with disabilities.
   b. not mentioned in special education law.
   c. required under the law for all secondary students with disabilities.
   d. only required for students with disabilities going into competitive employment.
   e. only required for secondary students with disabilities in work-study programs.

8. Students are eligible for special education services through age
   a. 18.
   b. 19.
   c. 20.
   d. 21.
   e. 23.

9. The most widely used delivery system for adolescents with learning disabilities is
   a. the resource room.
   b. peer tutoring.
   c. separate classes.
   d. work-study programs.
   e. separate schools.

10. Special education law requires that a transition plan be written for students with disabilities beginning at age
    a. 10.
    b. 12.
    c. 14.
    d. 19.
    e. 20.

11. High school requirements for graduation are
    a. not changing.
    b. decreasing.
    c. increasing.
    d. not known.
    e. none of the above.

12. What percentage of all students identified under the category of learning disabilities is in the 12 through 17-year-old group?
   a. 5 percent
   b. 11 percent
   c. 26 percent
   d. 51 percent
   e. 82 percent

13. The learning strategy in which students learn to review by saying aloud to themselves the main points of a lesson is called
   a. self-control training.
   b. social training.
   c. verbal rehearsal.
   d. error monitoring.
   e. drill and practice.

14. Learning strategies approaches have been found to be most effective with students who
   a. are above third-grade reading level.
   b. have average intelligence.
   c. can deal with symbolic as well as concrete learning tasks.
   d. All of the above.
   e. None of the above.

15. Which law guarantees that no qualified person with disabilities will be discriminated against because of the disability by programs receiving federal assistance?
   a. Section 504 of the Rehabilitation Act
   b. Individuals with Disabilities Education Act
   c. Perkins Vocational Act
   d. Public Law 94-142
   e. Public Law 101-476

16. About what percentage of all students with learning disabilities receives a high school diploma?
   a. 25 percent
   b. 50 percent
   c. 79 percent
   d. 89 percent
   e. 100 percent

17. What percentage of secondary students with learning disabilities receives at least some instruction in regular education classes?
   a. 25 percent
   b. 36 percent
   c. 51 percent
   d. 79 percent
   e. 96 percent

18. In which step of the strategies intervention model (SIM) does the teacher "think aloud" while students witness the entire process?
    a. Student verbally rehearses.
    b. Student practices with controlled material.
    c. Teacher pretests students.
    d. Teacher models the strategy.
    e. Teacher describes the strategy.

19. The number of college programs for adults with learning disabilities is
    a. unknown.
    b. decreasing.
    c. increasing.
    d. stable.
    e. none of the above.

20. The teaching method that helps students learn how to learn is
    a. learning strategies instruction.
    b. basic skills instruction.
    c. educational reform.
    d. collaboration.
    e. a work-study program.

21. What percentage of high school students with learning disabilities leaves high school with a high school diploma or certificate of completion?
    a. 30 percent
    b. 40 percent
    c. 50 percent
    d. 60 percent
    e. 70 percent

Test 9B

 1. George is receiving instruction designed to help him pass his regular history class examination. This is an example of
   a. basic skills instruction.
   b. functional instruction.
   c. tutorial instruction.
   d. a work-study program.
   e. learning strategies instruction.

2. Joyce receives daily instruction in rudimentary mathematics, which is not part of her regular algebra course. This is an example of
   a. basic skills instruction.
   b. functional instruction.
   c. tutorial instruction.
   d. a work-study program.
   e. learning strategies instruction.

3. Joe is learning how to complete applications for employment and how to compare prices in the supermarket. This is an example of
   a. basic skills instruction.
   b. functional instruction.
   c. tutorial instruction.
   d. a work-study program.
   e. learning strategies instruction.

4. Most secondary students with learning disabilities are served through
   a. separate schools.
   b. peer tutoring.
   c. work-study programs.
   d. separate classes.
   e. resource rooms.

5. The transition goal of most students with learning disabilities is
   a. vocational training.
   b. college attendance.
   c. competitive employment.
   d. supported employment.
   e. sheltered workshop.

6. Of all school students identified as having learning disabilities, what percentage is ages 12 through 17?
   a. 7 percent
   b. 12 percent
   c. 25 percent
   d. 51 percent
   e. 75 percent

7. Students are eligible for special education services *through* the age of
   a. 18 years.
   b. 19 years.
   c. 20 years.
   d. 21 years.
   e. 22 years.

8. In which step of the strategies intervention model (SIM) does the teacher "think aloud" as students witness the entire process?
   a. Teacher models the strategy.
   b. Teacher describes the strategy.
   c. Student verbally rehearses.
   d. Student practices with controlled material.
   e. Teacher pretests students.

9. The tendency of the education reform movement is to
   a. decrease the requirements of high school.
   b. give fewer tests to students in high school.
   c. increase the requirements of high school.
   d. lower the standards for high school graduation.
   e. do none of the above.

10. Which federal law requires that in programs receiving federal assistance no qualified handicapped person will be discriminated against because of the handicap?
    a. Section 504 of the Rehabilitation Act
    b. Technical Assistance Act
    c. Perkins Vocational Act
    d. Americans with Disabilities Act
    e. Individuals with Disabilities Education Act

11. Learning strategies approaches have been found to be most effective with students who
    a. have average intelligence.
    b. can deal with symbols as well as the concrete.
    c. are above third-grade reading level.
    d. have a commitment to learn.
    e. All of the above.

12. The number of college programs for adults with learning disabilities is
    a. unknown.
    b. decreasing.
    c. increasing.
    d. stable.
    e. none of the above.

13. What percentage of all high school students with learning disabilities receives a high school diploma?
    a. 15 percent
    b. 25 percent
    c. 50 percent
    d. 75 percent
    e. 90 percent

14. Under special education law, for secondary students with disabilities, transition plans
    a. are required for certain students.
    b. are suggested but not required.
    c. are only required for students in work-study programs.
    d. are required for all secondary students with disabilities.
    e. are not recommended.

15. The learning strategies approach is used to teach
    a. social skills.
    b. reading comprehension.
    c. mathematics calculation.
    d. study skills.
    e. all of the above.

16. What percentage of secondary students with learning disabilities receives services in separate classes?
    a. 10 percent
    b. 20 percent
    c. 30 percent
    d. 40 percent
    e. 50 percent

17. Colleges must make accommodations for students with disabilities under what law?
    a. Individuals with Disabilities Education Act.
    b. Head Start legislation.
    c. The Vocational Education Act.
    d. Title 1 legislation
    e. Section 504 of the Rehabilitation Act

18. What percentage of secondary students with learning disabilities leave high school because either they drop out or their status is unknown?
    a. 8 percent
    b. 20 percent
    c. 39 percent
    d. 50 percent
    e. 75 percent

19. What percentage of secondary students ages 12 through 17 with learning disabilities receives at least some instruction in the regular education programs (students in resource rooms plus students in regular classes)?
    a. 26 percent
    b. 51 percent
    c. 62 percent
    d. 79 percent
    e. 98 percent

20. The Individuals with Disabilities Education Act requires that transition plans for students with disabilities be included in the IEP by the time they reach what age?
    a. 10 years
    b. 12 years
    c. 14 years
    d. 19 years
    e. 21 years

21. What percentage of secondary students with learning disabilities receives a certificate of completion?
    a. 5 percent
    b. 10 percent
    c. 15 percent
    d. 20 percent
    e. 25 percent

CHAPTER 10

Developmental and Preacademic Learning

Test 10A

1. Which of the following persons has made a major contribution to a theory of deficits in motor development as related to learning disabilities?
   a. Chomsky
   b. Piaget
   c. Kephart
   d. Strauss
   e. Vygotsky

2. A fine-motor skill is
   a. running.
   b. jumping.
   c. hopping on one foot.
   d. walking.
   e. picking up a piece of candy.

3. Changing the physical education program to meet the needs of students with disabilities is
   a. sensory integration.
   b. adapted physical education.
   c. a physical education fitness program.
   d. an intramural sports program.
   e. all of the above.

 4. Children with developmental learning disabilities
   a. are mentally retarded.
   b. are slow learners.
   c. should have formal schooling delayed until they catch up.
   d. are deficient in precursor skills needed for academic learning.
   e. all of the above.

5. John has difficulty distinguishing between the printed letter *m* and the printed letter *n*. His problem is
   a. visual acuity.
   b. figure-ground discrimination.
   c. visual closure.
   d. visual discrimination.
   e. visual memory.

6. Alice is able to pronounce each letter in a word individually, but she cannot combine the sounds to pronounce the word. Her problem is
   a. auditory acuity.
   b. auditory blending.
   c. auditory closure.
   d. auditory memory.
   e. auditory sequencing.

7. The ability to hear discrete sounds in words is referred to as
   a. sound blending.
   b. decoding.
   c. phonetics.
   d. phonological awareness.
   e. phonics.

8. Which of the following is not usually considered an important sensory input channel for learning?
   a. Visual
   b. Gustatory
   c. Auditory
   d. Tactile
   e. Kinesthetic

9. Emphasis on games and playground activities for the purpose of improving the child's confidence and social responsibility is proposed by
   a. adapted physical education.
   b. perceptual-motor theory.
   c. sensory integration theory.
   d. perceptual modality theory.
   e. motor generalization theory.

10. Children who display difficulty in phonological awareness
    a. have difficulty in recognizing rhyming words.
    b. cannot recognize environmental sounds.
    c. have no oral language abilities.
    d. should only be taught with a sight word method.
    e. All of the above.

11. The notion that children have a greater facility to learn by using one perceptual way of learning than by using another reflects which concept?
    a. Sensory-motor concept
    b. Tactile perception concept
    c. Sensory integration concept
    d. Perceptual-motor concept
    e. Perceptual modality concept

12. Jim cannot copy a geometric shape because he cannot translate visual information into motor movement. From the viewpoint of integrating perceptual systems, his difficulties lie in the
    a. visual to motor system.
    b. visual to sound system.
    c. auditory to visual system.
    d. tactile to visual system.
    e. verbal to visual system.

13. Joan is briefly shown a geometric figure on a card. Then the stimulus picture is removed. Joan cannot pick out that same geometric figure from a group of geometric pictures. Her problem is
    a. visual acuity.
    b. figure-ground discrimination.
    c. visual closure.
    d. visual discrimination.
    e. visual memory.

14. When Alvin is given three things to do, he only does the last task because he usually forgets the first two. His problem could be identified as
    a. auditory acuity.
    b. auditory blending.
    c. auditory memory.
    d. auditory closure.
    e. auditory discrimination.

15. A small cutout of a geometric shape is placed in Terry's hand so that she feels the shape but cannot see it. She must then match this shape with one of several geometric shapes on a piece of paper. Terry must cross from one perceptual modality to another. She must go from
    a. tactile to visual.
    b. visual to motor.
    c. kinesthetic to motor.
    d. tactile to auditory.
    e. visual to auditory.

16. Phonological awareness
    a. is an essential precursor of learning to read.
    b. is related to auditory perception.
    c. includes the ability to recognize rhymes.
    d. includes the ability to hear sounds in words.
    e. is all of the above.

17. All of the following are activities to build phonological awareness *except*
    a. putting puzzles together.
    b. segmenting speech sounds.
    c. rhyming words.
    d. phonic substitutions.
    e. sound counting.

18. The skill of handwriting is most closely related to ability in
    a. gross-motor skills.
    b. auditory perception.
    c. the vestibular system.
    d. auditory sequencing.
    e. fine-motor skills.

19. Allie cannot recognize that words rhyme in songs and in nursery rhymes. Her problem might be identified as difficulty with
    a. phonological awareness.
    b. auditory blending.
    c. visual memory.
    d. auditory closure.
    e. visual-motor perception.

20. Deficits in precursor skills that a child needs in order to acquire academic skills are referred to as
    a. academic learning disabilities.
    b. specific learning disabilities.
    c. developmental learning disabilities.
    d. general learning disabilities.
    e. none of the above.

21. The sense of balance and the inner ear are parts of which system?
    a. Auditory
    b. Tactile
    c. Proprioceptive
    d. Visual
    e. Vestibular

Test 10B

1. Which of the following names is associated with motor theories in learning disabilities?
   a. Kephart
   b. Kirk
   c. Fernald
   d. Gillingham
   e. Orton

2. Which discipline modifies the physical education program to help students with learning disabilities who have problems in motor skills?
   a. Physical education fitness program
   b. Adapted physical education
   c. Occupational therapy
   d. Neuropsychology
   e. Intramural sports program

3. Sensory integration techniques for helping students with learning disabilities come from the field of
   a. developmental psychology.
   b. adapted physical education.
   c. occupational therapy.
   d. neuropsychology.
   e. cognitive psychology.

4. Haptic perception includes which of the following perceptual areas?
   a. Visual and auditory
   b. Visual and tactile
   c. Kinesthetic and visual
   d. Tactile and kinesthetic
   e. Tactile and auditory

5. Which of the following activities would *not* be used to build phonological awareness?
   a. Rhyming words
   b. Phonic substitutions
   c. Sound counting
   d. Matching geometric shapes
   e. Segmenting speech sounds

6. Jesse has difficulty distinguishing between the printed letters *b* and *d*. His problem lies in
   a. visual discrimination.
   b. figure-ground association.
   c. visual closure.
   d. visual acuity.
   e. auditory discrimination.

7. Six-year-old Donald cannot recognize that words rhyme in songs and in nursery rhymes. His problem might be identified as difficulty with
   a. visual memory.
   b. auditory closure.
   c. visual-motor perception.
   d. phonological awareness.
   e. auditory blending.

8. Which of the perceptual systems is *least* likely to be considered for educational purposes?
   a. Kinesthetic
   b. Tactile
   c. Visual
   d. Auditory
   e. Gustatory

9. Which of the following is a fine-motor skill?
   a. Jumping on a trampoline
   b. Doing jumping jacks
   c. Hopping on one foot
   d. Cutting with a knife and fork
   e. Walking on a balance beam

10. The system that involves stimulation from muscles or within the body and that engages in planned motor behavior is the
    a. vestibular system.
    b. proprioceptive system.
    c. information-processing system.
    d. delivery system.
    e. haptic system.

11. A sense of balance and the inner ear are parts of which system?
    a. Tactile system
    b. Ecological system
    c. Vestibular system
    d. Haptic system
    e. Proprioceptive system

12. Handwriting is a skill that is most closely related to ability in
    a. the vestibular system.
    b. auditory sequencing.
    c. fine-motor activities.
    d. gross-motor activities.
    e. auditory perception.

13. The perceptual modality concept is based on what belief?
    a. One method of teaching will be appropriate for all children.
    b. All children learn in the same way.
    c. All children with learning disabilities need tactile stimulation.
    d. All children with learning disabilities need visual perception training.
    e. Children have a preferred way of learning.

14. Difficulty in hearing discrete sounds in words is a problem in
    a. phonological awareness.
    b. phonics.
    c. sound blending.
    d. decoding.
    e. phonetics.

15. Fred is shown a geometric figure on a card for a few minutes, and then the stimulus picture is removed. When Fred is asked to pick that same figure from a group of geometric figures, he is unable to do so. His problem is
    a. figure-ground discrimination.
    b. visual closure.
    c. visual acuity.
    d. visual discrimination.
    e. visual memory.

16. Carla is told to do three things. She only does the last task because she forgets the first two. What is her problem?
    a. Auditory discrimination
    b. Auditory closure
    c. Auditory acuity
    d. Auditory blending
    e. Auditory memory

17. Mary cannot copy words from the blackboard onto a piece of paper. She has great difficulty translating visual information into motor movement. In terms of integrating perceptual systems, her difficulty is
    a. auditory to visual.
    b. tactile to visual.
    c. verbal to visual.
    d. visual to motor.
    e. visual to auditory.

18. A small plastic number 3 is placed in Jimmy's hand so that he feels the shape but cannot see it. He must then match this shape with one of several numbers on a piece of paper. Jimmy must integrate information from which sensory system to which other sensory system?
    a. Visual to motor
    b. Kinesthetic to motor
    c. Tactile to visual
    d. Tactile to auditory
    e. Visual to auditory

19. Tanya experiences discomfort when touched by other people or by clothing. She has problems with
    a. the proprioceptive system.
    b. tactile defensiveness.
    c. the vestibular system.
    d. the perceptual system.
    e. the auditory system.

20. Mike confuses the written letters *d* and *b,* as well as words such as *house* and *horse.* His difficulty is
    a. vestibular dysfunction.
    b. visual discrimination.
    c. visual closure.
    d. auditory blending.
    e. auditory memory.

21. Recognizing that the tree bark feels rough is an example of
    a. visual perception.
    b. auditory perception.
    c. kinesthetic perception.
    d. gustatory perception.
    e. tactile perception.

CHAPTER 11

Oral Language: Listening and Speaking

Test 11A

1. Children who display difficulty in phonological awareness
   a. should be taught only with a sight word method.
   b. cannot recognize environmental sounds.
   c. have receptive aphasia.
   d. have difficulty in recognizing rhyming words.
   e. have difficulty with the visual recognition of shapes.

2. The receptive language skills are
   a. speaking and writing.
   b. reading and speaking.
   c. writing and reading.
   d. listening and reading.
   e. listening and speaking.

3. James, at age 4, can follow verbal directions but does not talk. He does not have an organic or physiological abnormality. His problem can be described as
   a. an inner language disorder.
   b. receptive aphasia.
   c. expressive aphasia.
   d. acquired aphasia.
   e. a central language disorder.

4. The study of the system of speech sounds is called
   a. semantics.
   b. intonation.
   c. morphology.
   d. phonology.
   e. syntax.

5. The study of word meanings is called
   a. semantics.
   b. intonation.
   c. morphology.
   d. phonology.
   e. syntax.

6. Which of the following would *not* be used as a teaching activity for promoting "emergent literacy"?
   a. Teaching oral language
   b. Teaching concepts about print
   c. Teaching recognition of the alphabet
   d. Teaching syllable rules
   e. Teaching rhyming games

7. A distinction is made between a speech disorder and a language disorder. Which of the following is considered a *language disorder?*
   a. Lateral lisp
   b. Stuttering
   c. Articulation difficulties
   d. Saying "fank you" instead of "thank you"
   e. Delayed speech

8. A distinction is made between a speech disorder and a language disorder. Which of the following is a *speech disorder?*
   a. Saying "wabbit" for "rabbit"
   b. Delay in beginning to talk
   c. Limited vocabulary for the child's chronological age
   d. A problem with syntactics
   e. Dysnomia

9. The crucial skill that Helen Keller acquired at the age of 7 was how to
   a. finger-spell.
   b. speak.
   c. use words as symbols of objects and meanings.
   d. finger-spell the word *water.*
   e. control her behavior.

10. The study of the system of grammar or sentence order in language is called
    a. semantics.
    b. intonation.
    c. morphology.
    d. phonology.
    e. syntax.

11. An 11-month-old child's speech is described as
    a. first words.
    b. two-word sentences.
    c. babbling.
    d. jargon.
    e. none of the above.

12. The average child is able to understand and use language to communicate by age
    a. 1.
    b. 2.
    c. 3.
    d. 4.
    e. 5.

13. The approach for teaching children whose native language is other than English by instructing them in their native language for part of the school day and in English for part of the school day is called
    a. immersion instruction.
    b. English as a second language (ESL).
    c. bilingual instruction.
    d. the Berlitz method.
    e. none of the above.

14. When children speak a variant of standard English, such as black English, this is referred to as
    a. a language disorder.
    b. congenital aphasia.
    c. a language difference.
    d. a language disturbance.
    e. a language deficit.

15. Phonological awareness is demonstrated through the ability to
    a. segment sounds of language.
    b. count sounds in words.
    c. tap out the number of sounds in words.
    d. recognize rhymes.
    e. do all of the above.

16. The social side of language is called
    a. syntax.
    b. phonology.
    c. morphology.
    d. pragmatics.
    e. semantics.

17. The expressive language skills are
    a. writing and speaking.
    b. reading and writing.
    c. writing and listening.
    d. listening and reading.
    e. speaking and reading.

18. Maurice says "bathketball" for "basketball." He has
    a. a global language disorder.
    b. a receptive language disorder.
    c. a language difference.
    d. a speech disorder.
    e. developmental aphasia.

19. Tanya, at age 3, does not understand single words spoken to her, such as *milk* and *cookie.* English is the language of her home. Her problem is
    a. an articulation difficulty.
    b. a receptive language disorder.
    c. a language difference.
    d. a speech disorder.
    e. all of the above.

20. The theory of how children learn language that suggests that human beings have developed a natural or instinctive capacity for dealing with the linguistic universals common to all languages is
    a. behavioral theory.
    b. innatist theory.
    c. cognitive theory.
    d. psychoanalytic theory.
    e. information-processing theory.

21. James, at age 4, can follow verbal directions and understand what others say to him, but he does not talk. James does not have an organic or physiological abnormality. His problem can be described as
    a. expressive aphasia.
    b. preverbal language disorder.
    c. receptive aphasia.
    d. acquired aphasia.
    e. central language disorder.

Test 11B

1. Which theory of language learning emphasizes the reciprocal activities between the child and parent (or adult)?
   a. Behavioral theory
   b. Information-processing theory
   c. Developmental theory
   d. Innatist theory
   e. Social theory

2. "Emergent literacy" is recognized as an important stage for children. Teaching activities to promote "emergent literacy" would *not* include
   a. talking about stories.
   b. rhyming games.
   c. study skills.
   d. oral language activities.
   e. teaching about the alphabet.

3. The situation in which children speak a variant of standard English, such as black English, is referred to as
   a. language difference.
   b. language disturbance.
   c. language deficit.
   d. language disorder.
   e. bilingual language.

4. Which theory of language learning suggests that children have a natural or instinctive capacity for acquiring language?
   a. Innatist theory
   b. Visual-motor theory
   c. Information-processing theory
   d. Social theory
   e. Behavioral theory

5. Phonological awareness is demonstrated through
   a. the ability to tap out the number of sounds in words.
   b. the ability to recognize rhymes.
   c. the ability to segment the sounds of language.
   d. the ability to count sounds in words.
   e. all of the above.

6. A child who has difficulty talking or communicating ideas but understands what is said has what kind of language disorder?
   a. Global
   b. Expressive
   c. Receptive
   d. Acquired
   e. Preverbal

7. The social side of language is called
   a. morphology.
   b. pragmatics.
   c. semantics.
   d. syntax.
   e. phonology.

8. Name the expressive language skills.
   a. Reading and writing
   b. Writing and listening
   c. Writing and speaking
   d. Listening and reading
   e. Speaking and reading

9. Mike says "wide the horse" for "ride the horse." He has
   a. a language difference.
   b. a speech disorder.
   c. developmental aphasia.
   d. a global language disorder.
   e. a receptive language disorder.

10. Kimberly at age 3 does not understand single words spoken to her, such as *juice* and *cracker*. English is the language of her home. Her problem is
    a. a language difference.
    b. an articulation difficulty.
    c. a receptive language disorder.
    d. a speech disorder.
    e. a bilingual problem.

11. Which of the following is considered a language disorder?
    a. Articulation difficulties
    b. Stuttering
    c. Saying "fank you" for "thank you"
    d. Lateral lisp
    e. Childhood aphasia

12. The system of speech sounds is called
    a. morphology.
    b. phonology.
    c. semantics.
    d. intonation.
    e. syntax.

13. The system of vocabulary in a language is called
    a. phonology.
    b. syntax.
    c. semantics.
    d. intonation.
    e. morphology.

14. What is an 11-month-old child's speech called?
    a. Babbling
    b. First words
    c. Two-word sentences
    d. Jargon
    e. Gibberish

15. What method teaches children whose native language is other than English by providing instruction in their native language for part of the school day and in English for part of the school day?
    a. English as a second language (ESL)
    b. Bilingual instruction
    c. Immersion instruction
    d. Berlitz method
    e. None of the above

16. What method is used to teach children whose native language is other than English when there are many children in the school who speak many different languages? Instruction is in English, using careful control of English presentation and many repetitions.
    a. English as a second language (ESL)
    b. Bilingual instruction
    c. Immersion instruction
    d. Berlitz method
    e. None of the above

17. Name the receptive language skills.
    a. Writing and speaking
    b. Reading and writing
    c. Writing and listening
    d. Listening and reading
    e. Speaking and reading

18. Which of the following methods is used to evaluate a child's listening abilities?
    a. The teacher takes a sample of the child's oral language and analyzes the language sample.
    b. The teacher shows pictures and asks the child to identify objects in the pictures.
    c. The teacher reads a story out loud and asks questions about the story.
    d. The teacher gives an articulation test.
    e. The teacher gives a written language test.

19. Word-finding problems
    a. have little predictive significance.
    b. are not found among adults.
    c. are accurate predictors of reading problems.
    d. are not helpful assessment factors.
    e. are all of the above.

20. Vocalization during the first nine months of life is called
    a. babbling.
    b. jargon.
    c. gibberish.
    d. first words.
    e. none of the above.

21. A middle-ear infection that might affect language learning is
    a. limited English proficiency.
    b. otitis media.
    c. acquired aphasia.
    d. echolalia.
    e. dysnomia.

CHAPTER 12

Reading

Test 12A

1. What percentage of students with learning disabilities has reading problems?
   a. 40 percent
   b. 50 percent
   c. 60 percent
   d. 70 percent
   e. 80 percent

2. The condition of severe problems in reading that have a neurological basis is called
   a. dysgraphia.
   b. apraxia.
   c. dyslexia.
   d. aphasia.
   e. childhood aphasia.

3. Which of the following concepts is *not* part of the whole-language philosophy?
   a. The focus is on meaning.
   b. The various forms of language are integrated and are taught early.
   c. Learners are encouraged to guess at words.
   d. Children are introduced to literature early.
   e. Explicit phonics instruction is taught early.

4. In the informal reading inventory, the reading level at which the student can benefit from lessons with the teacher is called
   a. the instructional reading level.
   b. the independent reading level.
   c. the frustration reading level.
   d. the listening reading level.
   e. none of the above.

5. In figuring out words, readers use
   a. the sight word method.
   b. the phonics method.
   c. context clues.
   d. structural analysis.
   e. all of the above.

6. Identifying prefixes, suffixes, and roots to figure out words uses which method?
   a. Sight word method
   b. Phonics method
   c. Context clues
   d. Structural analysis
   e. Configuration

7. Which method involves recognizing a word from the meaning of surrounding text?
   a. Sight word method
   b. Phonics method
   c. Context clues
   d. Structural analysis
   e. Configuration

8. For fluent reading, what percentage of the text should be recognized as sight words?
   a. 50 percent
   b. 60 percent
   c. 70 percent
   d. 80 percent
   e. 90 percent

9. The special education law (the Individuals with Disabilities Education Act—IDEA) indicates that a student can be identified as having learning disabilities in what two areas of reading?
   a. Basic reading skills and reading comprehension
   b. Vocabulary and reading speed
   c. Phonological awareness and reading comprehension
   d. Reading speed and phonics
   e. Phonics and content-area reading

10. Explicit code-emphasis instruction emphasizes the teaching of
    a. comprehension.
    b. phonics.
    c. vocabulary.
    d. rapid reading.
    e. study reading.

11. A graphic organizer that is used to teach vocabulary by illustrating the word and linking concepts through a pictorial design consisting of circles or squares and connecting lines is
    a. VAKT.
    b. a cloze procedure.
    c. repeated reading.
    d. dialogue journals.
    e. a word web.

12. Which of the following is a formal test of reading?
    a. Informal reading inventory
    b. Portfolio assessment
    c. Standardized reading test
    d. Observation of a student's reading
    e. Miscue analysis

13. Which special remedial approach is a multisensory method that teaches the entire word as a unit?
    a. VAKT
    b. Orton-Gillingham
    c. Fernald
    d. Linguistic
    e. Basal reader

14. Which special remedial approach is a multisensory method in which students first learn individual letters and sounds?
    a. Linguistic
    b. Orton-Gillingham
    c. Fernald
    d. Basal reader
    e. Language experience

15. Which philosophy of teaching reading views reading as a natural extension of oral language development?
    a. Whole-language
    b. Decoding
    c. Phonics
    d. Neurological impress
    e. Structural analysis

16. Which assessment technique analyzes the types of errors that a student makes in oral reading?
    a. Cloze procedure
    b. Portfolio assessment
    c. Standardized survey tests
    d. Miscue analysis
    e. Speed reading tests

17. The first step for building vocabulary is
    a. using a dictionary.
    b. memorizing word lists.
    c. having primary concrete experiences related to the new words.
    d. listening to speakers with large vocabularies.
    e. Copying new vocabulary words five times.

18. Which is an informal measure of reading that requires children to read orally in a graded set of reading materials?
    a. Portfolio assessment
    b. Curriculum-based assessment
    c. Miscue analysis
    d. Informal reading inventory
    e. Standardized reading test

19. The procedure in which words in a passage are deleted and the reader must fill in the missing word is
    a. the neurological impress method.
    b. a directed reading-thinking activity.
    c. phonological awareness.
    d. the cloze procedure.
    e. Reading Recovery.

20. An example of narrative reading materials is
    a. a geography textbook.
    b. a world history text.
    c. a computer manual.
    d. a fiction book.
    e. a mathematics textbook.

21. An example of expository reading materials is
    a. a mystery book.
    b. a short story.
    c. a biography of a famous athlete.
    d. a history textbook.
    e. a fairy tale.

22. The ability to recognize words quickly and to easily read sentences and longer passages is called
    a. phonics.
    b. whole language.
    c. the multisensory method.
    d. Reading Recovery.
    e. fluency.

Test 12B

1. Which of the following is a formal reading test?
   a. Informal reading inventory
   b. Miscue analysis
   c. Survey reading test
   d. Teacher-made test
   e. Portfolio analysis

2. In an informal reading inventory, at which level can the student function without teacher help?
   a. Instructional level
   b. Frustration level
   c. Hearing level
   d. Independent level
   e. None of the above

3. What method of teaching reading uses a refrain in a story over and over?
   a. Cloze procedure
   b. Language experience
   c. Predictable books
   d. VAKT
   e. Learning strategies

4. What method of teaching reading uses the student's own language and integrates the language modes of talking, writing, and reading?
   a. Directed reading-thinking activity
   b. Language experience
   c. Predictable books
   d. Cloze procedure
   e. Orton-Gillingham

5. All of the following are ways to build reading comprehension *except*
   a. a directed reading-thinking activity.
   b. the language experience method.
   c. the cloze procedure.
   d. learning strategies.
   e. phonics.

6. All of the following are learning strategies *except*
   a. phonological awareness.
   b. advanced organizers.
   c. verbal rehearsal.
   d. self-monitoring.
   e. self-questioning.

7. Computers for teaching reading *cannot*
   a. offer one-to-one instruction.
   b. offer private instruction.
   c. take the place of books.
   d. provide time to think about a passage.
   e. enhance the connection between reading and writing.

8. Which of the following words represents the most abstract concept?
   a. Fairness
   b. Chair
   c. Eat
   d. Hamburger
   e. Jumping

9. What reading method focuses on the match between a phoneme and a written letter grapheme?
   a. Whole-language instruction
   b. Language experience
   c. Phonics
   d. Directed reading-thinking activity
   e. Neurological impress

10. What percentage of the text should be recognized as sight words for fluent reading?
    a. 40 percent
    b. 60 percent
    c. 70 percent
    d. 80 percent
    e. 90 percent

11. Reading fluency depends on
    a. knowledge of cause-effect relationships in text.
    b. rapid recognition of words.
    c. superior spelling skills.
    d. the ability to use a computer.
    e. knowing the works of classical literature.

12. Which informal measure of reading has students read orally in a graded set of reading materials?
    a. Miscue analysis
    b. Phonological awareness test
    c. Standard reading test
    d. Portfolio assessment
    e. Informal reading inventory

13. What medical term is used to describe a severe reading disability related to an organic problem?
    a. Dyslexia
    b. Agraphia
    c. Aphasia
    d. Dysnomia
    e. Apraxia

14. What reading method uses carefully graded stories that increase in difficulty from the early stages of reading through grade six or eight?
    a. Phonics
    b. Language experience
    c. Orton-Gillingham
    d. Basal reader
    e. Cloze procedure

15. Which is a multisensory approach to teaching reading that uses a systematic and structured language procedure for teaching individual letters and sounds?
    a. Orton-Gillingham
    b. Fernald
    c. Language experience
    d. Linguistic
    e. All of the above

16. What percentage of students with learning disabilities has reading problems?
    a. 30 percent
    b. 50 percent
    c. 60 percent
    d. 80 percent
    e. 95 percent

17. All of the following are emphasized in the whole-language philosophy *except*
    a. students are encouraged to guess at words.
    b. literature is introduced to children in the early grades.
    c. phonics is considered a primary instructional focus.
    d. the emphasis is on meaning.
    e. writing is taught early.

18. The special education law (the Individuals with Disabilities Education Act—IDEA) indicates that a student can be identified as having learning disabilities in two areas of reading:
    a. phonological awareness and reading comprehension.
    b. phonics and content-area reading.
    c. vocabulary and reading speed.
    d. reading speed and phonics.
    e. basic reading skills and reading comprehension.

19. In figuring out words, readers use
    a. context clues.
    b. structural analysis.
    c. sight word clues.
    d. phonics clues.
    e. all of the above.

20. In which of the following methods does the reader use word parts (e.g., prefixes, suffixes, root words) to figure out a word?
    a. Phonics
    b. Neurological impress
    c. Structural analysis
    d. Whole-language
    e. Decoding

21. An example of expository reading material is
    a. a computer manual.
    b. a mystery story.
    c. a biographical novel.
    d. a love story.
    e. a fairy tale.

22. An example of narrative reading material is
    a. a calculus book.
    b. a fictional short story.
    c. a science textbook.
    d. an American history textbook.
    e. a biology book.

CHAPTER 13

Written Language:
Written Expression, Spelling, and Handwriting

Test 13A

1. The stage of the writing process in which the writer develops a working version is the
   a. sharing-with-an-audience stage.
   b. prewriting stage.
   c. writing (or drafting) stage.
   d. revising stage.
   e. None of the above.

2. Severe difficulty in handwriting is called
   a. dysgraphia.
   b. dyscalculia.
   c. alexia.
   d. dyslexia.
   e. aphasia.

3. The linguistic approach to spelling is based on which of the following presumptions?
   a. The English language has consistent and predictable spelling rules.
   b. The English language has inconsistent and unpredictable spelling rules.
   c. There are too many exceptions to use the rules.
   d. Words for spelling instruction should be selected on the basis of how frequently students use the words in writing.
   e. Words should be selected on the basis of use in subject areas.

4. The most frequent difficulty in the forms of language is in
   a. oral expression.
   b. listening.
   c. handwriting.
   d. written expression.
   e. spelling.

5. The special education law specifies that a child could have a learning disability in which of the following?
   a. Written expression
   b. Spelling
   c. Handwriting
   d. All of the above
   e. None of the above

6. The word-frequency approach to selecting spelling words is based on
   a. underlying rules of spelling.
   b. research of words used in the content or subject areas.
   c. research of words used in speech by teachers.
   d. research of words commonly used by children in writing.
   e. none of the above.

7. Left-handedness in children
   a. should never be permitted.
   b. requires the use of left-handed pencils and pens.
   c. is accepted as natural for some children.
   d. should be encouraged for all children.
   e. means that manuscript writing should not be taught.

8. Cursive writing typically is taught in
   a. first grade.
   b. second grade.
   c. third grade.
   d. fourth grade.
   e. fifth grade.

9. Donna writes "wate" for weight. This can be analyzed as
   a. dysphonetic dyslexia (phonetically inaccurate spelling).
   b. dyseidetic dyslexia (phonic-equivalent error).
   c. a reversal error.
   d. an omission error.
   e. none of the above.

10. Good writers
    a. typically sit down and produce a complete text without the need for revision.
    b. check on spelling and grammar in the initial writing attempt.
    c. do not consider the audience who will be reading the text.
    d. produce carefully written sentences and paragraphs during the prewriting stage.
    e. go through several stages in the process of writing a document.

11. Stage one of the writing process is
    a. sharing with an audience.
    b. writing (or drafting).
    c. revising.
    d. prewriting.
    e. none of the above.

12. In planning writing instruction, teachers should
    a. help students spend time in developing ideas during the prewriting stage.
    b. not concentrate too much on spelling and punctuation during the first draft stage.
    c. avoid excessive correction of the student's work.
    d. provide abundant input experiences to inspire ideas.
    e. do all of the above.

13. Research on children who use invented spelling shows that they
    a. do not learn to spell in later years.
    b. are discouraged from writing.
    c. become very confused.
    d. spell as well or better in later years as other children.
    e. do not like invented spelling.

14. When children use invented spelling,
    a. they write less.
    b. they write more.
    c. it does not influence their writing.
    d. All of the above.
    e. None of the above.

15. Keyboarding skills
    a. should be delayed until high school.
    b. require specific instruction.
    c. can usually be learned incidentally without instruction.
    d. are too difficult for most students with learning disabilities.
    e. can be acquired without drill and practice.

16. Emergent literacy is a stage of learning that should occur in
    a. the primary grades.
    b. the intermediate grades.
    c. middle school.
    d. senior high school.
    e. college.
    f. none of the above.

17. The first developmental stage of spelling is
    a. using letter names.
    b. prephonetic.
    c. using written patterns.
    d. beginning phonic strategies.
    e. using multisyllabic words.

18. Sixty percent of the writing of elementary students consists of
    a. 100 words.
    b. 200 words.
    c. 300 words.
    d. 400 words.
    e. 500 words.

19. Manuscript writing is usually taught in which grade?
    a. First
    b. Second
    c. Third
    d. Fourth
    e. Fifth

20. Handwriting is considered to be what kind of skill?
    a. Gross-motor
    b. Quantitative
    c. Learning strategy
    d. Fine-motor
    e. Computer

21. In the multisensory approach to spelling, the student
    a. writes the word.
    b. recalls the visual image of the word.
    c. looks at the word.
    d. pronounces the word.
    e. does all of the above.

Test 13B

1. The term *emergent literacy* refers to
   a. young children's early involvement with stories.
   b. introduction to Shakespeare in junior high school.
   c. learning the literature classics in senior high school.
   d. using the Great Books in college.
   e. becoming a literate adult.

2. At what grade level is cursive writing typically introduced?
   a. Second
   b. Third
   c. Fourth
   d. Fifth
   e. Sixth

3. In the Individuals with Disabilities Education Act, an individual can have a learning disability in which of the following areas?
   a. Spelling
   b. Handwriting
   c. Written expression
   d. Creative writing
   e. All of the above

4. The first developmental stage of spelling is
   a. beginning phonic strategies.
   b. prephonetic.
   c. using written patterns.
   d. using multisyllabic words.
   e. using letter names.

5. Sixty percent of the writing of elementary students consists of a maximum of
   a. 25 words.
   b. 100 words.
   c. 300 words.
   d. 400 words.
   e. 500 words.

6. Research on the use of invented spelling shows which of the following to be true?
   a. Children do not like it.
   b. It keeps children from learning how to spell words.
   c. It discourages writing.
   d. It confuses children.
   e. Children tend to write more.

7. A medical term for severe difficulty in handwriting is
   a. alexia.
   b. dyslexia.
   c. dyscalculia.
   d. dysgraphia.
   e. aphasia.

8. Stage two of the writing process is
   a. sharing with an audience.
   b. writing (or drafting).
   c. revising.
   d. prewriting.
   e. none of the above.

9. If a child writes "roaneg" for orange, this can be analyzed as
   a. dysphonetic dyslexia (phonetically inaccurate spelling).
   b. dyseidetic dyslexia (phonic-equivalent error).
   c. a reversal error.
   d. an omission error.
   e. none of the above.

10. The word-frequency approach to selecting spelling words is based on
    a. the selection of phonograms.
    b. underlying rules of spelling.
    c. words used in content-area subjects.
    d. words commonly used by speech teachers.
    e. words commonly used by children in writing.

11. The premise underlying the linguistic approach to selecting spelling words is that
    a. there are too many exceptions in English to use rules.
    b. English has reliable and predictable spelling rules.
    c. words that are most commonly used by children should be selected.
    d. English does not have consistent and predictable spelling rules.
    e. words that are most commonly used by teachers should be selected.

12. Manuscript writing is usually taught in
    a. first grade.
    b. second grade.
    c. third grade.
    d. fourth grade.
    e. fifth grade.

13. Which form of the integrated language system is generally most difficult to acquire?
    a. Spelling
    b. Listening
    c. Writing
    d. Reading
    e. Speaking

14. Children who are left-handed
    a. should not be taught cursive writing.
    b. should not be taught manuscript writing.
    c. should be changed to become right-handed writers.
    d. should be accepted as having a natural preference for that hand.
    e. need special pencils and pens.

15. Invented spelling
    a. should be encouraged in young children.
    b. represents a child's early attempts at spelling.
    c. helps young children produce more writing.
    d. allows a child to concentrate on the content of the writing.
    e. does all of the above.

16. Word processing
    a. can be accomplished on a typewriter.
    b. is not recommended for students who have fine-motor problems.
    c. makes it harder to make changes and corrections.
    d. eliminates the need to use the writing process.
    e. eliminates the need to recopy or retype an entire assignment to produce a final draft.

17. Learning keyboarding skills
    a. requires special instruction and practice.
    b. should not start until the high school years.
    c. is unnecessary, and students should be encouraged to use a two-finger method.
    d. is too difficult for most students with learning disabilities.
    e. is usually easy and accomplished without instruction.

18. In what stage of the writing process does the writer collect initial ideas?
    a. Sharing with the audience
    b. Prewriting
    c. Writing (or drafting)
    d. Revising
    e. None of the above

19. New views on writing instruction emphasize that
    a. writing is a process that occurs in stages.
    b. teachers should be careful to correct spelling and grammar on all drafts.
    c. the important outcome is the final product the student produces.
    d. children should write for the teacher.
    e. teachers should mark all errors with red ink.

20. The Fernald method for teaching spelling is what kind of method?
    a. Linguistic
    b. Multisensory
    c. Test study
    d. Computer technology
    e. Learning strategies

21. In the multisensory approach to spelling, the student
    a. pronounces the word.
    b. looks at the word visually.
    c. recalls the visual image of the word.
    d. writes the word.
    e. does all of the above.

CHAPTER 14

Mathematics

Test 14A

1. The "basic skills" movement emphasizes
   a. understanding of the number system.
   b. advanced mathematics.
   c. preschool number learning.
   d. calculation abilities.
   e. modern math concepts.

2. Multiplication facts through the nines are normally taught in what grade?
   a. First
   b. Second
   c. Third
   d. Fourth
   e. Fifth

3. Nathan is setting the table for a snack in his preschool class. There are 6 children. He sets out 6 plates and pairs them with 6 cookies. Nathan demonstrated which precursor skill?
   a. Visual perception
   b. One-to-one correspondence
   c. Writing numbers skill
   d. Language skill
   e. Knowing place value

4. According to the special education law, IDEA, a student could have a learning disability in the area of mathematics in
   a. mathematics calculation or mathematics reasoning.
   b. problem solving or precursor math skills.
   c. estimating or problem solving.
   d. algebra or math calculation.
   e. using number lines.

5. Studies of the mathematics textbook series used in general education classes show that, for students with mathematics disabilities, the math books
   a. present concepts at an appropriate rate.
   b. present concepts too rapidly.
   c. provide sufficient review.
   d. provide sufficient guided practice.
   e. provide assessments of the students' prior knowledge.

6. A student makes the following error on an arithmetic test: 12 – 6 = 18. This can be analyzed as what kind of error?
   a. Place value
   b. Wrong process
   c. Poor writing skills
   d. Working from left to right
   e. None of the above

7. A student makes the following error: 55 + 29 = 74. This is what kind of error?
   a. Place value
   b. Wrong process
   c. Poor writing skills
   d. Working from left to right
   e. None of the above

8. The emphasis in modern math was on
   a. learning computation facts.
   b. giving practice in basic math skills.
   c. gaining an understanding of the number system.
   d. fast and efficient computing in mathematics.
   e. mastery development.

9. All of the following are required precursor abilities for math learning for preschool children *except*
   a. one-to-one correspondence.
   b. classification skills.
   c. sufficient experience with manipulating objects.
   d. good reading skills.
   e. understanding the order of numbers.

10. A mathematics instructional method with the goal of having students achieve mastery of computation skills through explicit teacher instruction is
   a. discovery learning.
   b. constructive learning.
   c. direct instruction.
   d. learning strategies instruction.
   e. problem solving instruction.

11. One result of the education reform movement is that high schools are
   a. decreasing the required study in mathematics.
   b. maintaining the mathematics requirement.
   c. eliminating the mathematics requirement.
   d. increasing the mathematics requirement.
   e. keeping the current mathematics requirements.

12. The National Council of Supervisors of Mathematics recommends that calculators
   a. should never be used.
   b. should be used instead of teaching computation skills.
   c. should be taught to students.
   d. should not be allowed in testing situations.
   e. have no place in school.

13. Dona has the following math error on her test: $5 \times 7 = 38$. How would you analyze this error?
    a. Place value
    b. Computation facts
    c. Wrong process
    d. Working from right to left
    e. Not lining up the numbers

14. Fractions are taught in grade
    a. 3.
    b. 4.
    c. 5.
    d. 6.
    e. 7.

15. Paula makes circles on her paper to figure out an answer to a math addition problem. She is using
    a. concrete math learning.
    b. representational math learning.
    c. abstract math learning.
    d. intuitive learning.
    e. none of the above.

16. Constructive learning theory in mathematics
    a. discourages children from counting.
    b. encourages children to count.
    c. does not discuss counting.
    d. emphasizes drill and practice.
    e. emphasizes rote learning and memory skills.

17. Severe problems in mathematics are referred to as
    a. dysgraphia.
    b. aphasia.
    c. dyscalculia.
    d. dyslexia.
    e. apraxia.

18. The word *product* is used in which computation process?
    a. Addition
    b. Subtraction
    c. Multiplication
    d. Division
    e. Estimation

19. Denise uses blocks to figure out addition and subtraction problems. This is
    a. concrete math learning.
    b. representational math learning.
    c. abstract math learning.
    d. intuitive learning.
    e. none of the above.

20. Bonita does well in class during mathematics instruction. But she does poorly in major mathematics tests given by the school because she is so nervous that she cannot concentrate. Bonita's problem is
    a. poor sense of body image.
    b. disorders in visual perception.
    c. memory problems.
    d. math anxiety.
    e. poor sense of direction and time.

21. Which of the following is a formal mathematics assessment measure?
    a. Clinical interview
    b. Teacher-made tests
    c. Group survey test
    d. Informal inventory
    e. Curriculum-based assessment

22. Mr. Collins makes up many math story problems and has his students make up more problems and exchange them. What teaching principle is he following?
    a. Teaching precursor skills
    b. Going from abstract to concrete
    c. Giving drill practice
    d. Teaching basic facts
    e. Generalizing to new situations

Test 14B

1. Billy counts poker chips to figure out problems in addition and subtraction. He is using
   a. abstract math learning.
   b. intuitive learning.
   c. concrete math learning.
   d. representational math learning.
   e. drill.

2. Which theory of mathematics instruction emphasizes teaching basic math facts through explicit teaching that is structured and carefully sequenced.
   a. Discovery learning
   b. Direct instruction
   c. Learning strategies
   d. Problem solving
   e. Constructive learning

3. The following is typical of Mohan's mathematics errors: $23 + 91 = 15$. His problem can be analyzed as errors in
   a. the wrong process.
   b. computation facts.
   c. place value.
   d. working from left to right.
   e. not lining up the problem.

4. Minnie makes the following error: $52 - 18 = 44$. Her problem is an error in
   a. the wrong process.
   b. computation facts.
   c. place value.
   d. working from left to right.
   e. not lining up the problem.

5. Mike makes the following error: $18 - 3 = 21$. His problem is an error in
   a. the wrong process.
   b. computation facts.
   c. place value.
   d. working from left to right.
   e. not lining up the problem.

6. All of the following are informal measures of mathematics performance *except*
   a. standardized mathematics survey tests.
   b. informal inventories.
   c. curriculum-based assessment.
   d. analysis of mathematics errors.
   e. diagnostic teaching.

7. Subtraction facts through 20 are usually taught in which grade?
   a. Kindergarten
   b. First
   c. Second
   d. Third
   e. Fourth

8. Fractions are usually taught in grade
   a. 3.
   b. 5.
   c. 7.
   d. 9.
   e. 11.

9. Modern math emphasized which facet of mathematics learning?
   a. Drill and practice
   b. Learning computation facts
   c. Computer technology
   d. Readiness for mathematics
   e. Understanding the underlying number system

10. In this first grade, children are encouraged to figure out their own ways of solving mathematics problems. This is
    a. direct instruction.
    b. constructive learning.
    c. learning strategies instruction.
    d. basic skills instruction.
    e. mastery learning.

11. High schools today are
    a. increasing mathematics requirements.
    b. decreasing mathematics requirements.
    c. not changing mathematics requirements.
    d. eliminating mathematics requirements.
    e. keeping the same mathematics requirements.

12. Which of the following is emphasized in basic skills instruction?
    a. Modern math concepts
    b. Understanding of the number system
    c. Advanced mathematics
    d. Preschool number learning
    e. Calculation abilities

13. What is the medical term for severe problems in mathematics?
    a. Apraxia
    b. Dyslexia
    c. Dyscalculia
    d. Dysgraphia
    e. Aphasia

14. The word *minuend* is used in which mathematics operation?
    a. Addition
    b. Subtraction
    c. Multiplication
    d. Division
    e. Calculus

15. Addition and subtraction of facts through 100 is taught in grade
    a. 1.
    b. 2.
    c. 3.
    d. 4.
    e. 5.

16. When Sarah makes lines on her paper to figure out an answer to a math addition problem, she is using
    a. abstract math learning.
    b. concrete math learning.
    c. representational math learning.
    d. intuitive learning.
    e. rote learning.

17. In applying theories of constructive learning in mathematics, students are
    a. encouraged to count.
    b. discouraged from counting.
    c. not permitted to use their fingers to count.
    d. taught through drill and practice.
    e. encouraged to learn through memorization.

18. The National Council of Supervisors of Mathematics recommends which of the following about using calculators?
    a. Calculators should never be used in school.
    b. Calculator usage should be taught to students.
    c. Calculators should not be used to complete homework.
    d. Calculators should be used instead of teaching computation skills.
    e. Calculators should not be used in testing situations.

19. Special education law, IDEA, specifies that a student could have a mathematics learning disability in
    a. algebra or precursor math skills.
    b. mathematics reasoning or mathematics calculation.
    c. geometry or mathematics calculation.
    d. estimating or mathematics reasoning.
    e. quantitative thinking or estimating.

20. Ms. Zee has a goal of developing automaticity in computation skills. Which of the following principles of mathematics teaching is she following?
    a. Teach students to generalize skills.
    b. Progress from the concrete to the abstract.
    c. Teach precursor mathematics skills.
    d. Have students overlearn math concepts.
    e. Teach math vocabulary.

21. Jim has the following error on his mathematics paper: $5 \times 6 = 35$. An analysis of this error suggests that Jim's error is in
    a. wrong process.
    b. computation facts.
    c. not lining up numbers.
    d. working from right to left.
    e. place value.

22. Jeffrey is 8 years old. His teacher is teaching him one-to-one correspondence. What math principle is his teacher following?
    a. Teach precursor skills
    b. Go from concrete to abstract
    c. Give review and practice
    d. Teach basic math facts
    e. Generalize to new situations

CHAPTER 15

Social and Emotional Behavior

Test 15A

1. Social skills deficits are mentioned in the definition of learning disabilities in
   a. the Individuals with Disabilities Education Act.
   b. Section 504 of the Rehabilitation Act.
   c. the Interagency Committee on Learning Disabilities definition.
   d. Head Start legislation.
   e. the American with Disabilities Act.

2. Students with a social disability
   a. may also have difficulty in academic areas.
   b. are poor in detecting subtle social cues.
   c. may do well in academic areas.
   d. often have difficulty making friends.
   e. All of the above.

3. Behavior management methods do *not* require information about
   a. the antecedent event.
   b. the consequent event.
   c. the underlying emotional cause of the learning problem.
   d. the target behavior.
   e. the stimulus.

4. When Tony comes to school without his arithmetic homework, the teacher scolds him in class. To avoid the teacher's scolding, Tony now does his homework. This is an example of
   a. positive reinforcement.
   b. negative reinforcement.
   c. shaping behavior.
   d. extinction.
   e. the Premack principle.

5. Andrea has never spoken. When she grunts, she is given a piece of cereal. This is an example of
   a. negative reinforcement.
   b. punishment.
   c. response cost.
   d. shaping behavior.
   e. contingency contracting.

6. The use of reinforcements to change behavior is part of which theory?
   a. Family systems theory
   b. Attribution theory
   c. Personality theory
   d. Piagetian theory
   e. Behavior management theory

7. John is working hard to improve his keyboarding skills. The keyboarding software grading system indicated that John scored 100; he made no errors and increased his typing speed. John explained that his success was due to his effort and hard work. This is an example of
   a. contingency contracting.
   b. response cost.
   c. time out.
   d. attribution theory.
   e. successive approximation.

8. The teacher promised Lisa that if she completes her written composition, she will be allowed to paint at the easel. This is an example of
   a. successive approximation.
   b. negative reinforcement.
   c. modeling.
   d. shaping behavior.
   e. the Premack principle.

9. A systematic arrangement of environmental events to produce a specific change in observable behavior is a description of
   a. psychodynamic theory.
   b. behavior management.
   c. social cognitive theory.
   d. attribution theory.
   e. personality theory.

10. Mr. Thompson uses a system in his class in which students are given a small plastic chip at the end of each hour if there has been no disruptive behavior and work has been completed. At the end of each week, the chips can be turned in at a "store" for toys, books, puzzles, and so forth. This is known as
    a. the Premack principle.
    b. contingency contracting.
    c. a token economy.
    d. shaping behavior.
    e. curriculum-based assessment.

11. Consideration of where children place the cause for success or failure in their own performance is an aspect of
    a. attribution theory.
    b. learning strategies.
    c. psychological processing.
    d. maturational development.
    e. behavior management.

12. Bernice did not read the chapter or prepare for the social studies test. She failed the test and then said the test was not fair. Her explanation exemplifies
   a. successive approximation.
   b. token reinforcers.
   c. response cost.
   d. positive reinforcement.
   e. attribution theory.

13. Don has learning disabilities. He has wanted to become a doctor since grade school. In college last year, he failed the foreign language course and could not graduate. He passed the test after studying for it diligently. Now he has done poorly on the medical school entrance exam. He plans to spend three months studying for this test and retake it. Don exhibits qualities of
   a. resiliency.
   b. hyperactivity.
   c. learned helplessness.
   d. social skills deficits.
   e. poor self-concept.

14. The child's psychodynamic development and personality structure have important implications for understanding which aspect of the child?
   a. Language problems
   b. Mathematics problems
   c. Reading problems
   d. Emotional problems
   e. Visual-motor problems

15. Carla is running about the classroom, and her behavior disturbs other children. Carla's teacher asks her to go to a special corner of the room for 5 minutes. What behavior management strategy is the teacher using?
   a. Response cost
   b. Contingency contracting
   c. Ignoring
   d. Shaping
   e. Time out

16. In the components of the behavioral unit, the reinforcement is the
   a. antecedent event.
   b. target behavior.
   c. consequent event.
   d. stimulus event.
   e. None of the above.

17. Mona is in the process of writing a term paper. She tells herself that she must first develop an outline. She also tells herself that when the outline is completed, she will get herself a glass of root beer. As she is pouring the drink, she says to herself, "I did a good job on that outline." This is an example of
   a. negative reinforcement.
   b. contingency contracting.
   c. cognitive behavior modification.
   d. shaping behavior.
   e. token reinforcement.

18. An intrinsic reinforcer is
    a. a piece of candy.
    b. gold stars.
    c. smiling-faces stickers.
    d. the satisfaction of completing a task.
    e. a small toy.

19. The most direct way to assess a student's emotional behavior in the school setting is through
    a. psychiatric evaluation.
    b. neurological examination.
    c. observation of the student.
    d. tests of personality.
    e. projective tests.

20. In Ms. Carver's general education third-grade class, she permits students to get up to sharpen pencils, to leave their seats to put completed work in a special place, and to stand or kneel while they work. The purpose for making these accommodations is to help students
    a. increase attention.
    b. improve listening skills.
    c. manage time.
    d. provide opportunities for moving.
    e. limit distractions.

Test 15B

1. Which of the following documents mentions social skills deficits in its definition of learning disabilities?
   a. Interagency Committee on Learning Disabilities definition
   b. Head Start legislation
   c. Americans with Disabilities Act
   d. Individuals with Disabilities Education Act
   e. Section 504 of the Rehabilitation Act

2. Josh has attention deficit disorders (ADD) and cannot sit at his desk and work for 10 minutes at a time. His teacher gives him a token for kneeling at his desk, then for sitting for 30 seconds, then 1 minute, etc., until he can work for 10 minutes. This strategy is
   a. the Premack principle.
   b. contingency contracting.
   c. shaping behavior.
   d. cognitive behavior modification.
   e. time out.

3. In the components of the behavioral unit in behavior management, the event preceding the student's behavior is the
   a. antecedent event.
   b. target behavior.
   c. consequent event.
   d. reinforcement.
   e. major event.

4. What is the most direct way to assess a student's emotional status in the school setting?
   a. Tests of personality
   b. Projective tests
   c. Psychiatric evaluation
   d. Neurological examination
   e. Observation of the student

5. The theory of psychodynamic development or personality structure provides a way to analyze the child's
   a. motor skills.
   b. language abilities.
   c. emotional status.
   d. reading achievement.
   e. mathematics abilities.

6. In planning a behavior management method, it is necessary for teachers to know about
   a. the underlying psychological cause of a child's problem.
   b. the child's ego development.
   c. the child's early interactions with the mother.
   d. the reinforcements that change the student's behavior.
   e. the child's psychological processing disorders.

7. When Sarah completes her assignment in arithmetic, she is given time to work on the computer. This is an example of
    a. negative reinforcement.
    b. response cost.
    c. resilience.
    d. positive reinforcement.
    e. attribution.

8. Sammy did not study for the American history test, and he failed it. He said that he failed the test because it was unfair. His explanation exemplifies
    a. successive approximation.
    b. negative reinforcement.
    c. response cost.
    d. positive reinforcement.
    e. attribution theory.

9. Willie has very poor motor control for writing and has refused to put anything on paper. His teacher is trying to teach him to write his name. After he draws a circle on a piece of paper, his teacher gives him a dinosaur sticker. This is an example of
    a. contingency contracting.
    b. punishment.
    c. ignoring.
    d. negative reinforcement.
    e. shaping behavior.

10. Nancy's teacher told her that if she finished a book report, she could have fifteen minutes of free time. This is an example of
    a. modeling.
    b. the Premack principle.
    c. shaping behavior.
    d. negative reinforcement.
    e. cognitive behavior modification.

11. The use of reinforcement to change behavior is a part of which theory?
    a. Behavior management
    b. Personality
    c. Psychodynamic
    d. Attribution
    e. Social

12. Students in Mr. Gardner's class are given a ticket at the completion of each assignment. They can accumulate these tickets and exchange them at the end of the week for small rewards such as games, candy, and toys. This is known as
    a. time out.
    b. shaping behavior.
    c. contingency contracting.
    d. successive approximation.
    e. a token economy.

13. Which theory analyzes where children place the cause of their own successes or failures?
    a. Psychoanalytic theory
    b. Developmental theory
    c. Attribution theory
    d. Behavioral theory
    e. Psychodynamic theory

14. Dave was shouting out loud in class and disturbing other children. His teacher asked him to sit in a corner of the room for 5 minutes. This strategy is
    a. token economy.
    b. time out.
    c. shaping behavior.
    d. contingency contracting.
    e. cognitive behavior modification.

15. Mr. Jackson uses peer tutoring in his class with students who have social and behavior problems. The peer tutors are students who have attained good behavior and social skills. Mr. Jackson hopes the students being taught will emulate the good behavior of the peer tutors. This is an example of
    a. the Premack principle.
    b. modeling.
    c. negative reinforcement.
    d. successive approximation.
    e. a token economy.

16. Kendra makes funny noises in class to gain attention. Her teacher, believing that reprimanding her would reinforce Kendra's behavior, does not pay attention to it. He hopes this strategy will lead to the disappearance of Kendra's behavior. This method is known as
    a. positive reinforcement.
    b. contingency contracting.
    c. modeling.
    d. a token economy.
    e. ignoring.

17. Which of the following is an intrinsic reinforcer?
    a. Smiling-faces stamp
    b. Small toy
    c. Praise from the teacher
    d. Personal pleasure of doing a good job
    e. Gold stars

18. In Mr. Ross's class, students earn plastic chips for good behavior. Eddie hit another student and Mr. Ross took two chips away from Eddie. This strategy is
    a. positive reinforcement.
    b. time out.
    c. shaping behavior.
    d. cognitive behavior modification.
    e. response cost.

19. Naomi is working on word-recognition reading skills at home. She tells herself that when she is able to recognize 10 of the words, she will be able to play a computer game for 10 minutes. After she learned the 10 words, she told herself that she had done a good job. This strategy is
    a. cognitive behavior modification.
    b. time out.
    c. contingency contracting.
    d. successive approximations.
    e. token reinforcements.

20. Dave has a personal goal of passing a biology course so that he can be admitted to a pharmacy program at his college. Although Dave knows he has dyslexia and the reading in the biology course is very difficult for him, he has a great deal of confidence in himself. He has set aside double the amount of time other students spend studying for this course and intends to use a study method that has worked for other courses. How would you characterize Dave's attitude?
    a. Learned helplessness
    b. Passive learning style
    c. Resiliency
    d. Poor self-esteem
    e. Attributing success to random luck

Answers to Multiple-Choice Questions

Chapter 1   Learning Disabilities: A Field in Transition

Test 1A

1. d	7. d	13. b	18. e
2. d	8. e	14. d	19. a
3. e	9. a	15. c	20. e
4. b	10. b	16. c	21. e
5. c	11. e	17. c	22. c
6. a	12. a		

Test 1B

1. d	7. d	13. b	18. a
2. a	8. d	14. c	19. c
3. e	9. b	15. e	20. d
4. e	10. a	16. c	21. e
5. c	11. d	17. c	22. c
6. b	12. c		

Chapter 2   Historical Perspectives and Emerging Directions

Test 2A

1. c	7. d	13. e	18. a
2. c	8. e	14. e	19. e
3. c	9. b	15. e	20. b
4. d	10. c	16. d	21. c
5. c	11. c	17. e	22. d
6. a	12. c		

Test 2B

1. b	7. c	13. a	18. b
2. c	8. c	14. b	19. b
3. d	9. e	15. e	20. a
4. b	10. a	16. c	21. d
5. e	11. b	17. a	22. b
6. d	12. e		

Chapter 3   Assessment

Test 3A

1. c	7. b	13. b	18. c
2. b	8. e	14. c	19. a
3. d	9. e	15. e	20. c
4. a	10. d	16. b	21. e
5. a	11. b	17. e	22. e
6. d	12. c		

Test 3B

1. a	7. a	12. e	17. c
2. c	8. e	13. c	18. e
3. e	9. e	14. e	19. d
4. a	10. d	15. a	20. c
5. a	11. a	16. e	21. a
6. d			

Chapter 4   Clinical Teaching

Test 4A

1. d	7. d	12. e	17. b
2. c	8. a	13. b	18. c
3. d	9. e	14. a	19. a
4. e	10. a	15. c	20. d
5. c	11. e	16. b	21. d
6. d			

Test 4B

1. e	7. a	12. c	17. b
2. e	8. d	13. c	18. d
3. a	9. b	14. a	19. a
4. d	10. e	15. a	20. c
5. c	11. b	16. d	21. b
6. e			

Chapter 5   Systems for Delivering Educational Services

Test 5A

1. c	6. c	11. a	16. c
2. b	7. e	12. a	17. d
3. c	8. a	13. d	18. d
4. b	9. e	14. a	19. e
5. c	10. e	15. a	20. b

Test 5B

1. b	6. e	11. e	16. a
2. a	7. a	12. c	17. e
3. c	8. d	13. c	18. c
4. c	9. e	14. c	19. b
5. e	10. a	15. a	20. b

Chapter 6   Theories of Learning: Implications for Learning Disabilities

Test 6A

1. e	6. c	11. a	16. a
2. b	7. e	12. c	17. a
3. d	8. d	13. e	18. e
4. d	9. d	14. b	19. b
5. a	10. e	15. c	20. c

Test 6B

1. e	6. e	11. a	16. a
2. a	7. e	12. c	17. d
3. b	8. d	13. c	18. a
4. a	9. e	14. e	19. c
5. b	10. a	15. d	20. e

Chapter 7   Medical Aspects of Learning Disabilities

Test 7A

1. a	6. e	11. e	16. a
2. c	7. c	12. b	17. c
3. b	8. b	13. a	18. e
4. d	9. d	14. e	19. c
5. c	10. a	15. a	20. c

Test 7B

1. c	6. c	11. c	16. d
2. c	7. b	12. c	17. a
3. e	8. e	13. a	18. b
4. e	9. c	14. c	19. c
5. b	10. a	15. e	20. d

Chapter 8   Young Children with Disabilities

Test 8A

1. e	7. e	12. b	17. c
2. a	8. c	13. a	18. b
3. b	9. b	14. d	19. b
4. e	10. a	15. e	20. b
5. a	11. c	16. d	21. e
6. e			

Test 8B

1. d	7. c	12. c	17. b
2. a	8. a	13. b	18. a
3. a	9. d	14. d	19. b
4. b	10. d	15. e	20. c
5. e	11. e	16. d	21. b
6. a			

Chapter 9   Adolescents and Adults with Learning Disabilities

Test 9A

1. a	7. c	12. d	17. d
2. c	8. d	13. c	18. d
3. b	9. a	14. d	19. c
4. d	10. c	15. a	20. a
5. e	11. c	16. b	21. d
6. e			

Test 9B

1. c	7. d	12. c	17. e
2. a	8. a	13. c	18. c
3. b	9. c	14. d	19. d
4. e	10. a	15. e	20. c
5. c	11. e	16. b	21. b
6. d			

Chapter 10   Developmental and Preacademic Learning

Test 10A

1. c	7. d	12. a	17. a
2. e	8. b	13. e	18. e
3. b	9. a	14. c	19. a
4. d	10. a	15. a	20. c
5. d	11. e	16. e	21. e
6. b			

Test 10B

1. a	7. d	12. c	17. d
2. b	8. e	13. e	18. c
3. c	9. d	14. a	19. b
4. d	10. b	15. e	20. b
5. d	11. c	16. e	21. e
6. a			

Chapter 11   Oral Language: Listening and Speaking

Test 11A

1. d	7. e	12. c	17. a
2. d	8. a	13. c	18. d
3. c	9. c	14. c	19. b
4. d	10. e	15. e	20. b
5. a	11. d	16. d	21. a
6. d			

Test 11B

1. e	7. b	12. b	17. d
2. c	8. c	13. c	18. c
3. a	9. b	14. d	19. c
4. a	10. c	15. b	20. a
5. e	11. e	16. a	21. b
6. b			

Chapter 12   Reading

Test 12A

1. e	7. c	13. c	18. d
2. c	8. e	14. b	19. d
3. e	9. a	15. a	20. d
4. a	10. b	16. d	21. d
5. e	11. e	17. c	22. e
6. d	12. c		

Test 12B

1. c	7. c	13. a	18. e
2. d	8. a	14. d	19. e
3. c	9. c	15. a	20. c
4. b	10. e	16. d	21. a
5. e	11. b	17. c	22. b
6. a	12. e		

Chapter 13   Written Language:
Written Expression, Spelling, and Handwriting

Test 13A

1. c	7. c	12. e	17. b
2. a	8. c	13. d	18. a
3. a	9. b	14. b	19. a
4. d	10. e	15. b	20. d
5. a	11. d	16. a	21. e
6. d			

Test 13B

1. a	7. d	12. a	17. a
2. b	8. b	13. c	18. b
3. c	9. a	14. d	19. a
4. b	10. e	15. e	20. b
5. b	11. b	16. e	21. e
6. e			

Chapter 14   Mathematics

Test 14A

1. d	7. a	13. b	18. c
2. c	8. c	14. c	19. a
3. c	9. d	15. b	20. d
4. a	10. c	16. b	21. c
5. b	11. d	17. c	22. e
6. b	12. c		

Test 14B

1. c	7. b	13. c	18. b
2. b	8. b	14. b	19. b
3. d	9. e	15. b	20. d
4. c	10. b	16. c	21. b
5. a	11. a	17. a	22. a
6. a	12. e		

Chapter 15   Social and Emotional Behavior

Test 15A

1. c	6. e	11. a	16. c
2. e	7. d	12. e	17. c
3. c	8. e	13. a	18. d
4. b	9. b	14. d	19. c
5. d	10. c	15. e	20. d

Test 15B

1. a	6. d	11. a	16. e
2. c	7. d	12. e	17. d
3. a	8. e	13. c	18. e
4. e	9. e	14. b	19. a
5. c	10. b	15. b	20. c

PART FOUR
Additional Teaching Resources

1. Sample Syllabus
2. Sample Student Assignment: Informal Assessment of a Child
3. Videotapes
4. Learning Disabilities Organizations: E-mail and Web Sites, Addresses, FAX and Telephone Numbers
5. Selected References and Professional Journals

1. Sample Syllabus

This text can be used in a one-semester course or a two-semester course. The following syllabus is for a one-semester course. It covers the entire book and is designed for a 16-week semester course meeting twice a week.

For a two-semester course:

- The first course covers Chapters 1–7 and emphasizes characteristics and assessment of learning disabilities.

- The second course covers Chapters 8–15 and emphasizes teaching strategies and methods of instruction for children and youth with learning disabilities.

Course Description

The purpose of this course is to introduce students to the field of learning disabilities. The course covers characteristics of learning disabilities, definitions, history, assessment, medical aspects, teaching of preschoolers and adolescents, and teaching strategies for preacademic learning, oral language, reading, writing, mathematics, and social-emotional development.

Course Objectives

The students will

- Demonstrate knowledge of the definitions and characteristics of learning disabilities.

- Demonstrate knowledge of state and federal legislation relating to individuals with learning disabilities.

- Demonstrate understanding of the educational foundations of teaching children and youth with learning disabilities

- Demonstrate familiarity with the full range of placements for individuals with learning disabilities.

- Demonstrate understanding of the effects of learning disabilities upon academic, social, and vocational performance across the life span.

- Demonstrate knowledge of informal and formal assessment methods, of making decisions based on assessment information, and of writing IEPs.

- Demonstrate an appreciation for cultural diversity and its effects on all aspects of teaching children and youth with learning disabilities.

- Demonstrate knowledge of teaching strategies and methods for instructing children and youth.

- Demonstrate an understanding of precursors of learning disabilities and methods for intervention.

- Demonstrate knowledge of academic learning disabilities and teaching strategies of oral language, reading, writing, and mathematics.

- Demonstrate an understanding of the social and emotional problems of individuals with learning disabilities and strategies for meeting social and emotional needs.

Methods of Instruction

The methods for instruction will include lecture, discussion, student work groups, reading assignments, student presentations, audiovisual materials, and computer multimedia presentations.

Assignments

Required Assignments

1. Attend class lectures and participate in class discussions.

2. Complete all assigned readings.

3. Read one article about learning disabilities in a professional journal and write a two-page report on this reading. Include a brief description of the content and your personal reaction.

4. Write a 5-page term paper on some aspect of learning disabilities. Use APA style for this paper.

5. Give a series of informal tests to a child (or children) and write a report on your findings. (Follow sample student assignment to find the locations of the information assessments in the text.)

6. Take midterm and final examinations.

Optional Assignments

You can complete optional assignments to earn additional credit. The following are some suggested optional assignments.

1. Make a presentation to the class on an assessment method or a teaching method. (This presentation must first be discussed with your instructor.)

2. Attend a professional meeting on learning disabilities or a related area of education and report on this meeting in writing or to the class.

3. Read additional articles about learning disabilities in a professional journal.

4. Create a computer program for children with learning disabilities. (For example, use a multi-media program such as HyperStudio.)

5. Do a library computer search to find resources on a particular topic related to learning disabilities.

6. Browse the World Wide Web, using Web sites of learning disabilities organizations to find recent information about learning disabilities.

Grading

Midterm examination	30%	
Final examination	30%	
Required assignments (informal tests, attendance, journal article)	10%	
Term paper	20%	
Class participation	10%	
	100%	
Optional assignments	1–10	additional points

Course Outline and Calendar

This calendar is based on a 16-week session, with two class sessions per week. Adjustments will have to be made for holidays and vacation periods. The outline can be altered for two-semester courses; we suggest teaching Chapters 1–7 in the first course and Chapters 8–15 in the second course. The sessions can be modified for courses with different calendars.

Date Week	Activities	Readings Chapter
1. Session 1	Overview of the class, calendar, assignments, exam schedule.	
Session 2	Overview of learning disabilities, definitions, common elements.	1
2. Session 1	Characteristics, age span, prevalence, multidisciplines.	1
Session 2	History: phases—foundation, transition, integration, current.	2
3. Session 1	History, current phase and development. Legislation.	2
Session 2	Assessment. Uses of assessment information. Assessment and IEP. Stages.	3
4. Session 1	Assessment. Assessment decisions, obtaining information, discrepancy formula methods, testing pressure.	3
Session 2	Clinical teaching. Definition. Clinical teaching cycle. Classification of teaching methods.	4

Date		Activities	Readings
Week			Chapter
5.	Session 1	Clinical teaching. Building self-esteem. Trends for instruction. Task analysis.	4
	Session 2	Delivery systems. Concepts about placement. Placement options. Inclusion.	5
6.	Session 1	Journal report due.	
		Delivery systems. Methods for regular-special education partnerships. Competencies for LD teachers. Parents and Families.	5
	Session 2	Theories. Role of theory. Developmental psychology. Piaget. Behavioral psychology. Implications for learning disabilities.	6
7.	Session 1	Theories. Cognitive psychology. Information processing. Psychological processing.	6
	Session 2	Theories. Psychological processing, constructive learning. Learning strategies instruction. Styles of learning.	6
8.	Session 1	Medical. The brain. Neurological examination. Attention deficit disorders. Medical treatment. Medical specialists.	7
	Session 2	Midterm examination.	
9.	Session 1	Informal test assignment due.	
		Review of midterm examination.	
		Young Children. Importance of preschool years. Precursors of learning disabilities.	8
	Session 2	Young children. Legislation for young children. Assessment. Programs for young children. Placement options. Transition. Curriculum. Computers.	
10.	Session 1	Adolescents and adults. Characteristics. Problems at secondary level. Transition. Approaches for teaching.	9
	Session 2	Learning strategies instruction. Adults with learning disabilities. College programs.	9
11.	Session 1	Preacademic learning. Motor development. Perceptual systems. Teaching strategies for motor and perceptual learning. Phonological awareness.	10
	Session 2	Oral language. The integrated language systems. How children acquire language. Linguistic systems. Emergent literacy. Assessment of oral language. Teaching strategies for listening and speaking.	11
12.	Session 1	Reading. Consequences of reading disability. Dyslexia. The reading process. Whole-language philosophy. Explicit code-emphasis instruction. Word-recognition skills.	12
	Session 2	Reading. Reading comprehension. Assessment of reading. Strategies for word recognition, fluency, reading comprehension, special remedial methods.	12
13.	Session 1	Writing. Written expression. The writing process. Strategies for writing. Word processing. Assessment of written expression.	13
	Session 2	Writing. Spelling. Developmental stages. Spelling problems. Invented spelling. Approaches to teaching spelling. Assessment of spelling. Handwriting, manuscript, cursive, keyboarding. Strategies for teaching written expression, spelling, and handwriting.	13
14.	Session 1	Mathematics. Disabilities in mathematics. Indicators of math problems. Changing views about mathematics instruction.	14
	Session 2	Mathematics. Theories about mathematics learning. Assessment of mathematics.	14
15.	Session 1	Social-emotional problems. Social skills. Emotional problems. Behavior problems. Assessment.	15
	Session 2	Term paper due.	
		Social-emotional problems. Strategies for building social competencies, self-esteem. Behavior management strategies. Accommodations for inclusive classrooms.	15
		Review.	
16.	Session 1	Final exam.	
	Session 2	Review of examination and grading.	

PICTURE OF SUCCESS. An inspiring story of a successful artist who has dyslexia. Featuring Pat Buckley Moss and Dr. Larry Silver. 16 minutes. $25. Learning Disabilities Association of America.

REACH FOR THE STARS. An inspiring story for people with learning disabilities. Each year the Lab School of Washington, DC, presents awards to selected entertainers, athletes, scholars, and businesspeople, who have accomplished great success in their fields in spite of learning disabilities. 22 minutes. $22. Learning Disabilities Association of America.

WE CAN LEARN: UNDERSTANDING AND HELPING CHILDREN WITH LEARNING DISABILITIES. A 50-minute, 5-part video series about children with learning disabilities. Produced by the National Center for Learning Disabilities (NCLD), along with WNBC, New York. Includes manuals for parents, teachers, and professionals. $39.95 + $3.95 shipping and handling. NCLD, 381 Park Avenue South, Suite 1420, New York, NY 10016. Phone (212) 545-7510.

4. Learning Disabilities Organizations: E-mail and Web Sites, Addresses, FAX and Telephone Numbers

The Attention Deficit Information Network, Inc. 457 Hillside Avenue, Needham, MA 02194. Phone (617) 455-9895.

Children and Adults with ADD (CH.A.D.D.). 499 NW 70th Ave, #308, Plantation, FL 33317.

Council for Exceptional Children (CEC) and the Division of Learning Disabilities (DLD). 1920 Association Drive, Reston, VA 22091-1589. Phone (800) 328-0272 or (703) 620-3660. Web site: http://www.cec.sped.org.

Council for Learning Disabilities (CLD). P.O. Box 40303, Overland Park, KS 66204. Phone (913) 238-5721.

Future of Children. The David and Lucile Packard Foundation, 300 Second Street, Suite 102, Los Altos, CA 94022. FAX (415) 949-6498. E-mail: circulation@futureofchildren.org. Web site: http://www.futureofchildren.org.

International Reading Association. 800 Barksdale Rd., P.O. Box 8139, Newark, DE 19714-8139. Phone (302) 731-1600. FAX (302) 731-1057. E-mail: 74673.3641@compuserve.com.

Learning Disabilities Association of America (LDA). 4156 Library Road, Pittsburgh, PA 15234. Phone (412) 341-1515.

Learning Disabilities Association of Canada (LDAC). 323 Chapel Street, Ottawa, Ontario, Canada KIN 7Z2. Phone (613) 238-5721.

National Attention Deficit Disorder Association (ADDA). P.O. Box 972, Mentor, OH 44061. Phone (800) 847-2282.

National Center for Learning Disabilities. 381 Park Avenue South, Suite 1420, New York, NY 10016. Phone (212) 545-7510.

National Information Center for Children and Youth with Disabilities (NICHCY). 1875 Connecticut Avenue, 8th floor, Washington, DC 20009. Phone (703) 685-6763.

Orton Dyslexia Society (ODS). Chester Building, 8600 LaSalle Road, Suite 382, Baltimore, MD 21204. Phone (410) 296-0232. FAX (410) 321-5069. E-mail: ods@pie.org. Web site: http://www.pie.org./ods.

5. Selected References and Professional Journals

Selected References

Barkley, R. A. (1995). *Taking Charge of ADHD.* New York: Guilford Press.

Cardoni, B. (1990). *Living with a Learning Disability.* Carbondale, IL: Southern Illinois University Press.

Deshler, D. D., Ellis, E., & Lenz, K. (1996). *Teaching Adolescents with Learning Disabilities: Strategies and Methods.* Denver: Love Publishing Co.

The Future of Children: Special Education for Students with Disabilities. Vol. 6, Number 1. Los Altos, CA: The David and Lucile Packard Foundation, 300 Second Street, Suite 102.

Harris, G., & Kirk, W. (eds.). (1993). *The Foundations of Special Education: Selected Papers and Speeches of Samuel A. Kirk.* Reston, VA· Council for Exceptional Children.

Journal of Child Neurology. (1995). *Learning Disabilities* (entire issue). Vol 10. Supplement Number 1.

Latham, P. S., & Latham, P. H. (1993). *Learning Disabilities and the Law.* Washington, DC: JKL Communications.

Learning Disabilities Association of America (ed.). (1995). *Secondary Education and Beyond: Providing Opportunities for Students with Learning Disabilities.* Pittsburgh, PA: Learning Disabilities Association of America.

Lerner, J. W., Lowenthal, B., & Lerner, S. R. (1995). *Attention Deficit Disorders: Assessment and Teaching.* Pacific Grove, CA: Brooks/Cole.

Lloyd, J. W., Kameenui, E. J., & Chard, D. (eds.). (1997). *Issues in Educating Students with Disabilities.* New York: Lawrence Erlbaum Associates, Inc. Publishers.

Lyon, G. R. (1995). Toward a definition of dyslexia. *Annals of Dyslexia, 45,* 13–30.

Lyon, G. R. (ed.). (1994). *Frames of References for the Assessment of Learning Disabilities: New Views on Measurement Issues.* Baltimore: Paul H. Brookes Publishing Co.

Lyon, G. R., Gray, D. B., Kavanagh, J. F., & Krasnegor, N. A. (eds.). (1993). *Better Understand Learning Disabilities: New Views from Research and Their Implications for Education and Public Policies.* Baltimore, MD: Paul H. Brookes Publishing Co.

Richek, M., Caldwell, J., Jennings, J., & Lerner, J. (1996). *Reading Problems: Assessment and Teaching Strategies*. Needham Heights, MA: Allyn & Bacon.

Silver, L. B. (1991). *The Misunderstood Child: A Guide for Parents of Children with Learning Disabilities*. New York: McGraw-Hill.

Smith, S. L. (1991). *Succeeding Against the Odds*. Los Angeles, CA: Jeremy Tarcher, Inc., St. Martins Press.

Turnbull, H. R. (1993). *Free Appropriate Public Education: The Law and Children with Disabilities*. Denver: Love Publishing Co.

Vogel, S., & Adelman, P. (1993). *Success for College Students with Learning Disabilities*. New York: Springer-Verlag.

Selected Professional Journals

Annals of Dyslexia
Exceptional Children
Journal of Learning Disabilities
Intervention
Learning Disabilities: A Multidisciplinary Journal
Learning Disabilities Quarterly
Learning Disabilities Research and Practice
Teaching Exceptional Children